Island Home

Out and About on Vancouver Island

Anny Scoones

TOUCHWOOD

Interior and cover design by Colin Parks
Interior illustrations by Hillary Schell

LIBRARY AND ARCHIVES CANADA CATALOGUING IN PUBLICATION

Scoones, Anny, 1957–, author

Island home: out and about on Vancouver Island / Anny Scoones.

Issued in print and electronic formats.
ISBN 978-1-77151-258-9 (softcover).—ISBN 978-1-77151-259-6 (HTML).—
ISBN 978-1-77151-260-2 (PDF)

1. Vancouver Island (B.C.)—Humor—Anecdotes. I. Title.

FC3844.4.S36 2018   971.1'2   C2017-906619-6   C2017-906620-X

We acknowledge the financial support of the Government of Canada through the Canada
Book Fund and the Canada Council for the Arts, and of the Province of British Columbia
through the British Columbia Arts Council and the Book Publishing Tax Credit.

The interior pages of this book have been printed on 100% post-consumer
recycled paper, processed chlorine free, and printed with vegetable-based inks.

PRINTED IN CANADA AT FRIESENS

23 22 21 20 19   1 2 3 4 5

To Mother Nature, the beekeepers, the lighthouse preservationists, and the wildlife rehabilitators; to the island entrepreneurs, cheese makers, museum care-takers, artists, goat experts, seafarers, and wanderers; to the saloon-goers, the cake makers, the huggers, the friendly (and cranky) ferry workers, and the countless others who have made our island home the perfect place to embark on our journeys, both outward and inward, which enable our many little thinks.

And for Sarah Ronayne.

Contents

Introduction

TRAVEL IS ABOUT SO MUCH MORE THAN OUR PLANNED ITINER-
aries, activities, and destinations; it's about our observations, feelings,
and thoughts—not only when we arrive, but when we're in transit,
when we explore, or when we do nothing more than sit and think.
I believe that journeys are personal and that travel is *mainly* about
what happens when we sit and think, making it an intuitive, nonlinear
activity that can spark old memories while creating new ones.

It's been my experience that Vancouver Island and the Gulf Islands
are ideal locations for discovering and rediscovering both literal and
figurative landscapes. It is also where I have discovered, in countless,
profound ways, what it means to feel and be *at home* anywhere, whether
on Canada's East Coast, where I am originally from, or here on the
West Coast, where I have lived happily for many years.

We don't have to be lithe, lentil-eating yogis sitting in the lotus
position while watching the sun rise over the ocean to get the most out
of visiting or living here. The most significant benefit of exploring our
island home is how we process what crosses our path, paying attention
to not just beauty and tranquility, but also the mundane, the uncomfortable, the ridiculous, the ironic, and the melancholy. It's all part of
defining our lives, and thus, the inner journey.

What you hold in your hands is not a conventional travel book. Rather, it is a loose compilation of some of my personal recollections, reflections, and observations, the kind you'd have on a pleasant road trip, whether travelling alone or with a companion. I call these moments Little Thinks. They come when you least expect, and they are truly joyful—blissful, even. They offer a serene rest for the mind.

Little Thinks

I first heard the expression "Little Think" when I was working with a community theatre company based in Dorset, a charming and quaint county in southern England dotted with hedgerows, meadows, thatched roof cottages, bluebell woods, golden fields of canola, and mossy stone bridges, which arched over clear bubbling streams straight out of *The Wind in the Willows* or a Wordsworth poem

Rather than produce conventional plays, this theatre company posed questions to the audience and then acted out the answers, thus allowing the audience to create the story. I suppose it was, at the time, "alternative" theatre, organized by a couple of sad hippies who resided in a mildewed brick house on a hill near Bournemouth. I lived with them and had a tiny, upstairs bedroom with slanted ceilings that overlooked a lush lawn and a tangle of rose bushes. In that room, I salvaged an old record player from the damp closet and played Kate Bush records as I wrote letters home to Mum in Canada.

Phillip and Margaret, the elderly landlords and owners of the property, lived in a cottage next door; they were very kind to me. Phillip was retired and painted as a hobby; he used to invite me over for tea in the afternoon and ask if he could draw me naked on the windowsill, but I always politely refused.

The founder of the theatre troupe—Nick, an intense, balding, older man—had thin lips and the early signs of what would undoubtedly become a humped back. Beth, his partner (noticeably younger than Nick), had thick, blotchy ankles, a pronounced lisp, and a head full of dull curly hair and smelled rather musty as if she had a sluggish constitution. All she wanted was a baby.

I was young and from Canada, but they hired me, and we all lived in this damp sprawling brick house, which had a magnificent, prolific fig tree just outside the living room window. We took turns cooking dinner in the humid little kitchen on the gas stove below the peeling green paint; they were vegetarians, and I recall Nick's dinners of massive cauliflowers and chips surrounded by numerous legumes, all covered in cheddar cheese.

We went on tour around England and Europe in a small, white car, which was rusted and cold, and performed Nick's creative theatrical endeavours at schools, pubs, and community centres. The British government supported such projects at the time, and our company was provided with minimal grants.

As part of the tour, we visited a school in a gritty town in Yorkshire on a bleak, raw autumn day. The students, all about twelve years old, lumbered into the musty gym and sat in a circle, their ill-fitting, dingy grey uniforms with stretched sweaters, untucked white shirts, and scuffed shoes splayed across the worn wooden floor. They were rosy-cheeked and messy haired, at that "sticky" stage, poised to discard belief in fantasy, though not quite yet. The students, with mild enthusiasm, chose to retell the story of *Jack and the Beanstalk* while our troupe asked questions and acted out the responses in our alternative style.

Nick, unshaven, tired, and wearing old blue jeans and a tattered sweater, began the questioning process (this was his role), jabbing his stubby fingers in the air for effect.

"And what did Jack do at the top of the beanstalk?" he bellowed with a subtle spray of spittle.

"He sat on a rock!" yelled a pale little girl in the back row.

"And then what did he do?" Nick continued.

Nobody answered; the audience was silent. But then a little boy, wearing shorts that revealed chubby legs and bruised, muddy knees, murmured, "He 'ad a lit-ill think."

Despite my youth (and, perhaps, my immaturity and naïveté), I understood exactly what this boy meant by "a Little Think": a brief time to relax and ponder what to do. And I have never forgotten this wonderful, simple phrase.

As I age, I take many Little Thinks, little pauses, little daydreams, little moments to drift off and experience a gentle, relaxed thought. Sometimes a Little Think leads only to a meditative blissful state; other times a Little Think can be invigorating, giving rise to entirely new thoughts and feelings. That's a moment of greatness, of movement, of personal journey.

The mysterious thing about these Little Thinks and realizations is that you cannot predict or manufacture them. They're often unexpected and not built on logic; they are simply what you feel and think and realize at the moment. Mum, who was an artist and had a grand studio in the attic of her house in Fredericton, described these unpredicted thoughts when she was in the middle of a huge oil painting of a Queen Street parade; she said, "Something just floated by, and I caught it."

It's like that in life, and to catch that perfect fleeting 'something,' whether it be a thought in a book, a golf swing, or a simple idea that just floats by is the greatest feeling in the world!

Sometimes Little Thinks can solve problems; sometimes they help you see things in a different way; or sometimes they just give you a little rest. And how do they end? Sometimes they gently float away; other times they provide a sense of completeness that tells you they are finished.

So, how to create optimal conditions for your own Little Think to occur?

- **Don't try to actively think**. Little Thinks happen spontaneously if you allow yourself to drift. Throughout this book, I suggest places and situations that will encourage productive Little Thinks.

- **Turn off your technology.** Little Thinks are precious and personal; they are not meant to be compulsively broadcast to the world via social networking sites, although sometimes it's lovely to share them with a friend over a cup of tea or a martini.

- **Allow your mind to go wherever it desires, even if that means nowhere.** There will indeed be times your mind goes to places that will astound you; your Little Think may turn into a Big Think.

Throughout this book, I suggest activities that could enhance your Little Thinks, while also inspiring and entertaining you as I take you on a virtual road trip of sorts around Vancouver Island and some of the Gulf Islands. If you're so moved, you can write down your thoughts while on your own journeys and perhaps even accompany them with a photograph or sketch or souvenir of some sort, crafting your collection of Little Thinks into a private journal. You may be surprised what this brings up and where it takes you.

Throughout the book, Little Thinks are indicated by the 🖋 *icon.*

My attraction to the West Coast

The other day, as I was cleaning out the basement and going through all sorts of boxes, I came across two lovely snapshots of the very frozen Saint John River in Fredericton, just a block from where Mum and Dad's house was on Lansdowne Street, where I was raised. Dad was the artist-in-residence at the university, just up the hill; he had a small studio in an old brownstone building, and one time he nearly burned the place down by leaving turpentine-soaked rags in a drawer. Most of the university buildings are of new, red brick—large solid boxes with white trimmed windows and huge old maple trees overlooking the meandering river below. The photographs I discovered were taken on a bright winter's day; the river was frozen and covered in snow, but it was the riverbank that was most interesting. The frozen shore was a ribbon of ice shelves surrounding brown grasses, with a tinge of sunlit turquoise between the crusty layers.

Those eastern winters were beautiful and remain as among my defining memories of Fredericton. But throughout my childhood years, I felt a very strong pull to the West Coast. I was born in North Vancouver and spent every summer with my Gran on the Gulf Islands. The deep blue-grey-green sea, white clamshell beaches, cedar forests, drooping with rain in the winter, and Gran's sweet peas from her garden lured me to the place of joyful childhood memories. I did not even wait for my high school graduation in Fredericton. (No prom for me—I'm not a prom type of person. It is frightening for me to even picture myself in one of those dresses.) Instead, Mum and Dad drove me out to the little train station in Fredericton Junction on a warm, dusky evening.

The train whistled as it rounded the corner and sluggishly came to a halt. As I climbed aboard, Mum said, "Remember, Anny, you can always come home," but in truth, I had a deep and contented feeling that I was, in fact, heading home. Mum had made me a rather wet and sloppy egg sandwich, which I ate on my grey seat, my little blue suitcase at my feet, looking out at the black, treed expanse of the Canadian wilderness.

When I arrived out west, I first lived on Galiano Island, where I worked at the local hotel. Before I knew it, my Gulf Island life was full! I even had to go to court in the little town of Sidney on Vancouver Island as I had witnessed horse thievery. Mum visited me once or twice a year, and I always went back to Fredericton at Christmas. Eventually I moved to Glamorgan Farm near Victoria.

Mum loved the farm. She'd dig up worms for the chickens and wander through the tangled, abandoned wood at the Sandown

Racetrack across the road and paint the wildflowers. We'd take road trips to Tofino, where she found those immense and shifting skies of Long Beach absolutely breathtaking, or up to Yellow Point to see her old friend Bunty, who used to work with Mum at Yellow Point Lodge when they were teenagers (Mum's tasks were of the hospitality nature and included cleaning the outhouses. Bunty was tougher, having to wring the chickens' necks for the guests' dinners). At night, we spent many happy hours by the fire, Mum with her Scotch, me with a martini, both of us watching the original Russian version of the film *War and Peace*. Mum would swoon over the prince and weep for "poor little Natasha." And when we went to bed, we'd hear the frog chorus from the pond in the meadow behind the huge red barn.

Alas, Mum became too frail to travel, and the farm became too much for me to handle, so my partner Mikki and I downsized to a lovely little house in Victoria, and Mum and I took our road trips (and our vermouth) throughout the Maritimes instead

And so today, when I look at the old, wrinkled photos of the frozen Saint John River, memories of all the neighbours skating under that huge, bright, cold sky, the iron railway bridge and the three massive Irving oil tanks in the distance come rushing back: Mum skiing under the winter moon through the black bare trees, and me fishing with Dad in his little aluminum boat, bobbing up and down the brackish, dark amber Saint John River during the humid summers. But then there were the times on Galiano Island, out west, which were spent under Gran's plum tree in my little tent, with my trolls, and an old feral cat named Gracie, the whiff of the sea blowing gently through Gran's flower garden of sweet peas on a languid summer night. Whether I'm back east or out west, I learned that home is truly inside us; no matter where you are on this planet, where we feel happy, where we settle is where we belong. Destinations are only part of the journey. It is the parts in between that are rich and rewarding, as are the Little Thinks that stay with you forever; *that* is the essence of home, of travel, and of being—it's an inward journey.

Even the wintering birds know this. Every autumn, on the beaches of Victoria's Dallas Road, elegant, shy little wood ducks appear, bobbing in the surf throughout the wet and dismal months, along with a flock of buffleheads and a massive merganser convention. Come spring, they return to their woodland residences. They make their home where they are, in any conditions.

Quintessential island characteristics

The islands are well known for their craft shops, galleries, and artisan studios; indeed, such endeavours are the lifeblood of many of the Gulf Islands. These enchanting, whimsical shops are typically small and quaint, with the aromas of old wood, sheep's wool, and mild natural fragrances, and represent what our Gulf Islands, both northern and southern, are all about: an imaginative, dreamy lifestyle that is often fringe or offbeat and perhaps isolated.

Two of my favourite examples are found at the gallery shop near the ferry wharf on Quadra Island and the village shops on Mayne Island.

The collections of crafts, curios, and concoctions are a visual and often flavourful and tactile treat. One feels as if they have entered an artisanal fairyland of sorts, a cocoon of fanciful items that dangle gently from elegant arbutus branches, drape over vintage pink velvet chairs, or hang on colourfully painted walls. Many such shops are connected to tucked-away coffee corners that serve wonderful local pastries and savoury snacks; most are within walking distance of the ferry and are often accessible by bike.

There are also many artisans on the Gulf Islands, and numerous galleries and studios, often in hobbit-like abodes tucked within country lanes, on rocky, windswept points, or in quiet bays.

Artisan is a relatively modern word and is often incorrectly used interchangeably with *artist*. (For example, Vincent van Gogh was not an artisan.) An artisan is what we used to know as a craftsperson, one who creates beautiful gift-type goods such as soap, candles, glass starfish, and homemade paper that contains flower petals and herbs.

The term *craft* has now been given to beer makers (as in craft breweries), which are in growing abundance over Vancouver Island, many of them using local ingredients such as barley. (At one time, hops grew well in North Saanich and were a major industry.) And then there are the islands' artisanal wines and cheeses.

The words *craft, artisan,* and *artisanal* to describe food convey an elevated level of thoughtfulness and careful preparation with an organic or local component; it is a pleasant and gentle method of rejecting highly commercialized, chemical household products and processed foods.

Living on the Gulf Islands

On all the Gulf Islands, you must generate your own income, entertainment, and sense of community if you desire to lead the island life. This is often more creatively challenging than city living where you may receive a regular paycheque, have a choice of films to see, restaurants to visit, or self-help groups to attend. Still, there is no end to surprising and delightful creativity. Where else but on the Gulf Islands would you see a CPR (Canadian Pacific Railway) caboose wedged between arbutus trees and converted into a bed and breakfast, or a double-decker bus turned into a café? Even more inventive are the thrift shops combined with recycling centres; you'll notice the word *vintage* is used quite extensively in many Gulf Island shops. Many islands also include a free store.

Poking around these retail facilities is great fun, and you may discover a treasure or a funny knick-knack. A trip to one of the Gulf Islands found me in a vintage shop, rummaging through a crammed shelf of scratched vinyl records, musty 1945 gardening books, and tarnished ashtrays. I came across a hilarious ceramic turkey candle holder for all of one dollar. Since it was close to Thanksgiving, I purchased it for my hostess who thought it was the greatest gift she'd ever received. She sets it up and lights it every Christmas, too. When lit, the turkey glows with warmth and humour among the mashed potatoes and Brussels sprouts.

As the name suggests, the goods in a free store are free, although some ask that you bring an item to swap. These shops originated as a socio-political statement, a reaction to our capitalist monetary economic system. One of the first organizations to establish the free stores were known as the Diggers, a sixties-era American group with anarchist tendencies; everything was free, including food and, in some cases, money itself.

Today, Gulf Island free stores serve a different purpose: reusing, recycling, and assisting lower-income citizens. An offshoot of the free store is the barter system which several island communities have developed; for example, you can trade a basket of salad greens for a haircut, or a car wash for a flute lesson.

And then there are the people who make this part of the world so distinctive. Who chooses to reside on the Gulf Islands? An eclectic mix of people: a blend of sixties folk, New Age enthusiasts, and educated environmentalist hippies; midwives, eccentric artists, and artisans; young, skilled builders and tradespeople with young families, retired conservatives, and retired liberals; even retired senators choose to reside on the islands—they write books and partake in communities far gentler than those back in Ottawa! And, of course, there are the old-timers and island pioneers who know how to witch for water with a willow limb, build an outhouse that naturally composts, knit socks, keep the fire burning, and bake a pie and a venison stew all at the same time. This group often takes a cynical view of the government when a team of consultants arrive in their spotless Japanese hybrid vehicles carrying briefcases, tripods, GPS trackers, and computer tablets, recording their overtime if the ferry is late, and wearing the latest Gore-Tex jackets and fingerless gloves to take tree surveys, and groundwater tests, starfish counts, soil samples, archaeological analysis, midden photographs, and tidal measurements before they finally leave. Then, about three years later (says the typical old timer), "they come back and tell us how to live."

There was an explosion of deer on Pender Island at one point, and an elderly logger sputtered in frustration at the village café, "Just bring a couple of hungry cougars over here and the goddamn deer will be gone by nightfall." He continued his somewhat accurate rant while chewing his fresh jelly donut. "These bylaws and fancy consultants with their useless ten-year degrees who make us put our outhouse twenty feet from our well are a load of bunk, coming over here and telling me where to piss on my own property."

Numerous citizens who are attracted to the lifestyle on the Gulf Islands feel they are part of the natural world; some may feel uncomfortable in mainstream, conventional city life, and so—perhaps to become closer to the world in which they choose to live—they change their names. My observation is that the most common adopted name for any gender seems to be Sky. But I have also met River, Aspen, Saturn, and Tesla (imagine naming your children after cars!), and Moonbeam, plus an array of names from nature translated into Indian, Tibetan, or Peruvian. I had a massage once by Skylark.

So, yes, life is undoubtedly different on the Gulf Islands, and at times it is extraordinarily blissful; when the winter windstorms arrive, blowing down trees which knocks out the power, often for days, there is nothing cozier than living by wood heat and candlelight with no other choices to make except those that involve how to survive.

I remember one cold, dark January night on Mayne Island when I took my dogs out for their nightly ablutions. As we walked to the end of the lane, it was completely silent; all was still but for the lapping sea against the sandstone rock at the end of the road, and there was a faint aroma of woodsmoke hanging in the crisp air. It was so dark that I had to use a little flashlight to guide me along the lane, lined with towering cedars. Something compelled me to turn off my light and look up at the black sky. There I saw the heavens: billions of stars, some brighter than others, celestial jewels clustered in myriad constellations, the heavenly bodies that surround us and which we are all a part of—and I was incredibly moved. I did not feel small, or irrelevant, or insignificant, but rather part of the whole miracle of the universe, of creation; the feeling was overwhelming. I'll never forget it. Maybe that's what living on a little island can show you.

The Southern Gulf Islands

Galiano Island, Mayne Island, Pender Island,
Saturna Island, and Salt Spring Island

THE SOUTHERN GULF ISLANDS SIT BETWEEN VICTORIA AND Vancouver in what is known as the Salish Sea, a body of water that includes the Strait of Juan de Fuca and Puget Sound all the way up into the Strait of Georgia. This stunning and diverse marine landscape is collectively known as the Salish Sea, out of respect for the Coast Salish people who have hunted, gathered, and resided here for millennia.

When you take a ferry between Victoria and Vancouver, you'll experience what my late mum called "a beautiful free cruise." You may even see schools of white-sided dolphins or orcas swimming and breaching in the bottle-green surf. Occasionally, somebody jumps from the freshly painted white enamelled deck: In 2005, a fellow leaped into Active Pass and attempted to swim to the shore of Mayne Island to avoid missing a baseball game! The ferry crew, expertly trained in overboard emergencies, donned their red thermal survival suits and lowered their little rubber orange dingy into the swirling and treacherous sea below as the captain held the ferry at a standstill with its engines idle.

Galiano Island

When I was a child living with Gran on Galiano Island, just across from Mayne Island, a car drove off the ferry ramp into Active Pass and sank like a stone. It is a very deep and narrow pass with lethal currents; kayakers are advised not to paddle in those waters.

Every so often, a vessel (or even a ferry) will go aground on Collison Reef where there is a beacon on a shallow rock where seals and sea lions rest, bark, and lay about between meals. I remember sitting in Gran's living room playing with my trolls one morning; my favourite troll, Isabelle, told her best friend troll, Enid (who was, in fact, a car ornament), that she had a toothache and had woken up with a swollen cheek. Mum and Gran were having tea in the kitchen. Gran had just picked a bouquet of sweet peas for the table from her garden, and they had made bread, which was rising into a massive soft mound on the warm counter. This was the house that Gran had high on a bluff overlooking Active Pass. Suddenly there was a great shudder—the whole house shook.

"Molly, it's an earthquake," said Gran.

Then we heard much commotion outdoors on the little lane; people gathered and pointed towards the sea. A great Russian ship had collided and gone aground with a ferry by the beacon on Collison Reef. Mum rushed to grab her pencils and sketch pad.

It was both horrifying and fascinating—not so much the grounding, but the frantic behaviour of the neighbours. A few of them scrambled down the grassy bank to the small pebbled beach below, yelling and waving their arms as tiny, dark figures on the freighter, showing much greater calm and order, appeared in succession on the slanted upper decks like ants who have had their hill smashed with a rock by an angry child.

Gran stood by the side of the road, dressed in her blue cotton Sears smock. Jack, her husband, came out from his little workshop, buttoning up his cardigan, stooped from years of pulling in fishing nets. We all just watched in awe in the morning summer heat. Jack pulled out a matchstick and scratched his ear with it. Mum sketched furiously.

I spent many of my younger years on Galiano with Gran, mostly in the summer months. She and Jack had an old blue Austin, and every day after lunch we'd drive a short way to Montague Park and spend the warm afternoon hours on the white clamshell beach; Gran and Jack sat under a huge arbutus tree while I waded in the shallow azure water with the trolls who wore bathing caps made of balloons which I cut in half. Of all the beaches on the Gulf Islands, I have never seen water that colour, a shimmering golden blend of jade and turquoise.

I still occasionally visit the beach and stroll around the lagoon; it is a wonderful place to kayak and swim and is my favourite spot on Galiano. The arbutus tree remains, gently hanging out above the white shell bay, still providing shade and comfort for all those that choose to rest beneath it.

The last time I was there was with Mum, Gran had long since died, her ashes spread into Active Pass. Mum was out west, and we made a day trip to our old stomping grounds on Galiano; we'd packed a picnic, and Mum decided to swim. Her idea of swimming was simply to dash into the freezing water and then rush out—and that is what she did, except when she returned, all pink and invigorated from the frigid water, her big toe cramped to what looked like ninety degrees *backwards*. I recall reacting with alarm and panic. The toe eventually returned to its normal position after vigorous rubbing.

If you prefer magnificent views, then you must visit the bluffs. These high rock cliffs form the southern section of Galiano and look towards neighbouring Mayne Island just across Active Pass. You are able to drive up to this magnificent grassy knoll. It is dotted with coniferous vegetation which, in the summer heat, give off a lovely, warm fragrance of pine and sea. There's a shack at the top where, for decades, lovers have carved their initials.

Mayne Island

Mayne Island is less popular than Galiano, possibly because it's a bit farther from both Vancouver and Victoria's terminals; the experience is a little more austere, perhaps a little lonelier, although it has a rich history of discovery and multiculturalism. One significant difference between Galiano Island and Mayne Island is the location of the village: Galiano village is clustered at the long, iconic wooden ferry dock, which makes a day visit easily accessible on foot; there is a charming bookstore, a diverse variety of galleries and cafés, and the sandstone beach; scenic country lanes are close by, and serious walkers could make it to the bluffs. In contrast, the village on Mayne Island is in its centre, a few kilometres from the ferry by a winding road through the forest.

The village on Mayne was established at Miners Bay in Active Pass, across from the bluffs (on Galiano). Miners Bay was named after the boatloads of miners who passed through—and perhaps rested en route—in their search for gold on the mainland. The oldest operating pub hotel in the province is the Springwater Lodge at Miners Bay. There was a one-room jail as well (spelled *gaol*) which is still standing; it's painted a fading yellow with green trim around its one little window and stands up the hill next to the thrift shop. And, of course, every small historic community includes a country church, usually in a lovely pastoral setting; Mayne's sits in a small meadow of daisies and arbutus trees on a grassy slope overlooking the sea.

I attended a service on Mayne Island once—the Blessing of the Animals. (It took the theme of animals to entice me to a service, although I will admit that a comforting, traditional Christmas Eve service is alluring.) I took my five old dogs to the church! I loaded them into my van, which smelled pungent after a day at the beach and walking through the woods. Alice-Mary, a chubby black Labrador, sat in the front passenger seat. Ruby, her chocolate cousin, sat behind her; Ruby was my ex-husband's dog, but he had handed her over to me because she was getting old and was beginning to urinate on his new rugs. Then there were the two aging hairy girls, Daisy and Lily; I had adopted them from the SPCA after reading their sign, which declared, OLD GALS MUST STAY TOGETHER. (I think they were trailer park gals: First, they wouldn't do stairs; second, they became excited if they saw a mobile home, panting and wagging their tails; third, they loved the propane delivery man who came every month to fill the tank.) The only information the staff at the SPCA would give me was that they came from Smithers.

And finally, there was little, nervous Sammy, the saddest dog I ever knew.

Sammy also came from the SPCA. So abused had she been that she had nubs for teeth from gnawing at a cage to escape, and she hid in the nearest closet she could find if she heard a loud voice, defecating on herself in fear and despair. Over the years, Sammy had relaxed a little and would sometimes forget herself for a moment and play hysterically, tearing in circles around portly Alice-Mary, who was the kindest and most patient of dogs.

I have the most heartbreaking little photograph of Sammy, one I had patiently set up thinking it would be a charming shot. It shows her sitting in a green wooden wagon, looking terribly uncertain about the world, not knowing quite where to look.

All the dear dogs lived happy, grand, long lives—perhaps thanks to God and the Blessing of the Animals. Actually, it had been a slightly stressful disaster: In the church sat children with guinea pigs on their laps and ribbons in their hair; women in lovely hats held small, well-behaved, well-groomed dogs with collars of rhinestones and pink bling; there were several budgies in clean little cages, and one small boy had brought his Siamese fighting fish to be blessed.

We were late because Sammy had stopped dead on the little stone step. The old gals, still damp from the beach with bits of forest debris in their tangled hair, trundled in first, followed by Ruby, then Alice-Mary, who smelled strongly like a wet Labrador. I had to carry Sammy, who was terrified, and the only seat left was half a pew at the front. It was entirely humiliating, passing all the regular churchgoers who smelled so sweet and were all so well turned out. This had been a colossal mistake. When the organist began, Ruby urinated on the red carpet. The old gals were straining to meet the Yorkshire terriers with the pink bows on top of their tiny heads across the aisle. And Alice-Mary, who had either rolled in a dead fish or eaten it (or both), happily panting and enjoying the entire adventure, let out a foul odour.

Sammy just hid under the pew, shaking with terror.

Halfway through the hymn, I could bear it no longer, so we left, slowly retracing our steps back down the spotless red carpet and the polished wooden pews of singing patrons and their perfectly behaving companions. Outside was an unwashed man with a filthy ram with great balls of dried dung clinging to its rear, and a lady with two goats, udders bulging, as well as a donkey wearing a straw hat!

We waited under the shade of a beech tree for the service to finish, thinking that we might be able to be blessed outdoors with the other pungent livestock.

The minister came out in his white robe trimmed in gold and did indeed bless each dog on the stone step, touching each lightly on their forehead as the bells chimed above from the little wooden roof—while a ferry somewhere, its engines deeply humming below the waterline, passed in the distance.

There was another time I relied on the church, but more out of a desire for comfort, the reassuring security of tradition, and some peaceful moments. It was on a howling, rain-swept Christmas Eve. I was alone that evening, living on my little farm in North Saanich. I had finished my nightly chores and lit the fire. Mum had called from Fredericton to say Merry Christmas, and I had opened the currant cake she had mailed. The dogs and I were sitting around the wood stove as the rain pelted against the windows. Also with us on the couch that night was my dear old goat Merlin. He had been picked up by animal control on Salt Spring Island, and I had taken him in. He was very, very stout, with coarse white hair and a long, pungent-smelling beard. (Did you know that male goats urinate in their beards to attract females?)

Merlin had extremely stubby legs; one was especially deformed, so he had issues with climbing onto the couch, but on Christmas Eve, he made it. I know it seems strange that a smelly old billy goat would be invited into the living room to hear the Queen's annual Christmas address, have a morsel of currant cake, and hear Handel's *Messiah*, but there he was.

(Merlin had bonded to Alice-Mary, the portly black Labrador; he'd taken a shine to her in the chicken barn when Alice-Mary was pilfering a chicken egg, and they became inseparable. Merlin even ate dog food and had his own basket beside Alice-Mary's on the porch. He'd follow us for walks through the daffodil wood and around the old mill pond across the road in the tangled and overgrown back meadows of the Sandown racetrack. In fact, the dog catcher on patrol one day asked me if I had a licence for "that animal," and feeling very sassy at that moment—having just being elected to the local municipal council—I answered, "Here in North Saanich we do not license billy dogs.")

On this stormy, dismal Christmas Eve, Merlin fell off the couch when *It's a Wonderful Life* came on the television; his eyes rolled back in his little elegant face, then he gave a weak little bleat and expired, right there on my grandfather's Persian carpet.

Alice-Mary didn't even wake up from her doze; she continued to silently pass gas after her Christmas bone, even though Merlin's lovely curled horns had brought down a pink silk lampshade which, in turn, hit a Chagall print. I needed some time to compose myself but managed to wrap the old goat in a tarp and take him outside to place him under the plum tree on the lawn.

And that's when I decided to wander along the lane and down the grassy hill at the end of the airport runway and attend the midnight service at the little historic wooden church which overlooked the sea at Patricia Bay and, in daylight, offered a view of the red coast guard vessels bobbing at the government docks (including the famous Canadian icebreaker, the CCGS *Louis S. St. Laurent*). I sat in the back of the warm, cozy church among candlelight and thought about Merlin. I did not sing, repent, grieve, nor pray. In fact, I don't recall even saying Merry Christmas to anyone. But the ritual and the urns glinting among the flickering flames as the rain pelted against the dark stained glass gave me great comfort; it was a place where others had gathered, for their own deeply personal reasons, to do things that all humans do— and feel all that we do, together.

It was a melancholy evening, but at the same time, a celebratory one, as church often is, with this wonderful blend of dignity and solemn reflection. I find melancholia to be quite uplifting, perhaps because we are reaching for something within our soul; it is quite different from sadness.

I felt strangely, serenely elated, almost blissful, as if the end of Merlin's life was not a tragedy ending in death, but rather a wonderful, angelic finish (minus the pungent beard odour).

The West Coast MAMIL

Back on Mayne Island: If you are a fit, strong cyclist, the rural lanes and hills will be most pleasurable to pedal on while visiting the Gulf Islands, but if you're not, the topography is probably going to be too much of a challenge (especially on Mayne) for the casual cyclist who is seized once every few years with the urge to do something adventurous on a bike that's been rusting in the garage. I've seen couples out together for so-called quality time on the lovely Gulf Islands: One of them wheezes on an old, clunky CCM while the other (no doubt belonging to a cycling club, the kind that ride in packs) rides effortlessly with sinewy thighs and narrow, tight buttocks perched on a seat no wider than a dessert spoon over skinny tires. His sleek, streamlined helmet and wraparound blue-tinted sunglasses complete the look that identifies the peculiar species known as the MAMIL (middle-aged man in Lycra). And apparently, the MAMIL's sleek, lighter-than-air bicycles are much less expensive than red convertibles.

(Though it's not directly related to cycling, I must comment on another strange accessory I often see on men of a certain age: the rather rudely named "fanny pack," an overstuffed, bulging pouch worn just under the navel, hanging loosely like an ill-fitting codpiece, supposedly to keep one's money safe. Whatever happened to the wallet?)

At the top of a long and winding hill, the MAMIL—sucking electrolyte-infused water with great gusto from a nippled thermos held high—turns to face the sun, legs set wide as if he were a god sent by Zeus from Mount Olympus. Languidly picking a blackberry or two from the thick roadside hedges, his slim racing bike propped up against a NO OIL TANKERS sign, he waits.

About fifteen minutes later, pushing with dogged effort her heavy, soft-tired bike up the long hill, serious and red-faced and perspiring under her ill-fitting, bowl-shaped helmet, comes his partner. In her bicycle basket, she carries a thoughtfully prepared bounty of chicken salad sandwiches, lemon bars, brownies, and cans of ginger ale; her partner has been daintily nibbling on his bag of pumpkin seeds and cranberries, stored in his Lycra pouch, probably near his privates and within easy reach.

This couple, like many others, might want to rest at Mayne Island's Georgina Point lighthouse, which sits at the entrance to Active Pass (on the Vancouver side) in a little grassy meadow lined with salal, old gnarled apple trees, trumpet honeysuckle, and wild currant. The lighthouse was first lit in 1885 and was followed by a foghorn and a bell to warn the travellers and sailors of the unseen, lurking dangers of these deep currents they were about to enter.

It's easy to make it down to the smooth, pitted sandstone which gently slopes into the sea where sea lions, otters, and whales often venture among the great kelp beds. Tidal pools are full of life: little darting water insects, busy barnacles waving their wispy feelers for a passing morsel, emerald and burgundy sea lettuces and flora floating among them, and tiny snails and clusters of mussels holding fast next to purple starfish packed together in the darkest rock crevices, all waiting for a fresh supply of ocean nutrients to wash over them as the next tide rises.

I once had an unforgettable experience in those waters. I was swimming close to shore, but the water was deep. If the currents are right, the waters around the Gulf Islands are warm enough to venture into due to the Fraser River's outflow, which is carried across the strait. I'm not a strong swimmer, but I can float and tread water for hours, and on this sunny afternoon, as the water sparkled and lapped onto the heated sandstone shore, I cooled off and pondered what to do in my life. Suddenly, I felt a strong undertow, perhaps ten feet away in the deeper water, like a whoosh around my legs. And then, very quietly, without drama or speed, the side of a large, gleaming, white and black whale's face appeared on the surface, almost floating, mouth slightly open, so close that I could see her teeth and a smudge of her pink gums. She rolled a little, and her little eye met mine.

I was incredibly and deeply moved; my gaze met hers for no more than five seconds, but I felt as if her eye penetrated my soul. If this had been a Disney movie, I would have swum away into the deep on her back. But she was a wild animal; the experience was natural, not a fantasy, and soon she rolled away and slipped under the surf.

If I were a religious person, I might have felt that I had come close to God; I do feel that I came close to creation. While I was neither filled with awe nor with joy—it did not seem like a revelation or an epiphany—I did feel as if something extraordinary had touched a part of me that transcends this earth, something much larger.

This is one of my most powerful memories; I am sure I will think of it on my deathbed and it will provide me with great comfort, the type of comfort that reminds me that we are part of nature, part of the huge, fluctuating cycle of life, full of mysterious moments—only that and nothing more.

No human being has come as close to entering my innermost soul as that whale did, although I did have similar experiences with an old cat named Peter, my horse Valnah, and an ancient dog named Fernando.

I once was involved in a book reading with an author from Port Alberni; we were reading about animals we had known, and she read a story about a frog who she felt knew her, recognized her, and remembered her a year after she had rescued it from a life-threatening situation in a mud puddle. Twelve months later, it was clinging to her window on a rainy afternoon. Perhaps it returned to her safe haven; I believe this may be possible. And, I might add, there's something deeply compassionate about a person who rescues a frog.

In these mysterious experiences, there are no messages, no secret sort of communication. The experience is simply a connection, and it is terribly penetrating.

The amazing story of Fernando and FedEx

Speaking of such mysterious animal connections, I must share with you an extraordinary story about the aforementioned Fernando.

There was a time on my farm in North Saanich when I was feeling a bit low, a bit unsettled, without direction, or as I used to explain it, I felt I had no purpose in life, no reason to get out of bed.

My friend Lorna noticed my low mood, and we both agreed that there was one thing we could do to alleviate my distress: make a visit to the SPCA. And so we did just that on a hot, sultry, hazy afternoon after I had done my farm chores (which were extensive).

Two amazing events occurred that day. The first involved a bony, old cat who approached me gently and put his paw on my lap, so I had to simply adopt the old fellow. However, the sweet woman that worked there understood that I was possibly in search of an elderly dog; one had just come in and was sprawled on the beige linoleum floor in the office.

"Do you want this old guy?" the worker offered.

The grizzled, old dog raised his head slightly when I bent down to pat him. He had been abandoned, had only a few teeth left, and walked with a stiff arthritic limp, so, of course, I took him home. I had to lift him into the car, and he sat happily in the back seat. Lorna suggested Fernando as his name, and so it was.

Fernando became part of the farm, spending many lovely hours dozing under the honeysuckle bush or on the blue painted kitchen floor, or hobbling beside me around the farm, pausing when I fed the pigs their warm mash or made the chickens a fresh hay nest. Fernando was a serene and dignified gentleman—kind to the cats, never begging or stealing food, a true dear companion who gazed at me as he waited to move on to the next chore. At drink time, he lay at my feet, and at bedtime, he lay on his rug at the foot of the bed.

A few times a year, I travelled back to New Brunswick to visit Mum and Dad, never staying more than a few days, but long enough to have a few vermouths and some of Dad's delicious bass, which he caught in the lovely New Brunswick streams and lakes. In Fredericton, Dad would take me out in his little aluminum boat on the Saint John River and fish while I daydreamed, running my fingers through the brown murky water as his little engine putted upstream and passed under the old railway bridge. Mum and I would walk to the market on Saturday mornings and buy a slab of Sussex cheddar or a Polish sausage for Dad. In the evenings, we watched old episodes of *Fawlty Towers* and screamed with laughter.

Back in North Saanich, the farm was in good hands, the chores and tasks seen to by a good caretaker, an old hippie who had a herb garden on the farm and a little greenhouse where he smoked a lot of pot and contemplated life.

I always flew Air Canada, figuring our own airline would never crash (although it did once, and they've had a few close calls) even though they charge passengers for chips (pretzels are free on some flights but make everyone cough) and cram in too many seats.

From Fredericton I flew to Toronto and then directly to Victoria. The farm was very close to the airport, just a couple of kilometres from the terminal, down the road, past Patricia Bay, across a meadow, around behind the little historic church, up the hill and down Glamorgan Road to the old farm with the winding driveway lined with poplars.

I always took a taxi from the airport, and the dogs—at this time, I had several dear old dogs other than sweet Fernando: Daisy, Lilly, Alice-Mary, and Ruby—would lumber up to the cab, wagging their tails, their pink tongues hanging out the sides of their mouths, before returning to their baskets on the porch or shady nests under their preferred bushes around the old log house.

But on this return trip, there was no Fernando. He had been missing since the morning, which was only a few hours earlier, but still, very unusual as he was so elderly and crippled. I thought I'd wait a few hours more in case he was just sleeping somewhere and, being deaf, simply did not realize I was home.

The evening passed following my chores. I had unpacked and had a bath. I wandered the farm in my nightgown as the sun dipped behind the crumbling yellow grandstand covered in blackberries at the Sandown racetrack across the road. And still no Fernando. I went to bed listening to the wonderful familiar frog chorus and thought that maybe the old dog had wandered away to die, as dogs and cats often do in their final moments (as I am sure I will want to do—to be alone).

Morning came, and no Fernando. I gingerly searched under the drooping cedars and in the deep cool, dark crevices of the barn, but found no sign of him. Finally, I called the SPCA and asked if anyone had found an old, lame, scrawny, kind dog. Nobody had.

Four days passed. The mystery grew. If only the other dogs could talk! Maybe they knew where our Fernando was.

And then the call came in.

Fernando had been found—you won't believe this—at the end of the runway at the airport at exactly the time my flight arrived, by the women that worked at FedEx.

They had found him waiting, looking at the tarmac. He had remained there all day, and was sitting there the next morning, stoic and patient, in the long grass behind the chain-link fence, so they took him in. They gave him a bath (embarrassing!) and a chicken sandwich and, hoping he would never be claimed, named him FedRex.

When I went to pick him up at the FedEx offices, the women, dressed in their blue uniforms, gathered in the parking lot as Fernando staggered to the van with great dignity. He climbed in with his long, gangly, uncoordinated legs, briefly glancing back at his new friends. With tears in their eyes, the women waved goodbye.

I'll never forget the kindness of those employees at FedEx. Fernando and I took them muffins and chocolates a week later.

How did Fernando know I was on that Air Canada flight? How did he know the time? What made him raise his tired, bony body and lumber all the way to the FedEx offices (which are, in fact, close to where the planes land) within an hour of my plane arriving?

(It's worth adding that the flight was an hour late because of a strike by the baggage handlers at the Toronto airport, but Fernando was on time.)

Mayne Island's Japanese Gardens

On the west side of the island you will find the Japanese Gardens, created by the community to commemorate the Japanese citizens who resided on Mayne Island prior to the Second World War. Many Japanese families lived on Mayne Island and grew tomatoes and cucumbers in their greenhouses. Then, as we know, after the bombing of Pearl Harbour in Hawaii, fear spread, and Japanese Canadians became the focus of a witch hunt; the Japanese—even those on Mayne Island—were sent to internment camps on the mainland.

Leonard Frank, the son of a professional photographer, came from Germany via San Francisco, searching for gold like so many other young men at the turn of the century. He settled in Port Alberni and ran a shop, a general store, but then Leonard won a camera in a raffle, and like his father before him, photography became his life and career. He moved to Vancouver and took thousands of images depicting the hard life of the times—the railway yards and docks along Burrard Inlet, the warehouses, the city streets, the mining and logging camps of the interior, and then, the Japanese internment camps. The Nanaimo Museum presented an exhibition a few years ago of photographs by Ansel Adams and Leonard Frank, and their images revealed life at the Japanese camps, a subject dear to both men.

Nestled in a tranquil and contemplative little corner of paradise, the gardens can be found in Dinner Bay Park (next to the baseball diamond). Here you can enjoy a diversity of shrubs, trees, grasses, and flora surrounding a bubbling stream which flows into a central pond adorned with lilies and carefully placed stones on its central island, accessed by an elegant little arched bridge. Discover other little calming surprises as you quietly amble, as if you were a whisper of air, along the narrow, well-raked, pebbled pathways.

The entrance through the drooping cedar forest brings you to a latched gate with an attached note asking that you to keep the gate closed due to the abundance of deer on Mayne Island, which would love to enter and feast on the wide array of delectable treats carefully tended to by the volunteers.

One of the gardens' many interesting features is a Japanese charcoal kiln. Charcoal burns hotter and slower than conventional wood fuels and was sold to the fish canneries on the mainland as fuel. It was also burned by the Japanese residents throughout the Gulf Islands in these domed earth ovens. Creating charcoal in these ovens is a little-known historic venture; however, it is a very traditional and valued part of both Japanese and Canadian history. In the United States, the ovens have been preserved in specific, protected sites; the pictures are fascinating and reveal rows of little beehive-style structures that look like troll houses.

Charcoal is a key ingredient in gunpowder along with sulphur and saltpetre, the latter of which is a chemical compound more commonly known as potassium nitrate and is related to potash.

Activated charcoal can be taken in pill form to treat flatulence, but casually ingesting run-of-the-mill charcoal can also kill you. If you're feeling bloated, you should probably simply attempt the wind release yoga pose. I suggest trying this alone at home, perhaps with the windows open and the CBC playing loudly, rather than in a crowded, humid yoga studio where the environment can be fairly serious—especially during meditation, or worse, when trying to practise mindfulness.

In yoga, when they say, "Trust the mysterious unfolding of your life" and "Let it go," they're not kidding when it comes to the wind relief pose!

Dad used to sketch the New Brunswick countryside and do portraits with charcoal. When I was very young, I would sit with him, his pants legs rolled up to his knees, beside a river. His legs, pale and slender, dangled in the grasses on the muddy riverbank, which steamed after a rain, as he sketched.

He drew slowly, looking up and gazing at the dark stream, shallow in places exposing pebbled islands, the rolling meadows beyond, and the dark row of trees curving the horizon, folding in and out of the distant hills and billowing clouds moving in—oh, how he loved New Brunswick! I have a drawing of a hairy little horse, standing on a hill in a fierce and blustery wind, drawn by Dad on one of his sketching excursions on a stormy day.

One day, when we were sitting by the river, he gave me a stick of charcoal, perhaps to encourage me to be an artist like him—but instead I ate it. I never drew or sketched a thing in my life, but I am able to write about what Dad drew, and I have always had the best digestion of the family. Mum used to say, "Wherever did Anny get her strong constitution from?"

Pender Island

The closest of the Gulf Islands to Vancouver Island, Pender is the easiest to reach via BC Ferries. It is, in fact, made up of two islands, North Pender and South Pender, joined by a tiny bridge.

Years ago, I had the pleasure of being a guest in Pender Island's annual autumn parade; I was even invited to act as a judge in their pie competition! As enjoyable as that role was, I did find it stressful as the six pie makers hovered next to me in expectation, probably thinking, What does she know about pie, anyway? Undaunted, I chose a big, sloppy, delicious berry pie that had obviously been made by a child. I suspect the serious pie makers disapproved of my criteria; I was never invited back. But I did submit a bid in the silent auction and won a pole dancing lesson! Yes, Pender Island had a pole dancing instructor—such is the innovative entrepreneurship of the Gulf Islands. I happily claimed my prize, with visions of myself swinging off a pole, upside down, a twenty-dollar bill stuck between my breasts as a BC ferry tooted its horn while it passed in the distance.

Alas, when I attempted, months later, to redeem my prize, the pole dance instructor had since departed from the island, so I was never able to fulfill that particular dream (at least not yet).

Here is the most Canadian story ever: In 2017, it came to the attention of Parks Canada that our national animal, the beaver, had built a dam on a small lake (as beavers are wont to do); turns out their construction was interfering with the water flow to a nearby residential area. Parks Canada's proposed solution was to cull the little animals. But the people of Pender rose to the beavers' defence, and the beavers were saved (at least for now) until Parks Canada considered other options. If I had been on Pender Island, I too would have joined the ranks of those defending our semi-aquatic rodent island residents.

People are passionate everywhere, but on the Gulf Islands, that passion is focused, concentrated, organized, informed, and acted upon. This quality is revealed time and again in the everyday lives of those who inhabit these little gem-like islands, so close to the cities of Victoria and Vancouver—yet, in some respects, worlds away.

Saturna Island

Across the channel from Mayne is Pender Island, and farther south is Saturna Island. Saturna is relatively remote and, according to the island's website, is the least-populated Gulf Island. The extra ferry travel is delightful, with lovely views of both Mayne and Pender.

Saturna is best known for its Canada Day lamb barbecue, but there are other delightful surprises to discover. The prominent features here are the magnificent landscapes, parks, and views; it has an immense amount of public land to hike, camp, and picnic through, and the scenery is unique to Saturna, quite unlike the other islands—even the colours are different. The meadows are more golden, the groves of trees a deeper green, and even the sea seems more touched with a glimmer of silver when viewed from the island's high ridges.

I recall taking a beautiful stroll on Mount Warburton Pike one summer. The dry bleached amber meadow, randomly dotted with clusters of elegant long-needled pine trees, gave off a delicate fragrance in the light breeze, which travelled up from a sparkling sea peppered with endless little islands far below and into the horizon. The visit to these gorgeous landscapes and natural settings is worth a trip.

Salt Spring Island

Salt Spring Island, a short ferry trip from Vancouver Island, is well known for its large and fabulous summer outdoor Saturday market; it has a vibrant arts scene and is home to many writers and artists. A city bus will help you get around if you don't have a car—catch the shuttle bus when you disembark from the ferry in Fulford Harbour.

In 2017, there were news reports that the RCMP and the Ministry of Transportation attempted to implement a no-hitchhiking law. This was poor judgment—the islanders were up in arms (pardon the pun) as hitchhiking is an efficient method of transport for many residents. Everybody knows everybody on Salt Spring Island, and helping one another it is a way of life. Some even call hitchhiking an important part of the island's culture.

By far the largest of the Southern Gulf Islands, Salt Spring has a little town called Ganges, that is full of cafés, shops, galleries, insurance companies, bakeries, artisans, jewellery makers, a store that sells wood stoves, and a small hospital; midway across the island is the Fritz Movie Theatre, just a short drive from Ganges. Built in 1896, the building is also used as a small community hall.

For outdoor recreation, there are places to hike, parks and lakes to explore, and marinas. For food and accommodation, there are bed and breakfasts, pubs, and motels.

Known for its delicious lamb, Salt Spring has a well-deserved reputation for being a food lover's paradise—you can even purchase organic hops. There are also many orchards and apple producers, and one of the major annual events is the Salt Spring Apple Festival, a celebration of the vast array of apples grown on the island—over 450 varieties. Many of them are from heirloom (original) seed.

Apple farming on Salt Spring has a long history dating from the 1860s when the fruit was shipped to the mainland.

One of the reasons I love the apple industry is that it has a touch of the politically incorrect. Take tree classification, for example: You have your standard tree (the original tall tree in which a ladder is required to pick the fruit), but then you have dwarf trees—better yet, there are semi-dwarfs (half a dwarf) and some apples are referred to as giants.

Even more delightfully insulting: two varieties of apples clearly refer to age and gender, the Pink Lady or the Bloody Ploughman; the Granny Smith targets seniors.

And what about the names of the baked goods? The tart or the apple turnover. And don't forget the upside-down cake. It's subtle, but if you look closely, you can find the hidden, subliminal, secret language of the apple industry and a clever way to not be politically correct; nobody would suspect apples of carrying sexual messages.

Heirloom apple varieties are sometimes named after bodily imperfections, making subtle references to our flaws—consider the Knobby Russet, recognized by its welts and blemishes. But don't be fooled by the titles and descriptions! These heirloom varieties are absolutely flavourful and bursting with healthy, fruitful, natural elements.

So be sure to attend the fascinating Salt Spring Island Apple Festival in the autumn and taste a "real" apple; you may also be surprised at what you might decipher!

Southern Vancouver Island

Swartz Bay, Victoria, Metchosin, Sooke, Shirley,
Port Renfrew, Pacific Marine Circle Route,
Bamberton, Cowichan Valley, and Spectacle Lake

THE DEEP, RUMBLING FERRY ENGINES BELOW THE DECKS MAKES me feel like I'm being rocked into a gentle sleep, and the journey from the tranquil, unhurried pastoral Gulf Islands to the more populated Vancouver Island offers, without a doubt, an extraordinary experience of inner calm—an in-between place where one is neither here nor there, but rather in a space where place is quite irrelevant, like the moment just before you fall into dreaming. Even though we are in motion, we need not do anything. People pay fortunes for this feeling at very expensive retreats where meditation, de-stressing, and living in the moment often seem to be unreachable goals. For the mere cost of a ferry fare, you may be able to experience such a spiritual awakening!

A sense of place is vital, but it does come with a certain amount of stress. When we are connected to a place, it brings responsibility, an obligation of sorts, and it is very difficult to separate ourselves from our emotional commitments to our home and the place we feel we belong.

The vessels which sail among the Gulf Islands (and to Vancouver Island) are smaller than those colossal four-storied ships emblazoned with Olympic bobsledders (time to change the design— the Olympics were years ago). On these smaller vessels, there are no ferry workers wearing gas masks on two or three cold steel levels directing endless streams of vehicles into numerous dark lanes here, and no massive cafeteria with line-ups winding down the hall and past a gift shop full of turquoise sweatshirts and pink paperweights. The Gulf Island ferries have a mere hot dog counter, which also sells Nanaimo bars, and the ferry travellers are on first names with the vessel's engineer—the captain often says, "Hello folks, sorry for the delay."

Scruffy dogs wearing red bandanas sit in old pickup trucks, their owners heading into town to stock up on supplies.

My favourite little ferry is the *Mayne Queen*. She plows through the churning, turbulent bottle-green seas in all types of weather. When I lived on Galiano Island years ago, I commuted daily one winter, to the university where I was studying. Outside, the dark, pelting winter rains beat against her windows as she tossed on the stormy surf, her engines rumbling below as I struggled with algebra at the little orange Arborite table upstairs in the steamy warmth, the cashier offering to explain the difficult mathematical problems between her minimal sales. Often, there were only a few of us on board. Sometimes the seas were so rough that the toilet water splashed onto the old, blue linoleum floor.

At dawn, she would reliably appear from the cool sea mists under a steel sky, bobbing at the wharf between its dark wooden pilings, ready to embark on another day of chugging gently between the islands, from wharf to wharf, like a loyal, old friend.

In warmer months, the sunsets and sunrises are excruciatingly beautiful, a beauty we may be too distracted or busy to notice when not being transported from one world to another.

The dear *Mayne Queen* is sometimes in use, but she has mainly been replaced by a larger vessel called the *Queen of Cumberland*, which looks to me like the *Starship Enterprise* and has sleek, cream-coloured benches of moulded plastic, a turquoise carpet, and a Plexiglas display of the Cumberland coal mining history. I think on this ferry you can even purchase smokies (a step up from the old hot dogs).

Another way we can look at the ferry excursions is as a tourist. Think of the ferry ride like a cruise but without the endless revolting buffets, has-been entertainers, elderly men wandering about with no purpose in baggy shorts and compression stockings pulled up to their knobbly knees, and the sequined dinners with the captain.

Very occasionally, BC Ferries has an accident. As already mentioned, I can recall when the *Queen of Alberni* went aground on a reef just off Galiano Island, across from Mayne Island, a shallow area home to many sea lions; although there is a green warning beacon on that spot, it is a sharp turn! And another time the *Queen of Nanaimo*, a musty, mid-sized member of the fleet, lost its brakes and plowed through the dock on Mayne Island, crushing the operators' booth like a tin can and making a pile of splinters out of the split pilings.

Docking and disembarking at Swartz Day

If you're coming from one of the Gulf Islands, and not the mainland, it can take you a few moments to adjust to Vancouver Island when the ferry docks at Swartz Bay. First of all, after disembarking, you'll find yourself almost immediately on the highway, with its merging lanes and high speeds, traffic circles and overpasses, and signage that sends you into U-turns or into Sidney. This bombardment can be a bit of a shock if your mind has not yet adapted to a faster pace—it feels as though you have travelled a million miles and that the little Gulf Islands are on the other side of the world.

You might find it more relaxing, and a smoother transition, to begin your journey on the scenic coastal and rural route of Vancouver Island through North Saanich (then a bit beyond, through Central Saanich). If this is the case for you, turn right very soon after you drive out of the ferry compound—you'll see a sign to Lands End Road.

Whenever I disembark from the ferry and drive along the highway, I have a slight pang, a nostalgic ache for my dear old farm on Glamorgan Road, just beyond the terminal, near the airport. There it sits among the hawthorn hedgerows and overgrown grass, across from the crumbling, abandoned Sandown racetrack, it's numerous red tin roofs just barely visible through the tops of the old Garry oaks down Glamorgan Road—those were amazing, surreal days, walking around the farm in my pyjamas at night, checking all the animals and locking in my funny naked-neck chickens, lying in bed on summer evenings listening to the resounding frog chorus below, scratching the hairy, fresh-smelling backs of my wonderful affectionate sows—I try not to look in that direction as I drive towards town.

No matter what the time of year, there always seems to be some kind of construction going on, and the highway is littered with orange cones, barrels, flashing signs and rough-looking flag girls in oversized Day-Glo yellow pants, holding a cigarette in one hand and a SLOW sign in the other. An excavator is always digging somewhere, and meetings are always being held at local municipal halls in protest to the infrastructure changes, and there under the fluorescent lights, late into the night, developers in suits tell the community members in cardigans and corduroys the following:

"I cannot comment until all the numbers come in."

"We cannot provide the numbers until the consultant's report comes in."

"We are being as transparent as possible until we see the report."

"The berm will be a seven-foot-high concrete barrier to address noise concerns, and very few trees will be removed."

"This is something we need to address when we have more information."

"This is the conversation we need to have."

"The public will be informed as we move forward, but we are still waiting for the report."

"We cannot address that issue until we deal with other challenges which have arisen due to the rising cost of sand—we will have the updated cost evaluation shortly."

"We need to consult with our significant partners."

"We need to wait until the consultant's report is completed before we can give you the exact numbers, but we can say that there's no quick fix due to the fluctuating world markets."

"We will look at optional resources due to the unstable prices of raw materials in China—we may have to look to Poland; they've been excellent partners in the past with projects such as the BC Ferries."

And so it goes.

So, you may prefer to take the scenic route into town along West Saanich Road rather than to navigate the ever-changing highway infrastructure, although the rural community is not without its own controversies, such as the sludge transport and biosolids consultants' reports on the cabbage fields.

"They do it in China!" shout the proponents.

"What about the pharmaceuticals?" the naysayers shout back.

Then there's the looming threat of jam inspection by government officials on roadside stands, compost odours, and manure management.

In summer, the fertile, black earth of the Saanich Peninsula produces a rolling tapestry of purples and greens, and in the autumn, it's a patchwork of orange. Winter on the peninsula fields is often overlooked, but it is equally beautiful, if not more so—under the low winter clouds, acres of sleeping, rain-soaked land stubbly with crop remnants, old rotting stems and leaves, sinking back into the pooling furrows, dotted with migrating snow geese, resting their tired wings.

Victoria

I live in the historic and rather quirky neighbourhood of James Bay in downtown Victoria, near the sea where I walk my dog Archie along the beaches and say good morning to the eight oystercatchers who pick at morsels off the seaweed-covered rocks at low tide with their wonderful orange beaks. We often walk to Clover Point along the vast, grassy dog-allowed areas where Archie meets his friends: Cosmo, Cyrus, Fig, Toad, Rascal, and Hazel. (Hazel has three legs—she was a rescue dog from Kuwait and she has issues). On most days we pick up garbage on the beach—bits of plastic, bottle tops, cigarette lighters, half-chewed flip-flops, and deflated balloons on strings wound around the piles of entwined beached kelp.

One day I had a battle over a condom with an aggressive seagull; he wouldn't let go, and neither would I (perhaps he thought it was a delicious worm of sorts). Well, I finally relented and let the gull discover his disgusting and very grave mistake. You may be interested to know that the object in question stretched to a lengthy three feet or more.

I have never found a treasure on the beach, only some barnacle-encrusted dentures (uppers, I think), and a very strange message in a Chinese medicine bottle.

Sometimes I walk through Beacon Hill Park without Archie, just for a peaceful, reflective stroll. Here, there's a wise old resident owl who conceals himself in the high, shadowy branches in the woods. There are also the two eagles seen gazing out at the Strait of Juan de Fuca from the heights of the world's fourth-tallest freestanding totem pole, carved by the esteemed Kwakiutl tribal chief and renowned carver Mungo Martin and first erected in 1956. Restored in 2001 and repainted in 2011, the Story Pole, as it's known, is a famous Victoria landmark.

James Bay is Victoria's oldest neighbourhood and is known for its vibrant and decorative Victorian gingerbread-style houses, with their widow's walks and leaded windows. There's the iconic retro stucco Surf Motel on Dallas Road, the lighthouse at the end of Ogden Point, and the great concrete gunneries embedded into the sea wall which, at a high tide and on a stormy day, takes the volatile rhythmic slaps and hammering of the sea and sprays it over the turquoise cement railing and onto the road above.

The gem of the city, in my view, is the Legislative Building, especially at night when all its domes and balconies are alight; it looks like a giant, glittering palace with its lights reflected on the still, dark waters of the Inner Harbour.

At Christmas, the harbour is especially stunning with moored vessels of all shapes and sizes decorated with strings of colourful lights; if there happens to be a rare dusting of snow, the scene is absolutely breathtaking.

Every morning (after I walk with Archie on the beach) I walk along the Inner Harbour on the lower causeway to work; I teach English at a little language school downtown. The walk along the Inner Harbour is a wonderful stroll that takes me past bobbing boats and neatly pruned trees and box hedges.

A year ago I wrote to my mayor and city council about trash floating in the harbour's water. "It doesn't look good," I said, and about a month later, I received a very pleasant, lengthy, and informative letter back from the Harbour Authority. They gave me such a positive response about my concern; it may be my imagination, but from that day forward, I was sure there was less rubbish, plastic debris, and coffee cups floating out there among the docks and lapping up against the algae-covered stone wall. At low tide you can even see crabs crawling around in the mud. I also asked the city if it was really necessary for the worker to use a noisy, intrusive, fuel-spewing leaf blower to push two leaves and a cigarette butt the whole length of the causeway when a broom and dustpan would suffice. "It's so inefficient," I said, and lo and behold, the next week, there was a city worker using a broom in the Inner Harbour!

Although Victoria is my home—I've already written about my love of this city in *Hometown: Out and About in Victoria's Neighbourhoods*—I also love to venture farther afield to the outer rural areas, farmers' markets, hiking trails, and wilderness parks as I meander up the Island to explore its many communities and unique landscapes.

Two of my favourite nearby country excursions are to Metchosin and Sooke, so let's begin our journey there. These are two communities near Victoria; they're quite easy to reach—unless you embark at rush hour, in which case you'll be stuck in what's known locally as the Colwood Crawl. This takes place on the stretch of highway between Victoria (in the vicinity of the Victoria General Hospital) and the suburb of Colwood. I find venturing along this road is best done at five in the morning.

But once you make it through the new overpass construction, and masses of new wood-beamed and grey shingled houses high on the rocky ridges scarred with the vertical inlays from blasting through the land, past the strip malls, fast-food outlets, and car showrooms, you could turn left to the rural community of Metchosin, just a few minutes along, or veer right to the village of Sooke, approximately thirty minutes farther.

Metchosin

The name Metchosin is a rough translation from the Coast Salish word pronounced *smets-shosin*, meaning "place of stinking fish." The accepted story is that the stinking fish in question was in fact a deceased whale that had washed up on the shore.

Metchosin is delightfully rural and is seldom embroiled in any political disputes seen in numerous other municipalities—one of its most controversial issues was parking at the local trail to the beach. The community consists of small farms, many fronting the sea, and is home to many potters. Once a year, Metchosin puts on a pottery event called Fired Up! Held at the Metchosin Community Hall, this event is more than a showcase for moulded, amateur ceramic knick-knacks depicting donkeys pulling wagons or smiling, freckle-cheeked children—it is a full-on professional display of spectacular skill, design, and craftsmanship. These potters are artists well known for their distinct work, each item revealing exquisitely detailed texture and painstaking skill in glaze application and pottery technique.

Fired Up! has a new theme every year—for example, a few years ago, the pottery was created by the five-hundred-year-old method of salt firing, and in 2018 the theme was "Coastal Vessels—Romancing the Sea."

> Salt-fired pottery is a very old process dating back to the 1400s; it involves applying salt to the clay stoneware as it reaches extreme heat within the kiln where temperatures as high as 1,200 °C are achieved. The process originated in Germany and spread globally, including to England where the method was incorporated at the Royal Doulton factories.
>
> The salt gives the pottery a unique and sometimes glossy texture resembling an orange peel and the earthy colours of chocolates, creams, ochres, and—depending on mineral content of the clay—deep blues or purples.
>
> The salt-firing process has been largely discontinued within modern mass-production, although it is thought that India still uses the method to fire its sewer pipes.

After you view the beautiful unique pottery, you might like to visit My Chosen Café in the heart of the community. This is a popular spot—people drive out from town to eat there, and on a Sunday, the parking lot is jammed. I once had the most delicious, immense piece of layered carrot cake with thick cream cheese icing after a hike around nearby Matheson Lake.

If you are able to walk after your snack, amble through a serene wooded path down to the sea at Witty's Lagoon Park (on the main road leading to Metchosin). The park is diverse, and one of the main features is the so-called sitting lady waterfall. Believe it or not, the spewing rapids do indeed resemble an elegant sitting lady, though her hips are a bit wide, as if she were wearing a dress from the 1700s—depending on the flow of water, she at times seems to have bare knees.

The trail continues through towering maples, firs, and cedars and arrives at the lagoon surrounded by crimson and burnt-orange grasses, shrubs, and ancient fruit trees.

Farther along is the salt marsh. Washed by the sea, it is covered with two important plants with rather unattractive names: the glasswort and the dodder. Their names may be homely and clumsy sounding, but they are crucial as a feeding ground for many little marine creatures and for seabirds, especially during migration periods.

Finally, you will reach the beach! This is the destination, the wild storm-bruised sandy beach, churned and constantly rebuilt and rolled by turbulent and unrelenting ocean storms, currents, and winds, vulnerable to the open sea that lies just around the corner.

Sooke

An easy forty-minute drive west of Victoria will bring you to the community of Sooke (some would call it a village, others would call it a town, but either way it's growing). You may want to simply pass through on the way to the Island's west coast where, at the end of the road, you can have a drink at the Renfrew Pub, explore the tidal pools at Botanical Beach, or, if you're ambitious, fit, and well-prepared, hike the West Coast Trail.

Sooke feels like the last bastion of civilization before you enter the wilds where storms at sea come up hard against the rocky shores and coastal brush; where towering old-growth forests loom on the country's western shores; and where being medevacked out above a voracious, volatile, steel-grey surf is a common occurrence, usually due to an overturned kayak or a broken leg snagged on a tree root along coastal wooded paths.

If you want adventure but aren't quite up for challenging your survival skills, Sooke has an abundance of tame and lovely natural areas to hike, picnic, kayak, photograph, and explore on horseback. There is birdwatching, swimming, and just about anything else relaxing that you would like to do, including visiting Jeff and Jessica Abel's Saltwest Naturals, an artisanal facility that desalinates locally sourced ocean water to create pure sea salt for culinary use and more.

Saltwest is tucked away on a quiet, nondescript, paved road a few kilometres out of Sooke, off Otter Point Road, and has a small parking area. The buildings that comprise the different stages of the operation are small wooden structures. Trees surround the property, and feral cats peer from the scrub.

To retrieve the ocean water, Saltwest owner and salt artisan Jeff drives to the nearby shore with a tank on the back of his truck; from this water the salt is extracted, crystallizing the very basis of this intriguing operation. The only facility of its kind in Canada, Saltwest makes products both for your cocktails and for your aching muscles. It even offers purified, salt-free drinking water.

Jeff and Jess offer tours Tuesdays to Saturdays between April and October, happily showing off their sun houses, where solar heat is used in the evaporation process, and the back room, where local herbs and botanicals are mixed to create lovely flavoured salts such as Smashed Peppercorn, Rosemary Sage, and Applewood Smoked. It's literally a hands-on operation, as Jeff demonstrated during my tour while scooping up a handful of pristine sea salt in a huge vat, halfway through the transitioning process.

After my satisfying visit, Jeff and Jessica walked me to the parking lot, where we chatted for a few minutes like old friends. When I noticed one of the feral cats, Jeff told me that the cats don't accept canned food but prefer to forage like the wild little creatures they are; however, in the raw, dismal winters, they never turn down his offering of a dry bed in his various sheltered outbuildings tucked away in other areas of his large property.

I went home with some Raincoast Tree Hugger bath salts as gifts for my friends Geoff, Liz, and Tess, who work tirelessly on their farm in Saanich; they need a soak after a day of loading hundreds of bales of hay into the barn loft, shoeing horses, or harvesting garlic.

Sooke has an abundance of creative enterprises: a jewellery shop that designs and creates stunning silver fishing lures with First Nations symbols; a grocery store that sells homemade jams; local entrepreneurs who create socks, blankets, and hats from llama wool; artisans who brew mead and make sushi by hand. At Wild Hill Botanicals, you can find beautiful, natural skin products. (I use the nighttime eye cream and the coconut bath powder, which smells delicious enough to eat—I don't know if the cream makes my face look younger, but the routine helps me believe I'm under sixty. The Wild Hill Vanilla and Almond Lip Balm is equally delicious!) Farther down the road, gin is uniquely distilled with kelp and seaweed. And Sooke even has a theatre and its own philharmonic orchestra.

A long time ago, I visited a llama farm in the Sooke area. My friend and I drove up a long gravel lane with vast, grassy meadows on each side enclosed by split-rail fences and a tangle of blackberry and wild rose hedges with tufts of brown wool clinging to the brambles. There was a small white house in the clearing, and an old weathered barn out back, surrounded by a large paddock. There the elegant llamas stood, regal, heads held high and confident, nostrils flared, staring down their camel-like noses at us, almost as if they resented our presence. They were not friendly but were snobbish, and one spat a slimy, grassy spitball the size of a grapefruit in my direction from about twenty feet—reputedly a sign of dislike and disgust. Llamas are strange creatures; they always look as if they are in shock. They ride in the back seats of minivans and unfold like wooden chairs when they exit, then confidently swish and swagger around the Saanich Fairgrounds on rhinestone leashes. In competition, they tackle obstacle courses; many of them seem to be knock-kneed or pigeon-toed and have brown teeth.

Despite the unwelcome at the llama farm, I purchased a winter toque for Mum to keep her vulnerable little head warm in the cruel and bitter New Brunswick winter. It was the thickest and softest wool I have ever touched, and it wasn't cheap! Mum loved that hat—I would say that it was probably the best gift I ever gave her in my life. When she became very elderly and frail and lived on Priestman Street at the Veterans Health Unit in Fredericton, I would take her for little outings to Odell Park or a drive up the frozen river under a big blue cold sky. She'd wear her little red coat from Zellers and some old threadbare mittens, and before leaving her bedroom, she'd say, "Where's my llama hat? I need my llama hat." I'd find it in her closet, behind the bottle of vermouth.

That hat not only kept her warm, but it also acted as a security blanket of sorts. I like to think that maybe it was because I gave it to her—perhaps, for her, it was a connection to me. I believe we were a little detached but connected at the same time, mainly with our shared sense of humour and love of animals. For me, my connection to Mum could be seen in a selection of drawings and watercolours she did of my dear pets and rescued creatures when she was able to visit my farm, before she became too feeble or nervous to travel out west. (Mum would not accept assistance from Air Canada and would often say, "I don't trust those fly girls." I have noticed, however, in the last ten years or so, that the assistance in airports has very much improved.)

Sooke Potholes Provincial Park and East Sooke Regional Park

Two of the most spectacular natural sites in Sooke are the Sooke Potholes Provincial Park and, farther down on the coast, East Sooke Regional Park.

The potholes are a pleasant stroll up a lovely path through a sun-filtered wood. They are exactly what the name suggests: large hollows, carved-out rock formations and boulders formed by glacial action many years ago. Now they are full of crystal-clear water that gushes down from the Sooke Hills above in elegant waterfalls before forming the Sooke River; it's a fine spawning ground for salmon below the holes.

The potholes are separated by little beaches and clearings and large rock slabs that provide ideal places to picnic and sunbathe, and to dry off after a refreshing dip. Use caution! Occasionally the potholes are the sad scenes of tragedy; people have fallen or dived to disaster.

Farther along the trail, now gated and no longer accessible, was the site of Leechtown, the original small settlement of men who had dreams of finding gold. Logging was also practised in Leechtown, but only a few rusted remnants exist now, buried under the grass and disintegrating back into the earth.

The flora in these sensitive woods include the endangered Sierra Wood Fern which is on the Province's "Red List." The Red, Yellow, and Blue lists are conservation status rankings that classify plants and animals: Red indicates a serious risk of being lost; Blue is vulnerable; and Yellow is a lower risk.

The classification, status, and glossary of our ecosystems and all its species are massive but extremely informative and can be perused on the BC Conservation Data Centre website.

Below the Sooke Potholes and the river, down on the coast, is East Sooke Park. The park is 3,512 acres and is connected from one end to the other by a magnificent coastal path, which you can hike in approximately six or seven hours. I embarked on this day hike recently on a spectacular day with a huge clear blue sky. The warm sun beamed between the grand firs, and the ocean sparkled. Whales breached in the distance, and sea lions glided along the shore in and out of the kelp beds.

But be warned, the trail is rugged; on the day I hiked the trail, one participant hurt her ankle and had to be driven out. It's an up-and-down climb but with plenty of beautiful spots to rest—warm, sloping rock faces, little crystal bays in which to wade and cool your feet, pebble beaches where you can relax with your thermos of tea, and grassy clearings under a canopy of arbutus. If you travel with a Capital Regional District (CRD) guide, you will learn a variety of historic facts on mining, Indigenous fishing techniques, and how to identify an endangered slug or salamander. She will point out lichens, bear excrement (called scat), and a strange fungus that looks like a massive soggy cauliflower—and you will even have a chance to taste delicious salal berries.

Having praised the wonders of this hike (I read in a piece of literature that it is one of British Columbia's best day hikes), I must add that, for few days after, I could barely walk.

If lichen is present, the air is clean. Many of our forest and coastal lichens are very sensitive to air pollution and are, therefore, used to assess air quality due to their responses to airborne contaminants. There are approximately twenty thousand types of lichen. You may see the dry, rough grey-green species clinging to the gnarled bare branches on the edge of the woods—some people call these the "old man's beard." (The lichen is probably cleaner than a real old man's beard!)

There are two entrances to East Sooke Park; the most popular is at the old Aylard Farm, at the end closest to Victoria. There are no ancient farm buildings remaining, but you can tell it was a lovely pastoral homestead at one time. Being a Capital Regional District (CRD) park, there are plenty of signage and parking. The map of East Sooke Park is full of beautiful coastal and woodland trails, hikes up hills to breath-taking views, and peaceful mossy enclaves. There are historical sites such as miners' cabins and remnants of the first pioneers who attempted to settle on this harsh land. Even today it is thick with drooping cedars, dense underbrush, and bogs of skunk cabbage—drenched in the winter rains, whipped by the bitter sea storms.

One of the unique sites is the petroglyph carved onto the weathered boulder sitting impassively by the sea, pounded over time by the winds and salt spray; the lovely simple engraving is of a plump seal and can be seen after a short stroll across the meadow and along the beautiful coastal path that passes little sandy coves and windswept native shrubbery.

Petroglyphs are engravings onto rock, and pictographs are rock paintings. Both are enchanting. Numerous petroglyphs can be visited on other parts of the island.

The CRD watershed tour in Sooke

For many years I wanted to take the CRD (Capital Regional District) watershed tour, offered at no charge to the public in the early summer months.

I had taken an impressive CRD tour of the Hartland Landfill site in Saanich a few years previously, before environmental concerns were as well-known as they are today. We used to call a landfill a garbage dump, and that's exactly what it was—a dump. In the sixties, when we lived in New Brunswick, Dad loved rummaging through the garbage dumps in the country and often took me along to withering, gnarled apple orchards and abandoned disintegrating homesteads in search of treasure; indeed, he rescued and restored many pieces of antique furniture, leaded windows, bread bins, bottles, and even picture frames from the weathered farmsteads which were slowly returning into the earth. I still have an old stuffed bear I found under the brambles on one of Dad's excursions.

But today, landfill sites are a compilation of recycling areas, reclaimed wetlands, lakes, and hills of greenery. On the CRD landfill tour in Saanich, we were taken by bus up and over a man-made landscape of thriving native trees and shrubbery constructed out of treated trash. I was awestruck at the number of redwing blackbirds singing among the bulrushes planted on the many constructed ponds. Even the methane and other gases released in the treatment processes are diverted to create energy to nearby communities.

The watershed tours consist of lovely leisurely bus rides through the Sooke Hills to the lakes, dams, and spillways that provide Victoria with our beautiful clean drinking water. The vast area is a protected watershed that includes supply facilities and, therefore, is restricted to the public; it was an eye-opener both visually and in terms of knowledge gained.

The Sooke water system was constructed in 1915. Previously water had been pumped into town from Elk and Beaver Lake, now a popular recreational area, but there were numerous problems with the water—tadpoles, for one—which flowed through old wooden pipes.

The water from the Sooke Hills now serves 350,000 residents, and thanks to the abundant protected forest, their water is completely and naturally filtered.

The tour I embarked upon was called "Behind the Red Gate," one of the CRD's "Get to Know Your H_2O" offerings. Our keen and jovial little group—mostly elderly or retired men in Tilley hats and sensible shoes, a few with binoculars—met at the CRD Field Office parking lot at 2955 Sooke Lake Road, where we were greeted by our young, tanned, and enthusiastic guides. They were wearing hiking shorts and sporting ponytails sticking out from under their blue CRD caps like professional tennis players.

We boarded an old school bus that smelled of mild disinfectant and had windows that were a struggle to open, but it was serene and very calming sitting there on a worn seat of green, cracked vinyl, with my camera on my lap, as we drove at a snail's pace into the restricted area beyond the red gate and into the deep purple forested hills rising in layers in the distance. The calming effect of tours is in knowing that, for that time, you are free of responsibility—you only need to sit back and gain knowledge and look at the scenery. How restful!

En route, as the old bus made its way along a dirt road, we passed an abundance of beautiful wildflower meadows, where, from behind a rotting stump, appeared a curious bear.

We disembarked at two dam sites and strolled across the immaculate walkway on the top, where the crystal-clear lake lapped the side of the clean white concrete on one side while the overflow trickled over the man-made spillway on the other, gently replenishing the rivers and forest vegetation. The spillways were intriguing, impressively constructed to look natural—granite pools and bubbling brooks lined with daisies, lilies, and columbines, sloping stone banks of moss, sedums, and ferns—and were so cleverly built to divert the overflow into the natural rivers that run through the forest that I would even say they surpassed Mother Nature in beauty and efficiency. Not all that Mother Nature creates is as spectacular as depicted in a Disney movie; in fact, she can be ugly—even repulsive and, at times, cruel. And so, sometimes, we can help her create a richer and more beautiful, beneficial landscape with a little care, planning, and innovation.

We visited an abandoned caretaker's cottage belonging to a fellow who'd been tasked with guarding the new water containment area one hundred years ago. The slowly disintegrating log and board and batten cabin sat in a grassy clearing among the sweet-smelling pines overlooking the sparkling lake, its weathered roof covered in moss, the glass in the window frames long ago broken. The caretaker lived there year-round with his wife and young daughter, and so serious was his task of protecting the watershed that, if the daughter were to have a young guest stay, permission was required from the authorities. The family was strictly prohibited from swimming in the water, destined to be ingested by the population in the growing town of Victoria over the hills and beyond.

The Sooke Hills water we use in Victoria is treated. (Sometimes, when I am sitting in my bath, I am sure I can smell bleach). Our water is indeed disinfected by three methods: by ultraviolet light, by the addition of chlorine, and/or by a combination of chlorine and ammonia. This is a necessity as bacteria, mainly from wildlife debris, is present in the watershed. However, no fertilizers, chemicals, or pesticides are deployed in the forest or water facility. The CRD often takes great pains to protect and sustain the creatures and flora in these hills, including relocating beavers, removing invasive species, and carefully monitoring forest-fire potential.

> Through testing at the CRD laboratories, minuscule traces of copper, mercury, and arsenic have been detected in our water—but they are at levels far, far below hazardous amounts for human consumption.

The CRD strongly encourages us to conserve water—after all, we only have this wonderful lake. Their two major concerns are toilets and garden sprinklers, so keep your toilet running well, and limit your sprinkler activity. Speaking of toilets, specifically the low-flush variety: They work well and, true to their claim, use very little water; when you flush, I find it off-putting. I always wonder how so little water can take away more than its weight, more than its water displacement. I hope the pipes are not going to back up one day from such a minimal usage of water to push away the you-know-what!

The Sooke Hills Wilderness Trail

Just in time for summer, a wonderful new hiking/cycling trail was unveiled in 2017, linking the Sooke Hills area to the Lake Cowichan–Shawnigan Lake Trans Canada Trail to the north. The distance is thirteen kilometres and begins at the Humpback Reservoir (park at the Mount Wells Regional Park's main parking lot). With a forty-one-metre-long suspension bridge (near the beginning of the trail) that crosses over the Goldstream River, the trail crosses over part of the restricted area in the Sooke Hills Watershed.

One breezy, crisp autumn day, I walked a good length of this trail, feeling patriotic as I reflected on how it links both the west and east coasts. I wondered whether anyone would ever walk the entire length of Canada this way. Meandering under the quivering golden leaves streaked by the sunlight, it was like walking right into a painting of the Annunciation with the beams of light shimmering from heaven upon a pensive, humble Mary draped in her grey robes. The impeccably groomed trail made for an easy amble, with a variety of wooded landscapes, waterfalls, the old unused railway track, split-rail fencing, wildflowers, and the dim, pungent rainforest. At the suspension bridge, I turned back, satisfied that I had walked on a section of our great Canadian trail.

Fuel up!

Before heading farther west, top up your fuel in downtown Sooke at the Petro-Canada at the intersection of Otter Point and Sooke Road; it'll be your last chance for gas for 128 kilometres—you'll even see a sign saying so.

On the other side of Sooke, on the way to Port Renfrew, are several delightful surprises—especially if you enjoy local honey, lighthouses, camping in lovely West Coast landscapes, exploring magical tidal pools, and more.

Tugwell Creek Honey Farm & Meadery

The first meadery in Western Canada was established in 2003, just beyond Sooke, in a little community called Tugwell Creek. Bob Liptrot, expert beekeeper and mead producer, loves his bees and is devoted to his one hundred hives, which sit among the long grasses and wildflowers in his rolling meadows and fruit orchards. Bob has been working with bees since the tender age of six, which I find utterly endearing. The study of bees (both wild and domesticated), honey, mead production, and the extensive (and often neglected) history of flowers and pollination has been Bob's lifelong work.

When you visit Tugwell Creek Meadery, you will learn not only what mead consists of and how it tastes, but also how we all are connected to the earth's flora and fauna, dating back millennia, and how bees became essential in our development, linking humankind with food.

The Tugwell Creek Meadery is very accessible and has a thorough, informative website. Self-guided tours can be taken most days in the afternoons; Bob's mornings are full of chores and tasks, as well as nurturing his beloved bees, who are up early collecting pollen and nectar from the farm's flowers and fruit trees and the wild wood and meadows beyond which are rich in wild plants and blossoms.

The entrance to the farm and meadery is a typical rural scene: a winding gravel driveway up a slope that reveals a fruit orchard on one side, followed by a spacious pen of busy ducks and geese honking and quacking and pecking at their food; on the other side are the rolling, grassy meadows so typical of the area. At the top of the driveway is the meadery shop, a simple but beautiful wooden structure. Then there's the core of the whole enterprise: the hives, set a little farther down, surrounded by lavender shrubs, away from us humans and our interactions.

Due to my severe bee sting allergy, I cautiously restricted my tour, but between Bob's wonderful descriptions and pictorial charts, and our viewing of the operation from a short distance— observing each little dedicated bee performing its own specific job—it was clear that the mead and honey operation was a meticulous labour of love, devotion, and care for how we must behave with our valuable bees and plants. Despite the fact that one bee sting could swiftly end my life, bees—and the lovely people who care for them—are my heroes (hence the dedication at the beginning of this book). Visit the Tugwell Creek Meadery, and it will give you a new, compassionate perspective on humanity and our interaction with nature.

Most hives on Vancouver Island house the European honeybee, but there are over seven hundred species of bees, seven of which are bumblebees indigenous to Vancouver Island. Sadly, the wild bumblebee population is declining in many parts of the world; this is very bad news because bees not only give us honey, but also pollinate plants—edible plants, vegetation that creatures need to consume, orchards, and flowers. Bumblebees are especially beneficial pollinators due to their physical ability to reach deeply into a plant, deeper than the honeybee.

Honeybee and bumblebee conservation aside, you can't beat the quality of locally made honey and mead. The history and crafting of mead is fascinating in and of itself, but even more compelling is that Tugwell Creek Honey Farm & Meadery keeps bees who produce the honey for the mead.

The three types of honey produced at Tugwell are displayed in the lovely tasting room, on a clean polished counter constructed from reclaimed wood. The palest golden honey is from fireweed, a tall slender elegant wildflower that prefers to grow in disturbed land among the stumps, gravel, and brush of a logged hillside; we can also see an abundance of fireweed after a forest fire. The other honeys that bees produce are 'wildflower,' and the darkest of all, a rich ochre treacle known as 'field blossom.' According to Bob, bees do not have a strong preference for colours or specific flora—they select the easiest and closest source.

Tasting the mead was a delightful and delicious experience. As I indulged, Bob shared a wealth of historical facts about the history of alcohol: how sweet alcohol from the European north came to mix with the dry alcohol of the southern peoples due to exploration and the mixing of cultures, and how medicinal plants were incorporated in wines and the how the *Apis* (which is to say bees) became vegetarians. I was intrigued to learn that, at one time, there were very few flowers on our planet.

Bob brews metheglin, a traditional medicinal mead made from wildflower honey and ginger; he also offers a fortified berry mead named Mad Marion. I took home a bottle of Solstice Metheglin; the label described it as "from bee to bottle," and "spirited, with a hint of ginger and spice," which sounded very robust and warming—perfect after a medieval winter jousting match or when washing down a huge turkey drumstick while sitting beside a towering, elaborate iron candlestick in the great dining hall of some lofty lord. As wintry as the Solstice Metheglin sounded, I drank a mugful of the mead at a sweltering summer barbecue, and it was wonderfully refreshing over ice. Curiously, I not only tasted the kiss of the ginger, but also the smooth undertones of honey. Drinking it, I felt like Anne Boleyn (before she met her demise, of course).

Deserving of special mention is Tugwell's Kilt Twister, a unique mead created with honey, heather, and hops. This remarkable Scottish mead concoction is based on a legendary secret recipe for mead produced by the Picts, the ancient people of the Scottish Highlands. The beverage was said to impart great strength for attacks and invasions.

When the Celts invaded, they demanded the recipe, but to no avail; in the ensuing battle for the special brew, the recipe was lost, perhaps destroyed.

But today it has been revisited. Inspired by the medieval days of chivalry and celebrations following a jousting match, this historic beverage—made with local honey from happy, unstressed bees who forage in the wild meadows and forest glades from clean, unsprayed wild flora at the Tugwell Creek Honey Farm & Meadery—is yours for the tasting. Mead has been reputed from the time of Julius Caesar to be an aphrodisiac; in fact, the etymology of the word *honeymoon* hearkens back to the pagan tradition of drinking mead for the month following a wedding ceremony, so if ancient lore is to be believed, your fertility, if not your vitality, could very well be enhanced!

Shirley and the Sheringham Point Lighthouse

The drive west along the coast from the Tugwell Creek Meadery towards Port Renfrew is rugged, slow-paced, and wonderfully, wildly scenic. The shoreline gradually becomes more treacherous, the winds and surf more obvious, and the rock formations more ominous. Many a ship has met its demise along this coast, and the wrecks become more numerous as you round the tip of the Island. (You can visit numerous memorials and remnants of the wrecks in the Pacific Rim National Park Reserve, near Tofino and Ucluelet.)

The drive will take you through various little communities so small they can be missed if you blink. Shirley is one such nook, with its fire hall and the enchanting, delightful (and busy!) Shirley Delicious Café. There you can munch on house-made corn fritters, pumpkin muffins, and, as the server proudly declared, "the best sausage rolls in the world!"

My friend Lynn tells me there used to be a sign on the road that read ENTERING SHIRLEY. Road construction signage that immediately followed was equally amusing: PLEASE SLOW DOWN.

Lynn also recalled a time when her young son was to stay with her parents in Shirley for an evening while she and her husband went to Victoria for a night on the town. Her parents lived across a little wooden bridge, which, on this particular evening, could not be crossed by a car or by foot, as it was under repair. So one of the big, burly construction workers carried her young boy across the bridge to his waiting grandparents.

I would love to think that such a kind and innocent gesture is possible today, without fear (from either parents or workers) of inappropriate behaviour or accusations thereof. It seems to me that in dear little Shirley, a place so community minded, this kind of act is still possible—when the need arises, someone offers a unique and helpful solution, with kindness the sole objective.

The Sheringham Point Lighthouse, less than a ten-minute drive from the café, was built in 1912 and is one of twenty-one heritage lighthouses in the province. At one time manned, it guided and warned many a vessel entering the Strait of Juan de Fuca for more than seventy-seven years before it became automated.

Lighthouses evoke such romance, such rhythm and stability. They are a sign of life and assistance in a winter sea storm, the security of help, of solace, of location, as if it whispers, "I'm here, do not worry." But so many of our coastal lighthouses are becoming weary, rusted relics, abandoned and forgotten, their beacons fading, their red tops turning an aged, flaking brown, and their little salt-sprayed windows broken, the glass lying in the encroaching grass and weeds.

But there are angels looking out for the elegant but weather-beaten Sheringham. A donation of over half a million dollars was recently made to restore the lighthouse, which is watched over by group of concerned citizens whose aim it is to preserve, protect, and share this piece of maritime history.

The lighthouse sits, unyielding, on two hectares, where the Salish Sea meets the great Pacific. It is easy to find for a visit, a Little Think or stroll, a picnic, or a fabulous photograph. The view is spectacular—even "jaw-dropping," says John Walls, a member of the preservation society's board.

Canada's many heritage lighthouses are now protected by the Heritage Lighthouse Protection Act. First introduced by late senator Mike Forrestall of Nova Scotia in 2000, it was then re-introduced in 2006 by our own retired senator Pat Carney; the act, after re-readings, amendments, and other delays, was finally approved in 2008.

The act was triggered by a group of concerned citizens from Nova Scotia—the province with the most lighthouses—who, in 1999, became concerned that the many abandoned or neglected structures were doomed for demolition. Their concerns became a national effort to protect these beautiful and elegant crumbling relics. The act is easy and clear to read and begins with an almost moving, dignified preamble which honours our lighthouses, but touches on a human chord as well: "Whereas lighthouses have long graced our rugged coastlines and majestic shores, providing and symbolizing direction, hope, and safe harbour to generations of mariners . . ."

Camping and hiking

Beyond the town of Sooke there is much more to experience, such as the various parks and campsites along the shores and throughout the forests on the drive to Port Renfrew. Very popular is French Beach, followed by the Juan de Fuca Provincial Park, which include several beautiful beaches, hikes, and campsites, beginning with China Beach. What makes this area so popular with walkers, hikers, birdwatchers, campers, and nature lovers of all sorts is not only its sheer beauty and easy access, but the diversity of the landscape, which includes unexpected and mystical grottos, caves, and waterfalls. (I love the ambience of the word *grottos*—it always makes me think of elderly Italian artists sitting with glasses of red wine and plates of olives.) There's an end-of-the-road feeling here, a romantic sense that we are nearing the end shores of our immense country; there's something magical about dipping your toes into these waters.

French Beach—named after the Canadian pioneer James French, who settled in the area in 1885—is a lovely combination of sand and pebble; open year-round, it's a popular place to spend the day paddling, picnicking, strolling, or camping. Small campfires are usually permitted, but at certain times of the year, there may be fire bans, so it's important to check online for current bans or restrictions. Also, you must only burn wood that you've purchased: collecting beach or forest wood could land you a fine. Environmentally speaking, it is crucial to not disturb the forest floor by removing nutrients such as wood and brush debris, as they not only serve as a soil conditioner, but also as habitat and a food source for many creatures. Dead wood is a vital part of the forest food web.

If you are a strong hiker, you can walk the Juan de Fuca Marine Trail from China Beach all the way to Botanical Beach—a distance of forty-seven more kilometres—with opportunities to camp along the way. There are four trailheads with parking that allow you access to the trail: They are (from east to west) China Beach, Sombrio Beach, Parkinson Creek, and Botanical Beach, but there are also campsites available along the trail between these points.

Second-growth forests are defined as forested land that has regrown after the removal of trees, either by logging or forest fires. The most common second-growth trees you will walk among along the Juan de Fuca trail are Sitka spruce, western redcedar, Douglas fir and western hemlock.

> A nurse log is a fallen tree (or limb) left to break down on the forest floor among other woodland debris such as fungi, lichen, fruit, seeds, animal excrement, coniferous brush, mosses and leaves; it serves as a 'nurse,' or host for countless flora and fauna in the forest.

Seabirds

The parks along the Juan de Fuca Strait are home to abundant seabirds. One of the most interesting is the common murre, a black and white bird about the size of a crow; it paddles and swims to its migration grounds in the north, where it feasts on small fish such as herring.

The murre's wings are short, so flying is a bit of an effort; still, somehow it can fly to a rocky ledge and lay its one blue egg. It is believed the murre was given its name from the purring or murmuring sound it makes.

A few years ago, I came to love the ducks and seabirds along our shores. When Mum and Dad were frail and heading towards their maker back in Fredericton, I travelled back and forth to be with them and to do what needs doing when our parents near their final days. It was a strange time, a time of great reflection, and I found it profoundly helpful to take long beach walks and be with the seabirds who were there every day. I especially loved the six oystercatchers who made a peeping sound as they flew from one rockweed-covered islet to the next, and the two mergansers, the ducks with the swept-back hairstyles, who quietly paddled along the shoreline below the great sand cliffs of broom, gorse, and wild fennel, and the dear and beautifully marked wood ducks who visit every winter before leaving in the spring to travel inland where they will breed in the forest.

I must mention the rotund little buffleheads as well, who were tossed among the golden ochre globes of kelp in the waves, waiting for a few morsels brought in by the tides. To say that these creatures were my friends is too much of a cliché; I did not need friends, but rather quiet reflection, routine, and stability. In times of stress—or even in calm times—routine is a grand security blanket; it's something steady, a reliability.

If on a given day these lovely, peaceful, charming seabirds were not there, or if there were one or two less, I panicked, worrying that they had met their demise somehow. Happily, they always returned within a few days, bobbing once again in the grey-green surf or flying briskly in their small flock against the white winter sky.

The grey whale migration

Another rhythm of nature—an impressive, enormous one—is the annual grey whale migration. These massive filter feeders, baleen whales, make the trek from the warm breeding grounds off Mexico to the cold feeding grounds in the Bering Sea; this is known to be the longest migration of any animal at more than twenty thousand kilometres return. If you happen to be in the Pacific Rim National Park Reserve in March, you might see these immense but graceful transients travelling northward; Tofino and Ucluelet hold a lively festival to honour and celebrate the great journey. The majestic, dignified creatures then make the return journey south in the fall.

Grey whales can reach a weight of forty tons and may live to seventy years old. When observing them with binoculars, you may see the numerous white patches and blemishes on these whales' bodies. These are either parasites or other small sea creatures, such as barnacles, who have decided to make a whale's back their home.

I have never paid to go whale-watching but rather chose to experience the whales naturally and respectfully from a distance. I saw them once from the trail in East Sooke Park; far off in the haze, their sprays and splashes rose in the mist, and even though the sight was minuscule, it took my breath away. Sometimes we do not need to be right next to greatness to feel it; a small glimpse is equally awe-inspiring, a tease of sorts. I'm sure the whales prefer it that way, too.

> Did you know that the man for whom the Strait of Juan de Fuca was named was actually a Greek born in 1536? His real name was Ioannis Phokas, but he worked for Spain, hence the translation to Juan de Fuca.

It is approximately a hundred kilometres to the Pacific Ocean from Victoria travelling west along the Strait of Juan de Fuca. As you pass Port Renfrew you are poised to leave the Salish Sea behind and move into the largest body of water on the planet.

A recent newspaper opinion piece suggested that the Salish Sea should become a UNESCO World Heritage Site. This idea has the support of the Victoria municipal councillors (at the time of this writing). Heritage sites may be designated either natural or culturally relevant.

Although a world heritage designation is quite prestigious, it occasionally carries one concerning drawback: too much tourism. This can damage or compromise the site or deter animals, such as nesting birds, from inhabiting the location.

In addition to the Salish Sea, there are only two other UNESCO heritage sites in British Columbia: the Rocky Mountains, shared with Alberta, and the Gwaii Haanas National Park Reserve and Haida Heritage Site area, on the tip of Haida Gwaii. The four countries with the most UNESCO heritage sites are Italy, China, Spain, and France. There are 1,052 designated UNESCO heritage sites in the world.

Port Renfrew

Port Renfrew, a village at the end of the road (West Coast Road/Highway 14), is an interesting little place with a pub, accommodations, busy fishing charter businesses (the salmon and halibut fishing are superb), and a few small, funky shops. It borders on an old-growth rainforest where, as I was told by a grizzled local on the dock, I could find the world's largest Douglas fir (73.8 metres tall), Canada's tallest Sitka spruce (62.5 metres tall), and Canada's gnarliest tree (in Avatar Grove).

On a raw and drizzly day, my partner Mikki and I had a delicious oyster burger at the Renfrew Pub, which resembles a large lodge; it was of wooden construction, large and airy with high beams, a roaring fireplace, and a view of the activity on the dock. The fishermen came in, the kayakers headed out, and old scruffy dogs waited for their masters. It was interesting to observe the stark differences between the young and fit kayakers, so friendly and chatty, and the fishermen, remote and resigned, with bent backs and rough, red hands, coming home from the catch in their big boots. I thought it was best to watch these locals and not to engage in conversation; I had the impression that chit-chatting was the last thing they wanted to do, at least with strangers who had just gorged themselves on burgers and chips at their local pub.

A walk down the trail to Botanical Beach is well worth the effort. It's not too far, and at the bottom, at low tide, a vast and enchanting array of tidal pools full of colourful and diverse ocean life awaits, the creatures resting until the surf returns with their dinners. Our proximity to the awe-inspiring beauty of the delicate and vulnerable sea life in these pools is humbling when we realize that we are powerful enough to cause them damage. When I peer into these pools, I feel as if I am an outsider, not quite privy to the greatness within these private pools filled with life.

Port Renfrew is a company town, logging and forestry being the main industries. Below the road is the small neighbourhood of company homes, a collection of small houses built on what used to be the rail yard. Trucks rather than a train now carry the logs out of town.

Company towns conjure up an image of roughness, of hard tough work, of old geezers in grease-stained jeans, exhausted men in great rubber overalls smelling of fish guts, of calloused and splintered hands, arthritic backs, of bent men still working at eighty years old in the woods because they love it despite their cursing and swearing.

Many Vancouver Island towns began as company towns—the mining, logging, and fishing industries, as well as agriculture, brought prosperity to communities from one end to the other. Most of these towns adapted over the years to tourism and artisanal endeavours as the traditional resource industries began to fade—Ladysmith focuses on heritage, Duncan on totem poles and First Nation culture, Chemainus on its murals and theatre, Nanaimo on its waterfront and maritime activities, Port Alberni on its spectacular hiking ventures and scenic beauty. But Port Renfrew, its hub of little houses on a dusty lane down near the pebbled shore, remains the traditional company town, where logging and fishing are still a prominent way of life and the guiding economical force.

Port Renfrew sits on an estuary which has not been beautified; this is one feature that makes the place unique. It truly is a traditional working community with lumberjacks, truck drivers, log scalers, mechanics, and rough-skinned fishermen who do not give a hoot how many potholes are in the road, or whether the WELCOME TO PORT RENFREW sign needs a fresh coat of paint, or if the blackberries are encroaching over the beach, or if the dock has a loose board that could trip a tourist, or if there's a stray hubcap in the ditch. This is one town that says it like it is; it's got personality, and it's a refreshing take on community.

Speaking of community: Port Renfrew has a community association, and on its website, there are some interesting and relevant historical photos under "Jack Chester's Walk Through History." There is also a library, an ambulance service, and a church—yes, a dear little church right at the entrance to the neighbourhood. That took me by surprise! I often wonder where we would go in an emergency in one of these remote communities; I suppose if it was life threatening, you would be airlifted to the closest hospital, but otherwise, the local ambulance volunteers would patch you up the best they could and drive the long and winding road to the closest clinic or medical centre; it would be a bonus if there were a doctor in the village, or an old-timer who knew how to make splints or concoct remedies, which most likely would work wonders but be against the law these days.

The West Coast Trail

Port Renfrew is also the start (or the end, if you begin your journey at Bamfield) of the world-renowned West Coast Trail. The seventy-five kilometres traverses the traditional territory of the Pacheedaht, Ditidaht, Huu-ay-aht, and Nuu-chah-nulth peoples, who have inhabited the region for more than four millennia. It's well known that this is an arduous trail where people come face to face with bears, climb hundreds of feet up ladders, and cross narrow log bridges—all while carrying an enormous backpack—then setting up camp in the middle of a wild, West Coast storm. Sometimes these intrepid adventurers break their ankles and are evacuated by helicopter (though apparently hunger and exhaustion do not warrant evacuation). All of this sounds both terrifying and intriguing, and I must admit I have pondered whether or not I could successfully do this hike.

Now would be a good time for me to mention, to the shock and horror of many of my West Coast friends, that I had never been camping until 2017. When I was a child in New Brunswick, Dad attempted to take us camping once; someone had lent him a huge, blue, mildewed tent, which he had set up in the garden to air out, but we never made it out of the driveway. I think he had an emergency of some sort at the university where he was artist in residence; his studio caught fire, so the camping excursion never occurred.

I have the good fortune of being friends with an intrepid individual who has braved the West Coast Trail and could offer me a first-hand account of the experience. Tracey is tall and sinewy and vivacious, extremely outgoing, and very capable; she can read a marine map, go fishing, repair the boat motor, knows the difference between a flounder and a halibut, can identify fishing lures, fillet a fish for dinner and cook it over a campfire that she made herself with two sticks. She can also grow a huge garden and preserve all the food for winter after making pesto and pickles, and she can make her own splints if she breaks her ankle. This is the kind of person who should hike the stunning but arduous trail!

Tracey hiked the trail in seven days—covering an impressive ten kilometres a day over the challenging terrain—and reported that prospective hikers must obtain a permit and take an orientation session because weather and animal conditions fluctuate; hikers must also learn to identify animal tracks and be familiar with tsunami evacuation procedures.

So far, so good, I thought. I am most able to meet these requirements.

"Oh, and there's a lot of mud," she added. "*so* much mud! Everything was so slippery."

Mud and lots of it, I thought. A week without a warm bath, and my ever-increasing bunion may be an issue. I began to have doubts.

Tracey went on to tell me there had been a bear sighting on her trip—specifically, a brazen bear who had no fear of humans. It was caught on several occasions going through a woman's purse on the beach, and—to add insult to injury—when Tracey and her companions were finally able to chase away the bear, he lumbered into the bush, taking the purse with him. He sounded like a personable fellow with whom I could share my little boiled wieners on the beach as the sun set. But in truth, the story further deterred me from making the hike, though I must admit that my fear of the muddy ladders is greater than that of a pillaging old bear.

There are food lockers along the trail for campers to use, and I must say, there's nothing more sobering (and sometimes rather amusing) than seeing a bear trying to break into one, as they do with cars when they spot a cooler in the back seat. Although bears can appear comical in their human-like exploits, with their dexterous paws and curiosity, I cannot help but feel great empathy towards them. Our tasteful West Coast subdivisions encroach upon their territory, and we euthanize them for walking into a playground at a school built at the base of their mountain, when all they are doing is looking for a scrap or two, which we have left in the pretty trash cans beside the swings and monkey bars.

I also learned that hikers must pack enough food for seven days; if food lockers aren't available, it's important to store food away from sleeping areas and high up in a tree. As for potable water: You can pack it, but water can also be taken from the numerous forest steams, as long as it's filtered properly—usually with some sort of a little gizmo, many of which are available through camping supply stores.

Here's a tip: Purchase three-ounce air-tight "wine preservation system" wine packs. These are little rubber bags with sexy-looking spouts in which you may pour (or suck) your wine and pack it for safe travel. I am at a loss, however, as to why they are called systems, except to surmise that whenever we use the word *system*, it sounds very important and complex. For the average wine drinker, I believe you'd need a fair amount of these systems to carry you over seven days. (These wine packs very much resemble, in my limited medical view, some sort of hospital drainage gadget that might be attached to your nether-regions).

The selling of camping supplies seems to be a massively lucrative business. Apart from the endless backpack designs, dehydrated foods, socks, thermoses, ropes, hooks, and boot laces, there is an immense array of compact cooking gizmos, including a solar heated fold-up stove.

"Travel with the sun," Tracey went on. "Rise at dawn, rest at dusk. And pack strategically." She handed me a list of what she packed: mostly boil-in-a-bag dinners.

This brought me back to Dad fishing on his beloved Miramichi River in New Brunswick and the lovely, quiet sunsets we spent together at his fishing camp. Dad would eat wieners from a plastic bag while Mum ate a fresh piece of fish that Dad had caught; she'd insist that fresh food was better than Dad's plastic-bagged fare. At such times, their dissimilar taste in food caused a bit of stress, and dinners were eaten in total and seething silence. For Dad, the joy in fishing was often found not by eating his catch—he usually put the fish back in the river—but rather from standing in the Miramichi pools in his great bulky rubber hip waders, holding his fly rod with the patience of a stone.

After a little consideration, I decided I didn't feel ready to tackle the West Coast Trail. Perhaps I'll reconsider sometime when the prospect of being covered in mud, not bathing for days, and climbing rope ladders doesn't seem so daunting.

Pacific Marine Circle Route

At Port Renfrew, you can continue along the Pacific Marine Circle Route to Lake Cowichan, a two-hour drive on a newly paved but severely potholed logging road. To embark on this adventure, cross the bridge at Port Renfrew and set off through the forested slopes covered with great blankets of trees and sliced with ribbons of clear-cut activity—but, again, I can't overemphasize the need to watch out for potholes: Some of them are deep and will catch you unexpectedly as you come around a turn or make your way over a blind hill.

This day excursion could be completed as a loop, bringing you back to Victoria by heading south on the highway. However, you may wish to explore the Cowichan Valley with a visit to the village of Lake Cowichan, a refreshment in Youbou, or a swim at Honeymoon Bay; all three communities are on Cowichan Lake. There's a small wooded ecological reserve off the road at Honeymoon Bay at the north end of the lake. I happened to visit after a snowstorm in early spring, so I did not see the rare pink fawn lilies that bloom through the forest debris in the spring. Still, despite the weather, I enjoyed a stroll along a lovely forest path to the river.

> The inventory of unique and special Canadian ecological systems was established in the sixties and seventies via a global environmental concern and recognition of existing but threatened natural areas; these sensitive locations were not only to be identified and protected, but also kept as specific genetic research locations; these are the British Columbia Ecological Reserves.
>
> British Columbia's Ministry of the Environment lists hundreds of these special sites; numerous ecological reserves have been identified on Vancouver Island. Apart from Honeymoon Bay, ecological reserves are also recognized on Lasqueti Island (just off Qualicum Beach) for, among other things, their dry site plants, including the prickly pear cactus. The tiny community of Bowser, just south of Fanny Bay, has a small forested ecological reserve, and in the Nanaimo area, there is the Yellow Point Bog, where sedges, peat, and other endangered marsh flora thrive—including one with the most delightfully repugnant name, the humped bladderwort.

Bamberton

In the spirit of attempting new activities (while I still am able), and to soothe my West Coast friends who were aghast at my limited camping experience, I arranged to finally go camping with my friend Sarah in a real, non-mouldering tent pitched somewhere other than

Dad's driveway. Sarah is young and handy with propane. She also has a smart phone and a fine sense of humour, so I chose her as my camping companion as carefully as Justin Trudeau selected our new Governor General.

We decided to visit Bamberton, a pretty provincial campsite just on the other side of the Malahat as you drive down the hill, just before Mill Bay. Situated on the Saanich Inlet, there is a beach where campers can swim. I thought my first camping trip should happen fairly close to home, just in case something unexpected happened and I had to rush away. My first camping experience triggered a bit of anxiety—I felt so helpless standing in the trees without my usual comforts, and I started imagining all the things that could go wrong (medically, mostly).

My friend Lee—who is young, virile, amusing, and has camped all his life—gave me three major points to keep in mind when camping:

1. **Socializing is important.** Talk to other campers; camping is a social activity when done at an actual campsite. This will be extremely difficult as both Sarah and I are introverts, but we have practised our opening line: "Where are you folks from?" I figure we should use the word *folks* when speaking to people in hundred-thousand-dollar recreational vehicles, but I'm not sure tenters use the word *folks*.

2. **Hygiene is dubious.** After a day or two, you will be grubby and unwashed; you may even become a bit sticky, musty, and pungent, with a humid, woodsy, smoky bouquet. Accept it—embrace it, even! It's all about the joys of public porta-potties, cold-water taps, and leaving most toiletries at home. I believe the general philosophy is something along the lines of: "What's the use of changing your underwear if you can't have a bath?"

3. **Camp food is often unhealthy.**

Every so often, it's fun to consume real junk, so why not enjoy the experience? Food doesn't have to be virtuous and nutritious every day of our lives. We can't always eat serious food—dried cranberries, chickpeas, and this strange fermented concoction starting with a K. Camping food should be full of delicious sodium and unknown chemicals—think hot dogs, Bugles, Pop-Tarts, and squeezable cheese. Going camping and not eating pure junk is like buying a tabloid and skipping the pages that report on who is Prince Harry's real red-headed father. Every so often we *need* to do the wrong, albeit harmless, thing; the trick, however, is to know what you're doing and recognize that the next day you will return from Pop-Tarts to whole grains and the *Globe and Mail.*

So, when you're camping, know that you will most likely subsist on processed wieners (Sarah says that smokies are the way to go—I think of those as high-end wieners), white buns, chips, marshmallows, and s'mores. In case you do not know what a s'more is, here is a brief description: S'mores are a revolting, debauched mass of melted marshmallows and chocolate over graham crackers; apparently, this is a traditional camping food staple that hearkens back to Girl Scouts circa 1920. S'more—what does that even mean? Sarah mused that it might be a contraction of *some more.* Alas, a gooey s'more was not for me—it's just too sticky. (I'd make a lousy Girl Guide.)

I scrubbed a little blue cooler in which chilled glasses on ice and the ingredients for vodka mojitos were carried in with great care (though, I have to say, the thought of sipping a chilled glass of a minty mojito followed by s'mores made my stomach churn). The cooler, a small box with a white handle, reminded me of the emergency container that holds a cooled, fresh kidney or another vital human organ, which transplant staff run with from a helicopter on the roof of a hospital to a waiting transplant recipient on a ward below. As I scrubbed, I speculated that my mojitos would be just as precious. And as it turned out, there was in fact a superb match for my mojitos: Sarah's amazing, killer, camping guacamole:

SARAH'S AMAZING KILLER CAMPING GUACAMOLE

2 avocados

½ cup chopped red onion

3 Tbsp lemon juice

3 cloves minced garlic (or more, if you're feeling wild)

½ tsp chili powder

Salt and pepper to taste

1 or 2 Tbsp mayonnaise

Mix everything thoroughly. Serve with taco chips and on burgers or, for a true camping experience, on a leaf. Just make sure it's not a poisonous leaf! Oh, and be careful who you kiss—though the pungent garlicky aroma should take care of that for you.

Drinks alone weren't enough; we needed games too, so I packed Scrabble and a deck of cards, two folding chairs with drink holders, and a citronella candle from the dollar store. As it turned out, the candle created toxic smoke and made us choke rather than fulfilling its intended purpose, which is to say deterring mosquitoes.

The camping expedition commenced at precisely thirteen hundred hours on a warm Saturday morning as we embarked on the forty-minute journey out of town and over the Malahat towards our destination. Any anxiety I had vanished as soon as we set out—anxiety usually comes upon me in the planning stages of an adventure rather than during the event itself.

Archie, my affectionate, aging hound, accompanied us, wedged into the back seat between deflated air mattresses, towels, sleeping bags, pillows, and duffle bags filled with other sundry items. I felt a sense of serenity as my little car made its gentle turns around Goldstream Park and up towards the Malahat, where the views of Saanich and the inlet are splendid.

The turnoff to Bamberton and into the campsite was just off the highway as we approached Mill Bay going down the hill, and soon we found ourselves on a quiet country lane. On the south end of the lane stood the abandoned Bamberton cement factory—its huge, smooth, grey, concrete towers a well-known, historic landmark—as seen from the water and across the inlet from Brentwood across the bay. A little journey north took us to the turnoff that would lead us to the pretty wooded campsite.

The Bamberton Cement Company is a significant part of local history. It is connected to the Butchart quarry business across the inlet that was at one time a lucrative industry. Bamberton grew as a small community, much of it colonial and worker-based, despite its relative isolation, but the industry disrupted and displaced the Indigenous people who created, worshipped, and lived in their traditional ways along the inlet shores.

The Bamberton Cement facility, now abandoned, its cement structures and towering chimneys seen from almost every angle, clings to the shore against the forest backdrop, standing as a constant reminder of its history.

In 1904, across the inlet, the Butchart brick and cement works were in full operation; if you take a walk down to Tod Inlet today, you will see numerous relics and many remnants of the old industrial plant hidden under the wild lilacs and creeping vines.

Business boomed so well that the Bamberton cement industry, then the Associated Cement Company, joined the cement and brick production in 1912. The community grew (giving rise to several elegant British homes) to house the staff and the workers, who even had a community dance hall.

After the First World War, the demand for bricks and cement greatly declined, but at its peak, the factory employed 180 men and used 40,000 tons of coal annually to fire the industrial furnaces.

In 2015, the Malahat First Nation purchased the property and the site; although the cement factory remains, they have a variety of plans in store, including housing. There is a current debate as well over whether to have the property serve as an LNG (liquefied natural gas) facility in operation. This is quite a contentious and somewhat ongoing issue.

Sarah and I found our spot, site 48, a cozy, well-raked, shady nook on the edge of a steep ridge surrounded by salal shrubbery and large regal ferns. The woods were tinder-dry and brittle, the cedar boughs an arid copper colour. Campfires were banned due to the devastating wild infernos burning the province's forests, towns, and rural homesteads (that no doubt eliminates the cooking of the s'mores, I thought with relief), but Sarah had brought a tiny gas stove on which we could cook our smokies.

The two jovial female park rangers made routine journeys in a speedy golf cart–type vehicle; they were so jolly, with big hairstyles, pink lipstick, and beautifully manicured nails! They kept the place in fine order—in fact, Sarah, who had camped all her life all over the province, remarked that Bamberton had the cleanest outhouses of any campground she'd seen.

The campsite was filled with families, but to my surprise, the place was serene. Children quietly rode up and down the wooded lane on their bikes or lay in hammocks strung between the firs and hemlocks; some staggered up the forest path from the beach dragging inflated swans and pink life rings, and others carried little orange buckets and bright green spades. Sarah and I theorized that when children are within nature, their minds are calm; stress, hyperactivity, and obsession with video games dissipate. It was remarkable—we did not see one child using a technological device! One little girl was even collecting leaves; another read a real paper book.

Sarah and I set up her very retro tent, an old Eureka, which belonged to her partner's grandfather and came in a ripped and faded green nylon bag. "It's an A-frame," Sarah declared with a smirk as she proudly pulled out the tent's "storm shield." I looked around and noted that the tent was a spacious, sturdy structure compared to the surrounding orange domes, which, on one windy night, looked as if they might fly into the treetops.

Sarah also supplied the ground covers, which had to be inflated. These were also from the past and belonged to her elderly uncle who had used them while trekking through the Rockies; they came in a brown bag with brittle leather labels. It occurred to me that these older outdoor exploration necessities that Sarah had acquired were not only more durable than those of today, but lighter and far more compact, just not as attractive.

Sarah's supplies reminded me of the poignant and rather sad day that I took Mum (by her own choice) from her lovely airy house full of geraniums, art, pottery, and the smell of soup on the stove up the hill to the Veterans Health Unit. She carried only a little battered blue suitcase, the kind with a handle and snaps to close it. All she had packed were her threadbare nightgown, a few pairs of underpants, and a clean white blouse.

We backed out of the driveway on that bitterly cold, white winter day with her case on the back seat, and a New Brunswick liquor store bag containing a few toiletries on her lap: a toothbrush, an old bottle of Tums, a tube of Nivea face cream, and a comb with missing teeth that she had found on a wet country road in Denmark with me years before. She loved that comb!

That little blue suitcase has withstood the test of time, quite unlike the one I purchased two years ago: the wheels fell off on the escalator at Heathrow Airport, and the retractable handle fell apart in Istanbul security. In Toronto, on Pearson's tarmac, I once saw, from my little airplane window, the baggage handlers throwing luggage onto the conveyor belt; one piece of luggage— that hard, shell-like type—burst open, and a few unmentionables scattered themselves on the asphalt under the wing. If it had been my bag, I would have been terribly embarrassed: one item was an enormous brassiere.

After our campsite was organized, we ventured down to the beach; the forest path was a fair hike through the trees down to the sea, but what a beach it was! The sandy bay gradually became deep, and we plunged in the clear water and floated and bobbed in the green surf, enjoying the late afternoon warmth of the sun. Being in the inlet, it was not too chilly, and as we revelled in this delightful spot, we watched the little ferry cross from Mill Bay, just around the corner, over to Brentwood; white sails billowed in the distance.

Following our very pleasant dip, we hiked back up to our camp, made our mojitos, had chips and Sarah's *very* garlicky guacamole, and played Scrabble. Sarah was shocked but amused that I had packed genuine crystal glasses (hand-blown in Halifax): two for mojitos, and two for wine. I am a traditionalist, and I simply feel that picnics, camping, and other outdoor excursions should include a little class! Some would say the classic British tea ritual has historically defined the British Empire, with proper cups and saucers and teapots lugged and set up in the most remote locations. As far as I'm concerned, this principle should apply to the proper preparing and serving of cocktails—even in a campsite.

I think it's more respectful to nature to "use the good dishes" when eating and drinking in her midst—to drink out of plastic glasses among nature's magnificent flora and ocean vistas just rubs me the wrong way. In bygone eras, eating outdoors included a gentle hike through the country-side carrying neatly packed china tea cups and little cakes on silver plates in great baskets (albeit carried by a staggering servant lugging the load at the rear of the happy party ahead). And so, on our excursion, I carried our chilled mojito glasses into the forest and gently placed them on a rustic picnic table which I first covered with a linen tablecloth.

Marinated with mojitos and wine, and fragrant from the garlicky guacamole, we went for a stroll around the other sites and worked up our nerve to approach a man who was washing his calloused, gnarled feet under the drinking tap.

"Hi there!" we said, smiling brightly. "Where are you from?"

He looked up at us as if we were idiots (Sarah told me later that she thought he'd rolled his eyes).

"Victoria," he answered in an offhanded tone.

And that was the end of our so-where-are you-folks-from quest.

Back at our campsite, the smokies were a great success in those big white buns smothered in mustard; I gave Archie two as a treat. He loved camping, and the little girl in the next site befriended him. At dusk the two of them sat side by side on a large rock.

A wind came up, so we decided to do our evening ablutions and go to bed—and by ablutions, I mean a quick squeeze of toothpaste, a swipe of hand cream, and pulling on our pyjamas. We lay there for a while in silence, listening to our breathing as the wind swirled around in the trees above the Eureka. Archie lay at my feet and let out a sigh. The wind grew stronger. Sarah suddenly sat bolt upright.

"DEPLOY THE STORM SHIELD!" she firmly commanded with the authority and knowledge of a camper who has braved the Rockies.

We scurried outside, hastily pinned the storm shield over the tent for extra security, then returned to our warm, safe "fart sacks." (I had learned from Mum that, in the army, this was the elegant title given to sleeping bags.)

The Eureka held fast in the principle (I realized in the middle of the night that we were indeed on a sort of ledge). However, there was a different type of wind inside our abode: Archie's sensitive stomach endeavoured to digest the two smokies he had eaten earlier, resulting in one foul wind release after another throughout the night. So pungent was Archie's expulsion, we had to open the tent's side flaps. Even so, we all had a good sleep and woke in the pale early morning light, its patches of white patterned between the dark treetops.

To my pleasant surprise I was able to rise off the ground without a single twinge or ache. I made my way through the storm shield and emerged from the tent to find myself immersed in the quiet, woodsy ambience—a lovely finish to my first camping experience. Eureka indeed!

The Cowichan Valley

The Cowichan Valley is the traditional territory of the Hul'q'umi'num Mustimuhw, a Coast Salish people. The Hul'q'umi'num Mustimuhw use the word *Quw'utsun*, meaning "the warm land," for this region; it is believed that *Cowichan* is the anglicization of this name.

The name Cowichan seems to be everywhere, so if you're not from here, it's easy to become confused. There's the District of Cowichan, the vast area that encompasses much of the southern island beginning approximately at Mill Bay, just over the Malahat, and stretching northward towards Duncan and beyond. Within the district of Cowichan is the Cowichan River; then there's Lake Cowichan (at the eastern tip of Cowichan Lake), and Cowichan Bay down on the coast.

Cowichan is known for its sweaters. The famous garment is beloved all over Canada (and perhaps the world to many travellers) as the traditional identification of the region. It is so famous, in fact, that in 2012, the federal government declared the Cowichan sweater to have national historic significance on the advice of the Historic Sites and Monuments Board of Canada. Sadly, the patterns of the Cowichan sweaters have been appropriated by those seeking financial gain from knockoffs, so if you want to purchase a Cowichan sweater, it's important to be certain of its authenticity.

The First Nations people, who have inhabited the Cowichan territory for thousands of years, originally practised weaving their blankets, hats, and other clothing from natural fibres they foraged from the land. This included both plant material as well as hair from wild mountain goats and dogs, which they spun and wove using the spindle and whorl method. Two occurrences changed this traditional culture, which ultimately produced the Cowichan sweater: the introduction of sheep in the mid-1800s by the Europeans and the arrival of the Sisters of St. Ann, who came from Quebec on a mission to educate the children of the colony (which, as we know, included the Indigenous population via the residential school system).

The nuns shared their knowledge of knitting with wool; their knitting skills originated in the Shetland Islands where sweaters were knitted for the local fishermen. The Indigenous people soon began to knit their wonderful thick sweaters, toques, socks, and mittens from sheep wool; the original features, apart from the thickness, are the symbolic designs, the most popular patterns representing the eagle, whale, salmon, deer, and snowflake. It is interesting to note that the snowflake pattern is rarely seen in the First Nation culture except on these sweaters.

The colours are always natural—cream, grey, black, and dark brown—although I saw one with a touch of red, though it was possibly a copy, or a knitter attempting to break the tradition using dyed wool.

These wonderful, long-lasting sweaters have no seams; they are knitted in one piece. I purchased one for Mum a very long time ago (along with her llama wool hat and a Hudson's Bay blanket) to protect her in the bitter eastern winters; the sweater lasted for the rest of her life. She used to wear it as she skied along the frozen Saint John River under the moon and then tell me on our next phone call how warm it kept her. Whoever cleaned out her closets after she died discovered this beautiful, comforting garment, and they are a lucky person indeed: They inherited a much-beloved piece of West Coast Indigenous tradition.

The Cowichan Valley, although large and sprawling between the mountain ranges and the sea, is a hive of activity, energy, innovations, interesting people, cultures, and projects of all sorts; there is no shortage of music festivals, farmers' markets, and culinary events. If you want to find out what's going on in the region, the best thing to do is to have a coffee at one of the many cafés in one of the numerous communities and pick up a copy of *Cowichan Valley Voice*; it is an extremely informative, educational, and interesting magazine. (Or, if you're addicted to the Internet, you can find the magazine online). In this publication, you will meet chef Bill Jones, who gathers wild morel mushrooms and offers up his delicious recipes from his farm; if you love honey but cannot keep bees, you could support the "hive share" project, which provides you with a hive but also with a beekeeping expert; you may be interested to learn the many important reasons of planting heathers, where to volunteer to build a therapeutic garden; how yoga might rid you of pelvic pain; or how to obtain a rebate from a woodstove exchange initiative. Have you ever wished to listen to, or join, a pipers and drummers society, communicate with horses, or wear clothing made from hemp? You can do it all here in Cowichan—it's a veritable hive of activity.

Hemp is naturally resistant to mould and blocks out ultraviolet rays. It is a fast-growing annual plant and is used for the construction of ship sails. Hemp cloth for clothing is often combined with other fabrics to increase comfort.

I was impressed to learn that hemp can be used to produce fifty thousand products such as sunglasses, kitty litter, a soil nutrient, and protein powder. Apparently, hemp is the newest thing in nanomaterials, but when I investigated the meaning of nanomaterial, I was thrown off by terms like super capacitator, electrodes, and graphene—it all sounds too futuristic and technological, and it probably has something to do with batteries. All I know is that I love my cool and comfortable hemp T-shirt, and my friend Sarah loves her hemp sundress, and my partner Mikki loves her hemp sun hat—all of which are probably edible.

An interesting fact to note is that hemp is part of the cannabis family, and industrial hemp production is only recently becoming a legal industry in the United States. It strikes me as peculiar that a country that fears such a sustainable, wonderful plant has no problem marketing machine guns to the general public.

Spectacle Lake

Sometimes the more we see of something, the less visible it becomes. This is the case of the signage to Spectacle Lake, a lovely provincial park just off the Malahat (about thirty kilometres northwest of Victoria; take the Shawnigan Lake turnoff). I've driven past the sign to this enchanting little lake a million times, but strangely, I never thought to drive in and take the charming and easy forest stroll, have a swim, and enjoy a picnic on the little sandy beach, until one day, for no apparent reason, I was inspired to do it.

A lake is a perfect place for a picnic because you can rinse your hands in the water, and you don't have to worry about the tides coming in and swamping your towel and clothing. There are usually trees around a lake to provide shade, and the water is warmer than the ocean. What's a picnic without a swim or drifting on an air mattress among the lily pads?

I called my friend Regine, who loves to get out of town and enjoy nature and explore new parks as much as I do, and we set off with our beach towels and lunches. Once we settled in at Spectacle Lake, I noticed a man fishing off the rock at the far end and saw a little girl rowing around in a rubber dinghy. We had a lovely afternoon chatting on our towels with our feet in the water, eating classic picnic food—watermelon and devilled egg sandwiches—and ambling through the shady paths along the shore. I swam right across the lake (it was not very far), pushing the lily pads gently to the side with every stroke. I stopped to rest when I was halfway across, treading water and lying back in the sun's warmth, but then I realized that the lake was shallow and went only up to my waist. In fact, the lake is so shallow that, in the winter, if it gets sufficiently cold, Spectacle Lake freezes over, and the locals can safely go ice skating on its surface.

The word picnic began to be used throughout Europe around the reign of King George III and is thought by many to have its root from the old French term pique-nique.

Picnics were not originally purposeful pleasurable activities but rather baskets of food packed for weary travellers or something for the wealthy to feast upon after a day of hunting. The latter variety were huge meals served in the country-side, outdoors—cheese rounds, cakes, and meat pies, all carried by servants. Eventually, citizens adopted a toned-down version of this pleasant activity, and it became a very popular social event, often combined with leisure sports such as rowing, croquet, or badminton.

Many of us think of Europe when looking back at our social (or in this case, culinary) history, but countless cultures the world over have been cooking and eating outdoors for generations, and continue to do so today (for example, the Middle Eastern and North African nomads with their earth ovens, and the Maori and Hawaiians with pit ovens). Here, on our island home, the Coast Salish traditionally cooked in pits, feasting on shellfish, mammals, fish, reptiles, and more, with individual nations having their own distinct methods and recipes.

I'll never forget cooking chicken in foil at Cox Bay in Tofino. I had taken Mum on a road trip; at that time, beach fires were permitted, so we made a little fire in the sand using driftwood; then we sat on a log with our wine and watched an incredible sunset and the waves crashing onto the beach.

I put the chicken right into the fire, and Mum did a little sketch of the distant black figures of surfers catching the last of the pink light on the silver sand. When the chicken was cooked, we put it on our log, and quite suddenly, a greedy crow flew down, grabbed it, and flew off with it—plate and all!

Dining outdoors

Choose a lake or river that you could drive or bike to, perhaps one that you've never visited; Vancouver Island's provincial parks have an abundance of them while offering good parking, clean porta-potties, lovely forest paths, and safe beaches.

Then, plan a picnic and make it from scratch—bring along a tablecloth, cloth napkins, cutlery, and glasses. If you want an authentic, more traditional experience, pack everything in a basket. I bought one for two dollars at a garage sale, and it even had hinged flaps!

Thoughtful, unhurried preparation is calming and plays a large part in setting the tone for the day. Unplug from our convenience-food culture and include food that you make yourself, such as potato salad, or a cool mint iced tea. These two items are so easy to make—I just throw together cooked (and cooled) potatoes, mayonnaise, and green onion; no egg or paprika or mustard or celery are needed, as far as I'm concerned. The mint tea I make with my own fresh mint from the garden; it grows like a weed! Once it's all steeped in hot water, I add a bit of honey, and when the tea has cooled, I add ice. Then I shake it all up, pour it into a lovely tall glass, and add a wedge of lime. It looks as if it's right out of Victoria's *EAT* magazine.

On your picnic adventure, unplug from your devices. Not everything has to be shared on social media; there is something to be said for private time. Try a water activity: paddle boarding, kayaking, or simply floating or swimming are all good options. Plan one or two other diversions: read a book or magazine; take photographs; play Scrabble; write a letter or a card; try your hand at sketching, or just listen to the birdsongs. And if you're not too self-conscious, you could even do a few yoga poses for a quintessential West Coast experience (although I must admit that when I witness this practice of stretching and bending and flexing in a public space, such as at a ferry terminal, I wince—I find it bothersome). A sun salutation might be appropriate, or perhaps the butterfly pose, but if you do the cobra pose, or anything else on the ground, watch out for ticks!

Whether you enjoy lakes or rivers, saltwater or fresh water, woods or sandy beaches, a picnic is an enchanting activity to do in the warmer months. You'll feel refreshed and relaxed after a day of lying back and listening to the water, and it's way better than anything you would pay a fortune for at the spa.

Circumambulation

WHY DO WE PREFER TO TRAVEL IN LOOPS RATHER THAN ON linear paths? Walking in a curved, beginning-to-end route is a hard-wired human instinct, possibly to prevent us from wandering indefinitely in a straight line rather than returning to our place of departure. Scientific studies report blindfolded participants walking in a circle despite conscious intent to walk in a straight line; perhaps they were influenced by the shape of our inner ear, which is essentially a labyrinth. And we have all observed how water swirls into a drain instead of going straight down.

I'm not a scientist; however, I believe our instinct is to travel in circles. I find walking a linear route, then turning around to backtrack on the same path, immensely irritating. At the very least, I need to walk around a trash can or bench or even a rock—anything that requires me to make a small loop and take a turn.

Labyrinths and mazes

Popular in the ancient world, labyrinths are making a resurgence in our modern times. They are often found in parks or on church properties as well as in therapeutic facilities and healing gardens.

The history of these circular and beautiful symmetrical patterns is complex and diverse. Most countries around the world have included them, in some form, in spiritual and mythical origins and traditions. Labyrinths have been developed for ritual dances, to symbolize a path towards God (the entrance being birth, the centre being the divine), as refuges for good tricksters, as metaphors for discovery, and for meditation, to quiet the mind. There are approximately sixty labyrinths on Vancouver Island. I have visited a few, including a grass one in my own neighbourhood in James Bay, located in a small park. I find the philosophy, symbolism, design, and history more fascinating than walking one—though I can understand the benefits. There are times when the knowledge of something provides you with more value than experiencing the originally intended purpose.

Mazes, on the other hand, are distinct from labyrinths in that they provide the participant with optional routes rather than a single path to the centre. In Scandinavian mythology, mazes were used to entrap evil trolls in remote coastal fishing villages. The mazes of ancient Greece and Rome frequently depicted the minotaur, a monstrous creature with the head of a bull and a body of a man, in the centre of the design, unable to escape, destined to perish; this scene was especially revealed in Roman floor mosaics.

An added and modern twist on traditional mazes and pedestrian puzzles is the corn maze. This amusing masterpiece is common on agricultural lands and farms in the autumn, when the cornfields are thick with tall stalks ready to harvest. The farmer, with a tremendous amount of pre-planning, carves out the maze on their tractor in the cornfield.

The public then will have a wonderful adventure in the greenery attempting to find the centre and making their way back out again. Since this happens in autumn, many farms include a U-pick pumpkin patch as well, and some even organize a haunted farm experience in their barns.

Mazes and physical puzzles are not for everyone. Take, for example, the modern corn maze: While highly entertaining, it could create the opposite effect of what we experience in a more introspective labyrinth. Becoming disoriented in a cornfield, not knowing which way to go, feeling helpless and trapped, could be quite frightening for some people.

One of the largest corn mazes on Vancouver Island was at Pendray Farms in North Saanich. When I visited, the theme was Vancouver Island life, and the intricate, meticulous maze included our provincial bird and other Island features.

As we journey throughout Vancouver Island, criss-crossing the country lanes, taking ferries, hiking up mountains, strolling the trails, cycling or kayaking or stopping to check out an eagle's nest, we can see that it is not unlike the process of making our way through a labyrinth or maze. It becomes clear that the outer journey is also an inward journey, a collection of reflections, of process, of memory, and moments to savour (or discard). This is why the destination is often not the true destination at all—the journey is in the moment you experience it. Just like our Island terrain, nothing is linear within ourselves. That is the wonderful thing about travel: The curves and hills and dips and surprises of our internal landscape reveal that we contain an abundance of possibilities.

Circle routes

There are two spectacular circle routes you can take on Southern Vancouver Island; the first one journeys from Victoria to Whippletree Junction, Maple Bay, Crofton, and across to Salt Spring Island.

From Victoria, head north on the Trans-Canada Highway/BC Highway 1 and drive for about forty-five to fifty minutes; take the Whippletree Frontage Road exit on the right (just short of Duncan by about six kilometres). Here you'll find Whippletree Junction, a funky, quirky array of shops, nestled in with cafés and art studios, offering everything from quilts to fudge to wicker.

As you wander around the old grounds among the pink-and-turquoise clapboard and tired wooden structures, you'll soon see that the merchants have a sense of humour: There's a hand-painted sign that reads: WHIPPLETREE—POPULATION 14, and a teapot garden on a patio that is slowly being enveloped by creeping vines.

As I meandered towards the back of Whippletree's property, I noticed a sign nailed to a tree: HERB RICE, it stated. What a novel idea, I thought when I saw it, to mix herbs with rice. But as it turns out, Herb Rice is the name of a talented Coast Salish carver who is Whippletree's artist in residence. His art depicts traditional themes with some slight crossover to contemporary, which is daring, in my opinion. Mr. Rice's obvious skill, vision, and intuition make his pieces remarkable. Rice's studio hours vary, so if you have your heart set on seeing his work, you should make an appointment by visiting his website at coastsalishjourney.com.

With its rustic, historic, pioneer-era look—check out the nineteenth-century typewriter and the steampunk-themed fountain in the courtyard—complete with cobweb-festooned antique treasures tucked in stores waiting to be discovered, the Junction's down to earth appearance may fool you but make no mistake: The businesses that make up this community are high quality and offer exquisitely crafted items, such as wooden furniture, handmade spun and dyed fabrics, and patio adornments, which all make lovely household gifts.

The abundance of creative goods I've seen here (and all over the island, really) causes me to reflect on how residing in a small town, or on an island such as Vancouver Island, seems to encourage its citizens to become entrepreneurs; it gently forces us to ask, "What am I good at doing, at making, at creating, at offering?"

From Whippletree, there is easy access to the back roads, on which you can amble through the countryside to Cowichan Bay. When you're ready to leave the rattan shop and maple candy behind, take Bench Road and follow the signs to Maple Bay, Cowichan Bay, and Crofton. Before you know it, you'll find yourself surrounded by hedgerows full of Nootka rose entangled with honeysuckle, stands of willows, cotton-woods, and aspens, and meadows full of daisies with smudges of dark magenta clover. Breathe deeply the fresh sea breezes, feast your eyes on beautiful pastoral vistas dotted with barns and country homesteads, cross little wooden bridges over streams, and pass marshes and wetlands teeming with birdsong.

Eventually, you will come across the grass-surfaced South Cowichan Lawn Tennis Club. Established in 1887, it's one of the oldest tennis clubs in the world, and is the oldest club still playing on grass in Canada. It's seen its share of disaster, though: sitting at sea level as well as on the river, it was the victim of a great flood in 2006—the water was waist-high at the net! When the water receded, a thick silty layer of mud and debris remained.

Across the road is Maple Grove Park, a stunning natural site of huge old-growth maples and a bird habitat, with a pleasant walk to the edge of the Cowichan Estuary. As I stood quietly admiring a hundred-foot maple, one of thirty-nine, an excited woman, accompanied by her black Labrador, came lumbering out of the shrubbery with great gusto. She carried a walking stick and wore sensible leather shoes, and her greying hair poked out of her silk headscarf.

"I saw a pelican!" she declared, panting. "But there shouldn't be pelicans here—I should call the wildlife people immediately—it must be the result of global warming." Just before she reached her little smart car in the grassy parking area, she turned and breathlessly added, "The pelican is off course!"

Poor pelican, I thought, but before I could say it out loud, the woman was already gone, leaving me standing in the grass, alone with my thoughts. But even if she hadn't left so abruptly, I'm not sure what more I could have said as I also had never seen a pelican in these parts.

Onward from Maple Grove Park, you will come across Saint Ann's church, quaint and demure on the hill, followed by Providence Farm right next door. This fine enterprise is not only a working farm, but is also involved in many community endeavours, including numerous and diverse therapeutic programs; it is well known for its unique and striking main building built by the Sisters of Saint Ann.

The Sisters of Saint Ann contributed a large part towards the history on Vancouver Island. The first four to arrive in Victoria were known as "the pioneer nuns," arriving from Quebec in 1858. They ventured towards the Duncan area, and in 1864, purchased four hundred acres; this was Providence Farm, which they eventually donated to the community.

From Providence Farm, the pleasant drive continues through the Maple Bay community, which is basically just to the east of Duncan. The road twists through serene and shady neighbourhoods and parks; there's a little road to the left down to Genoa Bay where you might divert to enjoy a snack or lunch at the pub.

Historic convent and religious architecture is distinctive, evocative, and striking in its beauty as it reaches for the heavens with stone arches, flying buttresses, gothic steeples, and elaborate domes. I find it interesting and a bit sad that, in contemporary times, with religious attendance decreasing and many older country churches for sale, new sites of worship mostly resemble, plain boring boxes, with clear, double-glazed windows, aluminum siding, plywood altars, grey vinyl decking, and flat roofs. Nothing reaches up to heaven anymore. I understand that this may be a modern choice, but I can't help but wonder: What would God think? Does God have taste?

Mount Tzouhalem and the hike to the cross

After I turned sixty, I joined the Outdoor Club of Victoria, mainly to alleviate one of my greatest fears: taking the wrong turn when out on a hike. I never want to be seen on local television being airlifted out of the woods in a basket, swaddled in a red blanket while the audience thinks, Silly old woman—what was she thinking, trying to act so young and fit?

I love my hiking group—we venture onto beautiful mountain ridges, beaches, river routes and meadows; my companions will enthusiastically point out the rare chocolate lily or a special landmark in the hazy distance atop a nearby mountain. The group even has a tasteful badge depicting two pine cones; I have proudly sewn one of these badges on my backpack.

When we meet at a location and then travel by carpool, we must bring a plastic bag to put our sullied hiking boots in when the hike is finished so as not to sully the car's interior. My companions' cars are lovely—charcoal or silver grey, often a hybrid, all with the scent of newness. I usually do not offer to carpool as my car is a dog and horse vehicle infused with the pungent aroma of sweaty saddle pads and wet dog.

One of the hikers is eighty-two years old! Most of the members use sticks to manoeuvre over the rock crevices and down the occasional steep path; somebody always brings delicious berry squares, which we devour during our break following a breathless ascent to a lichen-covered, rocky ridge that offers an equally breathtaking view.

Their calendar on their website is extremely informative and lists each hike, its difficulty, and the club member who intends to guide it. I usually select the middle degree of difficulty and avoid the ones that say, "fast paced, steep, not stopping for lunch, no breaks . . ."

In that case, there would be no time to take photographs and certainly no home baking on that outing! My image of the guide who leads these hikes is one of pure sinew.

I experienced a fabulous hike in the Cowichan Valley with my new group; it took us to the top of Mount Tzouhalem. The directions to reach the parking lot wound us through several very new subdivisions with tasteful landscaping, ocean views, and wide, freshly paved streets. I found this peculiar—I expected a country drive through meadows and marshes rather than a trek through an asphalted labyrinth of sage green and burgundy split-level homes with floor-to-ceiling windows and wraparound decks.

The hike itself was lovely, though; it took us along shaded forest trails and through a glorious wildflower meadow covered with a soft magenta blanket of sea blush and shooting stars dotted with the deep blue purple of the camas. We climbed the incline to a rocky ridge where there had been erected a large white cross; we sat and marvelled at the spectacular and expansive view of Duncan and the Cowichan Estuary, the historic grass tennis courts, and the elegant Providence Farm structures below the steep drop.

Sitting on the outcrop, eating moist little cheese sandwich and apple slices, which I had prepared at dawn, I sat apart from the rest of the group as they gathered under the cross chatting amicably. I did not know them very well yet, and in my shyness a sense of aloneness came over me. How odd it is, I thought, that those of us who enjoy being alone may not, in fact, prefer separateness when among others or in a large social gathering. Being alone by choice is far easier with nobody around, but when others are around, it can bring melancholy upon a person, as if reminded that, even in a crowd, we are vulnerable, especially on a high cliff. In my experience, there's a wistfulness that looms within introverts.

While I was feeling all of these things, a tall, slender woman approached me. She looked gentle and had on a very nice pair of pants— dark blue, loose, made of some sort of rough cotton or linen. (Her very satisfying and practical pants made a lasting impression on me.)

We chatted about dogs—she'd had Labradors all her life, and I'd had a black lab named Alice-Mary, who used to eat Brillo pads off the barbecue. I learned that my new friend's Lab loved to eat shoes, as most dogs do. She went on to tell me about her very formal mother-in-law, who had given my new friend a oven. Subsequently (and quite logically), my new friend explained that she had invited her mother-in-law for dinner, prepared in the new stove. A succulent roast was served, and everyone sat down on the formal velvet chairs; in keeping with the mother-in-law's elegance, the table was set with crystal stemware, polished silver candlesticks, crisp cotton napkins, and I would guess, a neat little vase of roses in the centre.

The mother-in-law always had sore feet and had a habit of slipping out of her shoes while eating. On this occasion, she wore fancy high heels, which she gently and discreetly removed under the table. After the strawberries and cream, the demitasse of coffee, and perhaps a chocolate bonbon, the mother-in-law proceeded to slip her shoes back on, but found under her opulent chair only the lowly heels of her shoes, gnawed beyond recognition and left discarded like two tasteless bones.

After this invigorating climb to the great white cross, and down through the lovely forest paths back to the parking lot, our route continues towards Crofton, leaving the residential communities and subdivisions behind; the rural flora reappears, the rose campions sprouting out of the jagged, sun-warmed rock faces, pastures of fragrant, freshly mowed hay lying in neat rows ready to bale, market gardens, orchards and fruit farms, and horse riders enjoying a leisurely outing. Take your time and savour the scenery—this route to Crofton is an ideal country drive.

Crofton

The name of Crofton, for many people, brings to mind the Catalyst Mill spewing white smoke and steam from its several cylindrical chimneys while vessels below are loaded with freshly cut logs hauled in by the logging trucks we see rolling down the highway from the forests beyond.

But the village of Crofton itself is clean and delightful, with a beach, a pretty, scenic waterfront walkway, the Old School House Museum, places to eat, and a farmers' market near the ferry terminal.

Speaking of the ferry terminal: This is where you catch the Crofton–Vesuvius Bay ferry for a twenty-five-minute sail across the strait to Salt Spring Island, which is the last stop on the circle route before heading back to Victoria. While waiting for the crossing, I tried the lunch at the Crofton Hotel—the homemade clam chowder was fabulous. Originally built in 1902, the hotel is now modernized, and offers five rooms, each redecorated and fitted with queen-size beds and full bathrooms.

Salt Spring Island

After docking at Vesuvius Bay, the drive across Salt Spring towards Fulford Harbour and its charming shops and cafés affords scenery as enchanting as the previously described route through the backroads of Cowichan. There is far more activity here, but the rural setting has been retained (although I get the sense that the area is under enormous development pressure, especially along the shore). As you drive you will see numerous hand-painted roadside stands, small farms, and wineries.

While waiting for the ferry back to Victoria (to complete my journey's loop), I visited a vegan coffee shop in Fulford Harbour and had the best coffee—made with coconut milk—that I've ever tasted in my life. There are some funky shops at the ferry terminal, offering you one final, quintessential Salt Spring Island experience before you head back to the big island. The scent of patchouli oil, incense, and wool wafts onto the road from a small shop packed with clothing and jewellery—so much so that you'll barely be able to move between the endless racks of scarves, leather bags, beads, and bangles—they even had merchandise dangling from the ceiling beams! Another shop sells local crafts and gifts, including wonderful, colourful, handmade felt hats.

Circle Route Two: Shawnigan Lake, the Kinsol Trestle (Trans Canada Trail) to Cobble Hill, Cowichan Bay (Estuary), Cherry Point

This route from Victoria also begins as you head over the Malahat on the Trans-Canada Highway/BC Highway 1; however, for this route, we turn left to Shawnigan Lake.

The country road to Shawnigan Lake is lined with an abundance of broom, a beautiful yellow-blossomed shrub that, despite its beauty, is highly invasive and toxic. Introduced from England during colonization, this is a tough plant that loves our landscape and climate. Its cousin, the spiny gorse, is also found throughout Vancouver Island; environmental groups hold broom and ivy pulls to control these plants. English ivy is especially harmful, climbing and choking the light and nutrients from the trees in the forest. It is a shame that these two plants are relatively attractive; if they had a foul odour or were repulsive in some way, more volunteers might be willing to pull their hardy, stubborn roots from the rocky ground.

As you make your way along the lake, you'll notice summer cabins along the shore; the lake is a peculiar shape, rather like a limp finger. (Can you believe I once held the notion that lakes are always round?)

The village at the lake is well worth a visit; this could be your first stop. One of the first features you will see is the school sign that sets the tone for the students and the village: WHEREVER THERE IS A HUMAN BEING, THERE IS AN OPPORTUNITY FOR KINDNESS.

The corner store seems to be a hub of the community; it has everything you can imagine, including items such as beach balls, thread, dew worms, and foot cream. During my visit, the bulletin board outside had an advertisement for a pasta night fundraiser to support the expansion of the little museum, a flyer offering a calculus tutor, and a photograph of a sweet old cat with a serene face, the caption reading, HAVE YOU SEEN DAISY? This almost brought tears to my eyes—poor Daisy, where could she be? The notice was so much more tender than if it had the plain old standard heading of MISSING CAT.

Just a few steps up the road is a busy bakery, full of locals: men in overalls; new mothers in purple leotards and ponytails; older, toughened working women with long grey hair and work-worn hands. (My visit took place on a sunny day, and there was a group of cyclists in their clinging Italian Cinzano shirts and slick black tights with padded crotches, wraparound sunglasses, and little spiked shoes that forced them, with their sinewy thighs, to walk like ballerinas. The MAMILs are *everywhere!*) The ladies at the bakery, and other residents, make their own chocolates and treats with names such as Whiskey Dragon and Power Sphere, and there is lavender lemonade.

Next door to the bakery is a manicure and waxing salon; I noticed with astonishment that they also offer eyelash extensions. Upon this discovery, I realized I must expand—or at least reassess my view of the typical small town West Coaster. Admittedly, I've always (and perhaps wrongly) assumed that nature-loving, organic-living, free-thinking residents would never pull carrots with freshly manicured, glistening fingers, and soft cuticles, and certainly not with long, fluttering eyelashes. And hairless legs—who would even see hairless legs in rubber boots? But it seems the people of Shawnigan Lake have seen fit to add a bit of cosmetic flair to their country lifestyle. Perhaps being waxed, primped, and polished is appealing and a bit sexy no matter who or where you are. Come to think of it, who doesn't love to be freshly coiffed while winsomely shimmering with perspiration from all that weeding and plowing? And who wouldn't delight in shiny red lacquered nails when plunging a soft ivory hand into the rich Island soil?

Our route continues to the village of Cobble Hill, just down the road, but a spectacular detour that you simply must take is the short drive to the Kinsol Trestle; trust me, you don't want to pass this up. The trestle, a railway bridge, is nothing short of amazing—the intricacy of the architecture and the elegant construction is truly awe-inspiring.

Be warned, though: the signage on the way there is a bit confusing. This may be the only time in this book that I recommend the use of Google Maps or a GPS (or much patience) to avoid the conflicts and verbal obscenities exchanged in the car between navigator and driver when trying to read a paper map or follow signage that does not seem to make any sense. I'm sure you'll want to avoid comments such as, "Haven't we been past that rock three times?" –and– "Pull over! I need to think—which way is north?" –and– "None of this would have happened if you'd just let me plug in the GPS!" So I suggest that you succumb, just this one time, to technology if you do indeed prefer paper maps.

Once you park in the lovely, wooded lot with picnic tables placed among the leafy, deciduous trees at the fabulous Kinsol site, take the impeccably kept trail about a kilometre to the trestle; this is the Cowichan Valley Trail, part of the Trans Canada Trail (known since 2016 as the Great Trail), the longest trail in the world. You can walk the trail from Sooke, which is thirteen kilometres to the Cowichan section, but of course, you would need to arrange for a drive home, or plan to camp along the way.

There are eight trestles along the Cowichan Valley route, but the fabulous Kinsol Trestle is by far the most spectacular. Built in 1920, the trestle towers above the Koksilah River at 44 metres high and is

188 metres long; the last time a train crossed it was in 1979. But don't let the fact that it's nearly a century old worry you: $7.5 million was invested in the restoration of the structure, which was completed in 2011. A recreational site for walkers and cyclists, it is solid and safe.

The day I ventured across this magnificent construction was warm and breezy, and the scent of forest greenery and wildflowers floated through the great dark beams of the amazing, massive, criss-cross, geometric construction. Woodland birdsong and the sound of the gurgling river below provided a peace better than any piped-in nature music found in a pricey spa. The trestle is so solid and wide, with high rails as well, that it is not a frightening experience in the least; I can say this despite my fear of heights. (I have had heart palpitations over the Elk Falls suspension bridge up by Campbell River.) Even horses cross the trestle on forest trail rides.

When you've traversed the trestle, there's a steep but safe and well-maintained zigzag path down to the crystal-clear river beneath. The river looks safe at this spot, and after a walk, it's refreshing to cool your feet in as well as to experience the trestle from below, giving you another view of this impressive construction and fascinating piece of railway history.

The Kinsol Trestle, built for rail transport close to a small local mine, was named after King Solomon's Mines, a famous action adventure novel set in Africa, written by the British author Sir H. Rider Haggard. King Solomon himself, as described in the Bible, is a symbol of wealth, wisdom, and power, even though he lusted and made foolish choices (as so many of us do today).

I have a bucket list item (though I think bucket list is a ridiculous idiom—it's much clearer to say, "before I die"): My goal is to walk along part of the Great Trail in every Canadian province and territory.

Years ago, back east, I walked along the Great Trail in Fredericton, which takes its route along the Saint John River very near to where Mum and

Dad lived. It was a bitter winter, and the river and the ground were frozen solid with a thin layer of crusted, gritty snow. The sky was white, the trees were black and bare, and the only colour to be seen was found on the tall, pointed, copper-green steeple of the cathedral across the road from the cold steel railway bridge.

Mum, slowly on her way to meeting her maker, was up the hill in the hot Veterans Heath Unit; the place was excessively warm and stuffy as the aroma of overcooked food wafted through the orange corridor under the fluorescent light. Mum was tucked into her bed, flanked by the bed rails, and on a swivel tray sat an untouched, plastic cup of beige Boost. Gone were the days of her vermouth at lunch. Now, several years later, I once again strolled along the Great Trail—this time here, on the Island, making my way towards the Kinsol Trestle. I passed through filtering shafts of sunlight between the wild cherries and maples, gently touching the daisies and wild patches of cobalt lupines. The spindly alders looked elegant, their silver-grey trunks in the green shade, their fragile leaves quivering in the slight breeze; even the black slimy slugs on the forest floor earned my respect while absorbing the beauty and peacefulness of the trail on this special day.

In that moment, I could not help but feel a deep sense of love for Canada, walking on a path that joins us all together, in a beautiful, natural setting that belongs to all of us. I thought of how the First Nations people are known for their spiritual connection to the natural world. Perhaps if we all took the opportunity to discover the woods, the rivers, the tops of the trees, and felt their pulse and life force, we could all connect on a deeper, more understanding, and compassionate level.

When you've sufficiently enjoyed your detour to the trestle and you're ready to return to the circle route, you'll need to be on the road to Cobble Hill, which takes you north from Shawnigan Lake (and is much easier to return to and find!). The whole trip back to Shawnigan Lake and then onward to Cobble Hill should take about twenty minutes.

Cobble Hill (I'm not sure I recall an actual hill) is not on a lake nor on the sea, but it is a quaint village with the necessary facilities: a women-only fitness centre, a beautiful gift shop and antique store, and—lo and behold—another waxing and eyelash extension salon! The ladies of Shawnigan Lake and Cobble Hill must value smooth skin and beautiful eyes. I must admit, a service that offers both hair removal and hair additions seems peculiar to me, but I can only deduce that beauty is in strategic hair placement.

> Frances Oldham Kelsey, the brave pharmacologist who took on the American Food and Drug Association on the dangers of thalidomide (the drug given to pregnant women to lessen morning sickness, resulting in a generation of babies with severe birth defects) was born in Cobble Hill.

Our final stop on this road trip loop is Cowichan Bay, which is across the Trans-Canada Highway. Thankfully, the signage is excellent from Cobble Hill.

Cowichan Bay is a diminutive seaside village jammed with ice cream stands, pasta and seafood cafés, and quirky shops selling sun hats, herbal concoctions, crystals, and windup toys. There's even a body piercing studio and a psychic on hand if the spirit moves you—all this with the spectacular seaside backdrop that is the Cowichan Estuary.

Towards the end of the village is the nature centre, an informative little place in a small park. Here you can rest or read the brochures provided while watching the herons fish in the shallow, silty waters at low tide; you can also have a chuckle at the kayakers who get stuck in the nutritious, fertile mud.

Great blue herons inhabit rookeries in many locations on Vancouver Island, usually in high trees in huge nests that they create with sticks. (There are several related species of heron, including a white version residing only in the southern United States.)

Watch them feeding in the shallow tide waters; it is a study in tremendous patience. Motionless they wait, poised and statuesque with their long, wispy, elegant plumage draping over their slender bodies, until they spot the perfect unsuspecting morsel. Small fish are their preference, and at just the right time, they strike like a dart, swallowing their meal whole. They have even been known to sometimes choke!

Important Bird and Biodiversity Areas (IBAs) are found around the globe. Volunteer-run by Birdlife International, the organization protects, monitors, and maintains diverse wetlands and other migration, feeding, and resting locations.

Several IBA locations on and close to Vancouver Island include Active Pass (the deep, swirling channel between Galiano and Mayne Islands), Sidney Channel, the islands off Oak Bay (Victoria), Somenos Marsh in Duncan, Little Qualicum Estuary to Nanoose Bay, the Comox Valley, Tofino Mudflats Wildlife Management Area, and Strathcona Provincial Park.

According to Birdlife International, approximately 320 birds breed in British Columbia. This is more than anywhere else in North America except Texas.

If you enjoy birdwatching, Birdlife International suggests a few important viewing guidelines so as not to disturb the birds, especially when they are weak and weary from a long migration or protecting their young. These guidelines include common-sense suggestions: keeping a specific distance, remaining quiet, not leaving trash or other objects behind, and leaving your dog. (Brochures that contain guidelines for viewing wildlife can be found at bcnature.ca; there is one for Vancouver Island.)

If you're a serious nature enthusiast who wishes to enhance your caretaking and birding skills, you can become a caretaker of IBA sites. But be prepared: the responsibility is not light. The main tasks are to organize the restoration and protection of beaches and other bird habitats, monitor bird movement, and keep a lookout for looming threats, such as development of some sort, pollution, or intrusion by careless citizens. Community education is also a vital duty of the caretaker, who may visit schools, lead field trips, and describe a few common-sense guidelines to the public, especially during the birds' rest stops during their migration journey.

You may recall the good caring citizens who roped off the area around a moulting seal who was resting on a Victoria beach in the spring of 2018. Sadly, no guidelines could prevent the ignorant children and parents who harassed the animal by shouting, throwing objects, and even nudging the seal from her rest. There are enormous fines and penalties for disturbing wildlife, and for good reason: Apparently, the seal was fine, and she returned to her ocean following her spring rest.

The Cowichan Estuary Nature Centre has produced a lovely informative pamphlet of five birding areas in their vicinity, and it lists the birds you might see. I find the variety of bird names intriguing and sometimes amusing. Here are a few bird species you can see at the Cowichan locations: the northern harrier, which sounds like a military war plane; the mute swan, who is obviously the silent type; the Eurasian widgeon (isn't that a type of tool used to change a tire?); the marbled murrelet, which sounds as if it might be a Hollywood starlet; and the pipit, which is simply a delightful, sweet name.

The vast areas of watersheds, streams, lakes, water courses, and estuaries in the Cowichan region are cared for by many volunteers and organizations. A prominent group is the Cowichan Watershed Board, which works with the First Nations people to focus on water quality and estuary health.

*Whenever I see the wood duck, my heart leaps, for this little crea-
ture is a work of art, with its intricate design of teal, burnt orange,
and white. I once saw a watercolour painting of a wood duck by the late
Canadian artist Fenwick Lansdowne; it was beautifully observed, and I
kick myself for not purchasing it.*

*A member of the Royal Canadian Academy of Arts and a recipient of the
Order of British Columbia and the Order of Canada, Lansdowne was an
influential and brilliant artist. His work is understated due to the subject
matter—mainly birds and wildlife. It seems to me that artists who depict
great suffering or colourful scenes or abstracts receive more accolades than
those who capture the essence of, in this case, birds. Still, I believe Fenwick is
one of the greats of Canadian art due to his exceptional skills in observation,
discipline, and detail; he has been compared to the American artist Audubon
and received high praise from Prince Phillip. One of his major projects,
which took him ten years to complete, was a commission titled Rare Birds of
China; this can be seen at rarebirdsofchina.com, and many of his other works
can be found elsewhere online. His art is a treat, a pleasure not only to the
eyes but to the spirit as well.*

Following your visit to Cowichan Bay, you have two options to con-
clude your circle route: Continue along towards Crofton as described
earlier, or head south and return to Victoria; if the latter is your choice,
take one more charming country road trip via Cherry Point. This is
easy—simply take Cherry Point Road outside of Cowichan Bay and
meander along the rural winding road until you arrive back on the
highway to return to town.

Duncan

If there were ever a town woefully misrepresented by casual first impres-
sions, Duncan is that place. The view from the highway isn't glamorous:

It's lined with strip malls, insurance offices, pokey little pizza takeout joints, thrift stores, money marts, inkjet refill and photocopy depots, auto supply centres, and dollar stores, all adorned by plastic signage, flat roofs, and oil-slicked asphalt parking spaces. There's a faded sign on the gritty boulevard that reads, WELCOME TO DUNCAN, CITY OF TOTEMS, but no totems can be seen from that vantage point. Looming in the distance are big box stores and giant supermarkets. Gas stations and convenience stores are on every corner, and traffic is usually jammed and congested between street lights. But what a surprise awaits you if you venture along a side street and into the town itself! I cannot overstate this: What you drive through on the highway is *not* Duncan, so please do not judge this book by its cover as you sail along this ribbon of plastic and vinyl signage, concrete, and fast-food drive-thru restaurants. One day, it may provide a remarkable academic study on our present civilization!

Situated on the traditional lands of the Cowichan First Nation, Duncan is a quaint and charming town with pretty little shops, pocket parks, and public art. Here you can find restored historical buildings, including the original creamery, livery stable, blacksmith, wheelwright, and the Duncan opera house, to name a few. Mysterious and inviting alleyways lined with flower boxes, commemorative plaques, paving stones, garden beds, fountains, and statues honouring Duncan's history are tucked away among several of the main streets. You'll notice that the town's citizens are remarkably friendly—when was the last time you meandered down a street as shop personnel greeted you? As I strolled along, I passed some home decorating shop owners who were especially friendly as they cleaned their windows, which displayed pink chintz wingback chairs and cranberry glass candle holders. Even more charming is how the shops and services are effortlessly adorable and unpretentious—there's even a street sign that points to LOIS LANE behind the beautiful red brick, clock-towered City Hall. The contrast of the town to the highway strip malls a few blocks away is astonishing, and I must say that downtown Duncan is one of the most pleasant hidden gems on the island.

The work of erecting totem poles throughout Duncan began in 1985 (although there were already many poles present in the area). The western redcedar is the tree of choice for totem carving, and traditional tools are still used today, custom-made to fit the hands of the carver. Totem poles are records of First Nations culture and family history; each pole represents a deeply personal and cultural story, a traditional legend, or belief. This diverse and moving display includes over forty poles (at the time of this writing) and is the largest outdoor collection in the world. In the summer, there are free guided tours offered by the Cowichan Valley Museum (in the former E&N Railway Station, found at 130 Canada Avenue) but year-round you can pick up a booklet at the front desk of the museum, follow the painted yellow footprints on the sidewalk, and go on a self-guided walk—it's fascinating, educational, and the stroll around town is delightful in its own right. The booklet describes each pole, its symbols, and the carver. From this handy resource, I learned there's a totem that represents both the air (the raven) and the land (the beaver). Another totem that stood out was called Owl Spirit, which the carver, Tom LaFortune, crafted in honour of his mother. I also learned that a distinct feature on totem poles are the guardians, perched on top, looking out to sea. And there is a pole devoted to the legend of the raven who steals the sun and lights the earth.

A meaningful and beautiful aspect of First Nations culture is their tradition of selecting a cedar tree: They celebrate the use of the tree after they take it down, honouring its life and new purpose, almost as if they are thanking the tree for its use. And when a new pole is carved and raised, a great ceremony takes place; many First Nations people attend and perform dances, gift giving, drumming, and singing. This is in stark contrast to how non-Indigenous people usually regard the cutting down of trees. I believe we exploit nature to its fullest without sufficient appreciation of the natural world because we do not feel connected to, or part of, nature. In contrast, Indigenous artists often acknowledge their spiritual link to the natural world.

When I moved to Victoria from my old farm in North Saanich, I fell in love with my neighbourhood—the beach, the dog park, the local characters who feed the birds and collect bottles, the flowering cherry trees in spring, the park ponds full of ducks, the heron rookery, my village pub, and with a wonderful old gnarled apple tree in my small back garden. I adored its boughs, laden with firm red fruit, arched over the little deck and under the clothesline. I would hang out my fresh laundry there, admire the healthy, prolific old tree, and feel a deep sense of calm and joy. (I love doing laundry and hanging it out to dry, and I appreciate the freedom I have to do so, knowing there are some neighbourhoods with residents who find visible laundry offensive and do not allow for such a burlesquey exhibit.)

Now, there was another scrubby, sad, stunted apple tree in the corner of my garden, so I decided to have it removed to make room for a quince tree. The day the little tree was to be removed, I was at the dentist down the street. As I approached my house, I was horrified to see two young, strong arborists hauling out the great limbs of my big, beloved tree, its ripened apples dropping heavily on the sidewalk as they tossed the lush limbs into a giant chipper.

They had cut down the wrong tree.

I flew into a rabid rage, screaming at these men as if they had committed murder—and as far as I was concerned, they had: I loved that tree with all my heart. Words I had never used flew out of my mouth in despair, anguish, and fury as the two men made a rapid getaway in their truck, leaving their tools, ropes, and chainsaw behind, all of which I threw onto the street.

I grieved for weeks, and I still think about my dear tree daily; it was and still is a tremendous loss, both physically and spiritually. I will never forget my beautiful apple tree, which has now produced a thousand sprouts throughout the back lawn. It wants to live, to return. It has a life force, and in those sprouts I see that even though it was cut at its roots, that tree will endure in the form of sprouts. It possesses the fierce will to live.

E. J. Hughes

Duncan is home to the E. J. Hughes Gallery. One of the most well-known artists in Canada, E. J. Hughes (1913–2007) was born in Vancouver. He was a war artist in the Second World War (as were my parents, Molly Lamb-Bobak and Bruno Bobak), and after the war, he settled in the Cowichan Valley, where he painted the local landscapes, often in vivid colour. Mum knew him and adored his work—easy-to-enjoy imagery in realism style, depicting the beauty of Vancouver Island through its busy harbours and working coastal communities, wharves, inlets hung with arbutus trees, little red tugs, steamers, fish boats, rural villages, and golden meadows. An original Hughes oil painting is worth hundreds of thousands of dollars, and the E. J. Hughes Gallery on Duncan's Station Street sells numerous beautiful art cards and framed reproductions and prints. In 2018, Victoria artist and writer Robert Amos published *E. J. Hughes Paints Vancouver Island*, a retrospective on the book's namesake, featuring photographs and sketches from Hughes's estate.

I always thought Hughes looked like a dear old grandpa, like Matthew Cuthbert in CBC's eighties version of *Anne of Green Gables*.

The Malaspina Mural

Built in 1927, the old Malaspina Hotel in Nanaimo fell into disrepair. Though quite luxurious in its day, it became a bar and even a home-less shelter, and was finally was abandoned and left empty. (There's a wonderful but melancholy expression given to old, run-down urban architecture: demolition by neglect. This was the old hotel's fate.) It was officially demolished in 1996, and discovered in the dust and gritty debris, and hidden behind a wall, was a sizable mural (9 × 12 feet) painted by a young E. J. Hughes in 1938, who painted the hotel walls for his room and board. The subject, in six sections, was the history of our coastal exploration. Although much of the art was destroyed, damaged, or eaten away by fungus and mould, an intact and rescued piece depicted Captain Alessandro Malaspina standing on our shores flanked by his Italian and Spanish crew members. The mural was lovingly restored by art historian Cheryl Harrison and can be viewed today at the Vancouver Island Conference Centre in Nanaimo. Its worth is currently estimated at over four million dollars.

> Who was Alessandro Malaspina? The seventeenth-century explorer's name is well-known, but here are a few interesting facts about the Italian captain who mapped our shores following Captain Cook's voyages:
>
> Born in Tuscany, Italy, Malaspina sailed with the Spanish navy.
>
> Malaspina is also recognized for preventing scurvy on his ships; due to his knowledge of the disease, he carried citrus fruit aboard his vessels, and made spruce tea on our shores—a recipe probably learned from the First Nations people he met with in the coastal forests (although, admittedly, I have also read numerous accounts crediting Cook with a similar skill).
>
> Various articles note that he and the First Nations people of our coast were amicable—in fact, he is thought to have repaired a few bridges burned from earlier European explorers' attitudes and plundering.
>
> One of the more notable facts recorded about Malaspina states that he drew up plans for a canal through Panama, which was eventually constructed by the United States between 1903 and 1914.

Somenos Marsh

On your way out of Duncan, travelling north on the main highway, you will easily see the Somenos Marsh Conservation Area on the right.

There is a small parking lot to pull into, and it is well worth the stop.

The marsh surrounds the sixty-square-kilometre lake and is cared for by volunteers. They have built a lovely, discreet, unobtrusive boardwalk and viewing platforms in a circular route just beyond the parking lot. The boardwalk stroll takes only fifteen or twenty minutes, longer if you sit and listen to the sounds of the marsh or look for a blue heron or trumpeter swan.

There is numerous and colourful, informative signage poking up from the reeds, describing all who live in the lake—including beavers—and among the marsh foliage and bracken and black cottonwood trees. Although the yellow iris is beautiful and adds a warm splash of colour within the reeds of the marsh, it is considered invasive and must be controlled by hand.

Invasive plants present us with quite a dilemma! They are often not only attractive, such as English ivy, but also traditional. Yes, it is a charming and quaint sight to see a brick house with English ivy crawling up over its old walls, paned windows, and gables, but the truth is, ivy chokes out light and fertile space with its long and entwined root system, depriving native vegetation that provides habitat and food for our wildlife. The yellow iris chokes out pond life; holly and scotch broom are other invasive plants; and, despite the delicious pies we make from it, so is the Himalayan blackberry. I suppose the paradox is that invasive species seem to thrive in our environment, possibly since many are English in origin and we have a similar climate.

One looming invasive concern is the American bullfrog, a large, confident creature that can eat an entire duckling. It is believed that these bulbous pond inhabitants originally hopped across the country from New York where they had been imported from France for their delectable legs; perhaps this is their revenge! (And why is it that such elite food is often so sparse? After all, there's practically no meat on a frog's leg.)

One native shrub—the red osier dogwood, distinctive by its stiff red stalks—is abundant throughout the Somenos Marsh. There's a dear little bird who lives among its stalks: the marsh wren, which I speculate is named after Christopher Wren, the brilliant and innovative British architect who designed London after its terrible fire in the 1600s.

The marsh wren is also an amazing architect—well, at least most of the time. He will construct several nests from grasses, leaves, and marsh debris, carefully concealing them from predators and designing them for comfort and strength to endure winds, rains, and storms, all in the hopes of attracting a mate who will, after carefully inspecting the labour, location, stability, and nesting potential of each home, hopefully select him to be the father of her children. Can you imagine the anticipatory anxiety and then disappointment if all abodes are rejected by her?

The poor little fellow! Such humiliation and despair he'd feel watching her move on to another bachelor along the shore who included something more appealing in his construction—maybe a smaller entrance, or a softer bed, perhaps a better floor design or superior feng shui.

This is why I love the marsh wren: Rejection is always looming, always possible, but even so, you can hear his optimistic little song. Cheer him on when you visit this lovely marsh! The world needs such positive thinkers.

The Somenos Marsh represents a source of natural capital. This is the dollar value on the natural services that an ecosystem provides, as opposed to a man-made service of the same kind; I like to think of it as Nature's Bank. For example, a wetland such as the Somenos Marsh can provide flood control, water filtration, tourism, and carbon storage, thereby saving the community huge expenditures while maintaining a healthy environment.

At the north edge of the marsh is the BC Forest Discovery Centre. Its most prominent features are its beautiful museum, which provides education on trees and lumber to its visitors. The enchanting little train journey winds through the logging and sawmill remnants, old orchards, a shady woodland, and over a trestle above the marsh filled with ducks and succulent wetland reeds and rushes. Whether for a peaceful adult rest or for the amusement of children, this charming railway activity is lovely: the conductor blows the whistle and toots the horn, and the train stops for ten minutes midway in a park-like meadow where you can buy ice cream. Elsewhere on the grounds, explore a historic schoolhouse, a ranger station, a blacksmith shop, and the 1930s logging camp bunkhouses; then take a stroll through the forest trails and learn about trees from the informative signage. For example, did you know that the yew tree produces a chemical that is included in Taxol, which is used to treat cancer?

At the quaint little Alderlea train station, behind its white-painted railing and wooden platform, I noticed a poster on the wall; it was in the corner, rather hidden from all the other attractions, and described the so-called Hoo-Hoo organization. I was intrigued—what in the world is a Hoo-Hoo?

I learned that the International Concatenated Order of Hoo-Hoos are a little-known fraternal organization established in 1892. Its membership is restricted to men over the age of eighteen who, according to their values statement found online, "live by a code of ethics." Members are also typically associated with the lumber industry in some way. A lighthearted fraternity, its ruling council of nine supreme members take their titles from Lewis Carroll's nonsense poem "The Hunting of the Snark." These include the Bojun, the Jabberwocky (which replaced the Bandersnatch for some reason), and the Grand Snark himself. One of their rituals is known as the Embalming of the Snark, and it is through this rite that a new supreme leader is established (or perhaps retired). It is all in good fun, and one can't help but wonder if the embalming process involves alcohol. Not being a member of this fraternity (and not being very intrigued by paper products), I am not privy to their rituals, so I am unable to explain the *embalming* process in detail. However, I think I'll include "The Hunting of the Snark" on my future reading list.

But where, you ask, did the Hoo-Hoos get their name? Some say hoo-hoo is a slang term to describe lumbermen; others say a hoo-hoo is a lock of hair on a bald man and that the founder of this organization sported this prominent feature.

Reflections While Riding the Choo-Choo

A woodsman started a club called the Hoo-Hoo,
What it's about I don't have a clue-clue.
I am baffled and vexed—it seems rather koo-koo!
So if I write more, I could very well be sue-sued.

On the train, as it tooted and choo-chooed,
I pondered forest products, pencils, and pool cue-cues,
And paper goods that belong in the loo-loo:
These, and morality, bind Hoo-Hoos like glue-glue.

Butch or Kenny can be names in the Hoo-Hoo,
Not Dolly, nor Dottie, especially not Lulu.
And strictly forbidden are colourful tutus;
Such garments would be instantly poo-pooed.

This secret society exists—oh, who knew-knew?
It's quite elite, and no matter what you do-do,
If you're a lady, never shall you be a Hoo-Hoo—
So give up now—Hoo-Hoos shan't woo-woo (you!).

Chemainus

Art is usually the last thing people invest their faith and money in when pursuing financial growth. But Chemainus did it in spades and defied a threatening economic collapse (due to the flagging logging industry) with its famous murals, thus becoming an attractive tourist destination. After visiting this little whimsical town, you will find, as I did, its creative and artistic endeavours extremely admirable.

In 1858, as with numerous towns in our region, Chemainus's economy was driven by the lumber and forestry business and industry. Of course, we cannot always rely on business and industry, even in boom times when the money flows and there seems to be no end to resources and employment. However, the logging industry did slow in the 1970s; little Chemainus had to think of a way to survive, so some forward-thinking residents came up with the idea of creating a mural town and attracting tourists—and the strategy was successful and very lucrative!

Chemainus now has approximately forty-five outdoor murals as well as a diverse array of sculptures. The murals are connected by yellow-painted footsteps on the sidewalks, and are on the sides of shops and businesses, throughout back alleys, parks, and down the main street among ice cream parlours and credit unions. Depicting various scenes of Chemainus history, each mural is painted in a different style. The subjects range widely from the Hong Hing Waterfront Store, to the First School House, to the Chemainus Hospital, to the 1915 Telephone Company; my favourite mural is *Logging with Oxen* by Harold Lyon.

When in Chemainus, pick up a colourful brochure and mural map at the Chemainus Visitor Centre, just beside the museum, and stroll out for some marvellous mural meandering. The clever route also takes you through Old Town Chemainus down along the shore below a lovely shady park. There's a variety of little gift shops to explore and places to rest and indulge in refreshments, such as homemade caramel ice cream.

My cousin Elizabeth from England visited last summer. Her father, my uncle, had the most British of names: Willoughby Mortimer-Lamb (I called him Uncle

Abby when I was a child). He was a minister at the little church, right in the heart of Chemainus, from 1942 to 1947. The church, St. Michael's and All Angels, is delightfully restored and open often; visitors are very welcome to enter through the original inner door and sit quietly to have a Little Think or learn about several of the architectural or historical features. The font is from 1920, a gift from the Japanese community. I had no idea that Uncle Abby was ever in Chemainus—Mum never told me! I used to visit him in Chichester, England, and we'd have tea in his rose garden and a joint (a roast) on Sunday, and his wife Irene and I took brisk walks along the tow paths, over stiles, and across meadows throughout the English countryside with their little dog Muppet.

The murals of Chemainus

The Chemainus Festival of Murals Society oversees the mural program and maintenance of the art as well as the creation of new murals; since they're outdoors, you can imagine how the weather takes its toll on the paint. Building construction and renovation also impacts the murals—they are difficult to remove from the side of a crumbling stucco shop that needs to be replaced, so newer murals that may end up relocated in the future have been placed in removable frames. The scenes primarily depict First Nations, historical themes, and influential people from the past, including the artist Emily Carr.

Like poetry, art can be intimidating; people are often unsure what it's all about and wonder what they are supposed to feel or understand. This typically happens when people view abstract and conceptual art. When people look at, say, a huge oil painting of a red square between two yellow stripes, they may feel cynical and combative (thinking, *I can do that*) or shrink back from lack of confidence and feeling intellectually inferior. Either way, they may simply lack understanding about the art—if in fact there is anything to understand, especially in a gallery where one painting of a pink square hangs on a huge, bare, white wall, forcing you to look at what baffles you. There is no escape!

Even worse, the commentary often makes no sense to the average patron. I was in a gallery on the Island, viewing a collection of photographs of desperate-looking naked women doing strange things with logs; the accompanying, rambling commentary went a little like this:

"The pieces represent the disseminated juxtapositions of the ordinary." And . . .

"The examination and mapping of the interconnected practice of the documented creative practices." Plus . . .

"An exploration and investigation of a dichotomous collaboration between the active interaction and the detached disintegration of our maternal needs within the child among us."

I wondered: Are they speaking about the inner security of a person who has been breastfed? In such a setting, I'm either a fool or am being played the fool—regardless, I'm uncomfortable.

I believe if Chemainus had gone the traditional route to facilitate tourism, it would have failed. The reason the murals are, and continue to be, so successful is this: They are wonderfully simple. There is nothing wrong with simplicity; it is misguided to believe that complicated is superior, and even worse to create complication on purpose, attempting to sound so superior and intellectual. With these murals, what you see is straightforward; you are not being manipulated, and there is nothing artificial. Their purpose and pride is to encourage you to enjoy the community and embrace its history, the culture, and its citizens.

As the murals are all outdoors, the patrons are free to move on, not held as intellectual prisoners, heads tilted in analytical pondering; nor are they forced to feel they must stay because if they leave without pondering the subject it may indicate a lack of comprehension of the work and therefore, stupidity. Art should never lower your confidence in yourself! When I am in a gallery, I admit that I do feel slightly inferior if I move about too rapidly, wondering: Should I study each piece carefully, searching for the deep understanding of humanity as depicted in these works? Outdoor art holds nobody accountable to time limitations.

Finally, the murals in Chemainus tell a story. You can learn a few cultural and historical facts, and you can take those facts home and treasure them for a long time. A tourist might return home and recall a mural, and say, "Sweetheart, do you remember that lovely mural of the steam train crossing that bridge? Wow, those were the days, eh?" But I'll wager they would never say, "Sweetheart, do you remember that dichotic triptych collage juxtaposing pieces of the broken camera and the symbolism of the cracked lens within the three white circles?"

On two occasions, I've been awestruck or profoundly moved by art that is not of the traditional type. Similar to the Chemainus murals, both were quite simple, and both were installations. An installation, from my observation and understanding, is a piece of created art that is constructed, built, or applied, or consists of various parts put together to convey a message. It may be indoors or outdoors and can be dismantled, taken apart, packed away or, in some cases, left to disintegrate. Ultimately, an installation is installed and is usually created with the intent to leave a deep and lasting impression on the viewer.

One unforgettable installation has left me with vivid memories and a lingering case of the willies. I was at the MOMA (Museum of Modern Art) in New York many years ago with my dear friend Patsy; the installation was in an enormous, airy room, with high skylights, bare white walls, and a polished wooden floor. In the centre of this huge, echoing space was a long table; on the table were two rows of large silver jars, each about the size of a small garbage can. Each silver jar had a label on the side, written in beautiful calligraphy, with each jar displaying a different body fluid. The labels read as follows: SEMEN, MUCUS, VOMIT, SALIVA, SWEAT, EAR WAX, and so on. Oh, it just repulsed me! (Interestingly, I do not believe that BLOOD was there, perhaps because it is not as repulsive, or maybe because it did not mix with the other colour schemes of yellows and pearly whites.)

"Ugh, that's just revolting!" I said to Patsy.

"Are you ashamed of your own body?" she asked.

"When I see it like that, yes," I said.

After a good laugh, we headed upstairs to the bar and drank several mimosas (each).

But now, to this very day, whenever I use the sauna at the gym, the sight of people perspiring on the cedar benches has me cringing in the corner on my towel as I recall the rows of those silver jars all so neatly labelled in that great room with nothing else.

In contrast to this installation, I witnessed a profoundly powerful, moving, and brilliantly conceived piece by a Winnipeg-based Metis artist named Jaime Black. In 2010 she created the REDress Project (redressproject.org), which I first saw at The Museum of Human Rights in Winnipeg. The REDress installation at the museum was a collection of approximately thirty red dresses—representing over twelve hundred missing and murdered Indigenous women in Canada—hanging silently in a row in a small, dim alcove. But the installation has moved beyond that small, closeted area. Throughout our country, red dresses can be seen hanging in a variety of locations: in trees, on front porches, in gardens, on a beach. And in March 2017, the artist hung a hundred red dresses on the campus of the University of Toronto.

One cold autumn evening in 2017, on the shores of the Comox Estuary, a cluster of small, flimsy red dresses hung on a line between two wooden posts, flapping and snapping in the bitter wind as the sun slipped behind the deep purple-grey mountains under a dark, yellow sky. A storm was looming; the water was still and black, and the seabirds were quietly nesting. By midnight, the wind thrashed the first cold autumn rains against the windows of my beach cabin at nearby Kye Bay where I was nestled beside the wood stove (unlike the sad, drenched, threadbare dresses, so vulnerable to the storm) and tore any remaining leaves from near-bare tree branches. The following morning was calm and silent when I was on my way to purchase a few supplies in town; the white dawn turned into the misty drizzle of the new day. The only colour to be seen along the grey estuary came from the soggy red dresses, twisted and mangled on the line that held them so high. The effect of the wild weather enhanced the installation with stark simplicity; the dresses were left, in disarray, to the mercy of the elements—brilliant symbolism.

So it is in Chemainus that art, in ways we can all understand, feel, and respond to, has shaped the little town that was almost forgotten. Perhaps in our own lives there are times when art can help us cope, understand, and endure. These moments are precious and rare, and to a certain degree they must come by our own choosing. But we can be sure that the powerful effects wrought by art are more valuable than the financial gain of lumber and gold. What art gives us is transcendent and lasting; even if the experience itself is fleeting, we have the images within us to recall when needed.

Five interesting and often-unknown facts gathered from my stroll among the murals:

- Chemainus had the first rail logging industry in the province.

- The Company Store, which operated in 1917, accepted one of the first credit card transaction systems, using coupons and paycheque deductions.

- In 1929, the first all-Japanese Boy Scout troop in Canada was established in Chemainus.

- Telephone service began in 1908 and served thirty telephones.

- The nearby Lenora Mine produced gold, silver, and copper, all extracted by hand.

Ladysmith and the Road North to Nanaimo

IF, WHEN DRIVING FROM CHEMAINUS TO LADYSMITH, YOU'D like a pleasant diversion off the Trans-Canada Highway, try one of the area's prettiest but most underrated seaside drives. Mikki and I took this charming fifteen-minute route along Chemainus Road one day—she'd won a quilt in a raffle, and we had to pick up her prize at the quilter's home, which was tucked down a little lane leading to the waterfront.

The winding road took us past modest little homes, the sea glinting between the trees as we passed the settlement of Saltair, and when we approached Ladysmith, we were struck by the unrushed, uncontrived sense of the area. Driving past a school, a local store, and people strolling along the road with their dogs, we had a strong impression of a lovely, close-knit community.

Ladysmith, situated precisely on the 49th parallel, is a charming, quiet small town that prides itself on its historical features and countless heritage awards: As you travel both south and north, the town's welcome signs proudly proclaim its status as a repeated heritage award-winner. Here is just a partial list of the town's many restoration and heritage awards:

- The Agricultural Hall, built in 1922: "Outstanding Achievement" 2000

- Railway Machine Shop, built in 1940: "Award of Honour" 2002

- Maritime Museum: "Award of Honour" 2008

- Ladysmith Archives: "Award of Honour" 2009

- Main Street Canada: "National Communities in Bloom Award" 2003

- Metal Collage, display of historical artifacts and photographs: "Award of Honour" 1991

If I were mayor of a small town on Vancouver Island, I would not even bother entering the competition if I knew Ladysmith had applied. This is clearly a town that excels at heritage preservation. They are untouchable, unstoppable, unbeatable.

Many of the town's restoration projects and heritage awards celebrate their agricultural hall, railway machine warehouses, maritime museum, and their famous heritage main street, especially amazing at Christmastime when they hold the grand light-up. Several blocks transform into a dazzling, festive winter wonderland. Local history and heritage, as displayed in their artifacts and venues and older buildings, are so important to Ladysmith that the Tourism Ladysmith website offers not one but two different self-guided walking tours that cover a surprising number of stops worth checking out as you meander along their historic streets. A massive ship's anchor in the city's roundabout, a big old water pump, a whaling ship's harpoon gun, the 49th Parallel Cairn, and the amusingly named "steam donkey" are only a few items of interest scattered around town.

Ladysmith's little main street up on the hill and its heritage are inseparable; this is, in fact, what Ladysmith is currently best known for. Moreover, the town has an important Indigenous and industrial past: For thousands of years, the shores were a rich source of shellfish for the Stz'uminus First Nation people; much later, the coal mining industry's use of Ladysmith Harbour, as endorsed by James Dunsmuir, and commercial oyster farming, also made the little town a significant business community. A volatile coal miners' strike took place between 1912 and 1914, which ironically ended with the start of the First World War, shifting the focus of fighting from Ladysmith to Europe.

If, from our vantage point on the hill, we shift our gaze to below the highway and down to the waterfront, there are a few lovely surprises in store. There is a wonderful art gallery in the original railway maintenance warehouse used in the 1940s by the Comox Logging and Railway Company. Outside are aging, rotund, black engines sitting on rusted tracks enveloped by grass and weeds; it has a rustic and historic feel and should not be mowed and tidied—the vegetative growth combined with the dying age of rail creates a lovely, slightly melancholy presence. The interior of the repair shop is immense and when fully operational could house seven logging trucks; two trains could also enter the building for repair.

Today, many talented and professional artists exhibit here; the gallery is bright and airy, painted white with vast views, through a row of paned windows, of the harbour often jammed with log booms at the mill below. The stairway up to the gallery is quirky, with a huge chandelier hanging in the bright, bare, whitewashed lobby. The admission is free, and the variety of exhibits changes frequently; subjects range from doors to water themes, beachcombing, and textile skills. One of the gallery's primary projects was to raise money to install an elevator up to the exhibition room—the members believe that art should be accessible to all, which is a wonderful aim, and they even display art in the waiting room of the local medical clinic.

The idea of art being free for all can be traced back to the Golden Age of the Elizabethan era. Yes, Queen Elizabeth I may have relished the revolting punishment of public castration and disembowelling—performed on the victim while they were still able to see their own innards—but she also felt that all people, rich or poor, should be able to enjoy art.

(I find her support of these two pursuits perplexing as they are so opposite . . . or are they?)

At any rate, England has carried on this tradition (not the public castration and disembowelling!) to this day. There are specific times in the week when many, if not all, public art galleries are open, free of admission, to all citizens.

I will always remember being in the aging, concrete-columned Tate Gallery in London on the muddy Thames. As I contemplated the array of Turner master-pieces, a man and his children entered the large room, with its polished floors and impeccably hung, gilt-framed oils of seascapes and the foggy, smoky, steamy streets of London. From the look of his ragged coat and baggy pants, dishevelled hair, and floppy shoes, it seemed he was quite poor, and the children looked like thin, pale waifs in stretched threadbare sweaters (right out of a Dickens story), but their enthusiasm for the paintings was remarkable. I'll never forget them, whispering in excited gasps at Turner's murky, energetic, ochre skies, the pale blue-grey misty hazes, and his elegant seagoing vessels, leaning into the ocean wind, sails billowing on the sweeping whitecaps, as the children's father gently guided them through the great echoing marble halls of the galleries.

The effect of art does not discriminate between rich and poor; it is not solely the domain of the privileged. It can latch itself on to you, or anyone, at the least-expected moment, perhaps presenting you with an epiphany, which could possibly alter your perspective on life. Thus, there should be no fee for this opportunity, this chance, this fate that may be found in the art, waiting for you.

Also along the waterfront of Ladysmith is the very popular five-star Transfer Beach, a sweeping green space dotted with glades of trees and picnic tables. The beach is also home to Sealegs Kayaking Adventures, a rental outfitter on the sandy cove. The vast park is completely accessible for all—whether on scooters, wheelchairs, or in baby prams—with large open parking areas and a wide paved road. There are no strenuous hills to climb and paved paths wind throughout to large shady trees and lovely West Coast vistas.

The Ladysmith Community Marina is a hub of activity as well and offers a variety of events, ocean knowledge, harbour tours, restored wooden boats, and sailing lessons for those who live with disabilities. Marinas have certainly changed over the years—they used to be not much more than makeshift docks where people with boats would tie up for a day to refuel and buy a fresh supply of toilet paper and fishing bait. Nowadays, marinas are small, friendly communities; at the Ladysmith Community Marina, the wharves welcome you with lush, overflowing flower baskets, and there's a shop that sells gift items and practical but fashionable naval clothing such as navy fleece vests and yellow rubber boots. There are spotless showers and a lovely café with homemade muffins.

Many marinas are eco-certified; these green facilities comply with the criteria proposed by Clean Marine BC, a Georgia Strait Alliance program. This vital group lists six major boating and marina concerns: sewage and grey water disposal; oil spill response; waste and recycling; control of toxic paint and maintenance products; wildlife interaction; and derelict vessels.

Best practices for boaters include washing the boat thoroughly before sailing to another location to avoid transporting invasive ocean plants or animals; boats also should not anchor in nor speed through nutrient-rich eelgrass, a valuable ocean plant that looks like long grass and provides hundreds of little creatures, including the Pacific herring, with habitat, protection, spawning areas, and food. Eelgrass beds also maintain the ocean floor by preventing runoff and erosion.

The Pacific herring run takes place every March, close to the time that the brant geese return from their southern wintering. Both exciting marine events occur on the Island's long stretches of pebbled and sandy shores and is one of the first welcoming signs of spring; the herring run is especially dense around Parksville-Qualicum, Deep Bay, and Denman Island.

The herring appear in huge shoals to spawn among the kelp beds and eelgrass, and the sea is suddenly dotted with hundreds of fish boats, their aluminum hulls glinting in the glare of the spring sun. Then an amazing phenomenon occurs: The colour of the ocean turns to a milky azure and turquoise blue. Data on various websites differ on the cause of the colour change, but a common belief is that the water is milky due to the massive amount of herring sperm released to fertilize the female herring's eggs; the blue is a combination of the silver of the fish reflecting off the sun's rays, the blue-green sea water, and the blooms of phytoplankton on which the herring feed.

The herring roe—minuscule little jellies, a favourite food of the grey whale—wash upon the shore, creating waves of what looks like pale yellow ridges of cream of wheat. The initial odour is fresh, like a sea breeze, similar to what you'd smell in a fish store, but when the roe begins to dry, it is fairly pungent—some would even say revolting. A female herring lays anywhere between twenty thousand and forty thousand eggs; adult herring may live up to fifteen years.

A large part of the herring caught is sold to the Japanese seafood sector; the roe, collected separately and commercially, is considered a delicacy, although our local fisherman use herring as baitfish.

PICKLED HERRING WITH WINE, SPICES, AND HERBS

GENEROUSLY PROVIDED BY CHEF AND AUTHOR BILL JONES
OF DEERHOLME FARM IN COWICHAN

1 cup white wine

1 cup distilled white vinegar (or apple cider vinegar)

1 cup granulated cane sugar (or ½ cup honey)

1 tsp whole allspice

1 Tbsp black pepper

1 tsp sea salt

1 Tbsp grainy mustard

1 tsp whole coriander seeds

Juice and zest of 1 lemon

¼ cup chopped dill (or fennel)

1 large carrot, julienned

1 small red onion, thinly sliced

2 lbs fresh herring fillets

In a stainless saucepan, combine the wine, vinegar, sugar, allspice, pepper, salt, mustard, coriander seeds, lemon juice and zest, dill, carrot, and red onion. Bring to a boil, remove from heat, and allow to cool.

Roll herring and fasten with a toothpick (or cut into large chunks). Place the fish in a glass or nonreactive container and pour the cooled pickling solution over the fish. Cover with lid (or plastic wrap) and refrigerate at least overnight and ideally for 24 hours.

Serve with toasted rye bread as an appetizer or over boiled new potatoes.

> A herring ball occurs when a large group of herring form a massive school near the surface of the ocean to escape from predators. They then become an excellent and accessible food source for diving seabirds and gulls as well as larger prey such as sea lions.

The Ladysmith Community Marina is eco-rated as a green marina with Clean Marine BC, but it goes above and beyond to provide more to the community. The marina has established the largest purple martin nesting colony on Vancouver Island by building and erecting nesting boxes on the poles and dock pilings throughout the marina. The purple martin prefers wide-open spaces, so a marina is an ideal location to perch their nesting boxes. For this endeavour, the marina was awarded a certificate of recognition in 2014 by the Ministry of Forests, Lands and Natural Resource Operations. In 1985 there were only five breeding pairs of the purple martins; today there are over one thousand.

> The purple martin is North America's largest swallow. This flighty little bird feeds on high-flying insects; the mosquito, which is low-flying, may not make up a large part of the martin's diet, but they do enjoy the invasive flying fire ant.

> The purple martin migrates annually to South America and then returns, building a nest in three layers, the top layer being fresh green leaves. Their home may be in a natural setting, such as a tree cavity, but also, artificially built nesting boxes and hollowed-out gourds.

Their two main enemies are the European starling (non-native) and the house sparrow, who find it tempting to invade the little martin's nest and at times, even kill the young.

The house sparrow especially is brutal with its pillage.

The female martin hatches her eggs with her warm "brood patch," which is the part of her body that transfers her heat to the eggs.

The Ladysmith Community Marina includes a charming little museum as well as two beautifully restored heritage vessels which you can visit: the retired tug *Saravan,* built in 1938, and the *C.A. Kirkegaard,* an elegant twenty-nine-foot vessel originally used to transport seafarers and loggers throughout the local waters when industry on the sea was dominant. The marina's restored wooden boats have won numerous awards at local boat festivals held in Victoria, Maple Bay, and Salt Spring Island.

In the little museum, there is a sweet and cozy re-creation of a captain's cabin, with a leather-bound Bible beside the narrow cot; a brass candlestick; a photograph of the captain's wife and children; a pot of ink beside a sepia chart of local waters; a delicate, typically British watercolour painting of a stone church among rolling meadows; and a beautiful, elegant desk, originally on the ss *Beaver*, the first steamer to cruise our coast. (In 1888, it ran aground at Stanley Park in the vicinity of the famous Siwash Rock.)

An additional feature of Ladysmith is the "living reef," an intriguing concept to which I was introduced while listening to a CBC interview on our local morning program. The fellow being interviewed explained that a living reef is a created spot in the ocean in which you may place the ashes, or "cremains," of a deceased person. What a fascinating idea to be able to return to the sea, to become memorialized with the creatures of the ocean and become part of the grand circle of life in that manner!

The living reef idea is described as a green burial at sea. According to various websites, the cremains of the deceased are placed in a mould (which could weigh up to five hundred pounds), which takes about thirty days to cast. The mould then is lowered into the ocean (they use the word *deploy*, which sounds as if they are launching a bomb and reminds me of the Royal Canadian Air Farce's chicken cannon skit) whereby countless sea creatures attach themselves to the memorial and thus create a living reef, with you still inside! What a paradox—the deceased providing life. Prices vary, but all deployments include a certificate, a video of deployment, and a GPS location to allow you to visit your reef. There are several deployment locations around Vancouver Island, Ladysmith being one.

I like the idea of a man-made reef providing our ocean creatures a habitat and surface to cling to, but I also like the idea of my ashes being free and loose—not encased, but rather rolling and churning in the surf, in the kelp, through the eelgrass, perhaps swirling in a herring ball, or filtering through the pebbles, sea glass, sand, and mud, with the tube worms, washing over the spines of the urchins, slipping through the anemone's tentacles, and gliding among the sea stars and little snails to simply become part of the wonderful ocean's cyclic food chain. I want to be part of the vast movement of the ocean when I die, not locked into a cement cast, deployed, and located by a GPS app. I do not wish for people to know where I am in death—*especially* in death.

I'll never forget the day I threw (yes, threw, not spread) Mum's ashes into the Bay of Fundy on a blustery winter day from the shores of Saint Andrews, New Brunswick.

I carried her down to the shore in a plush blue velvet bag the funeral home had supplied; she was surprisingly heavy for being such a tiny person! I stumbled over the seaweed-covered rocks in front of a quaint old inn called the Gleason Arms. Many years before, Mum spent time there writing her book Wildflowers of Canada, *and she had told me it was the happiest time of her life. The weathered wooden inn still stands and now houses a hair salon. Across the street is a cozy lobster café Mum and I used to visit on our road trips; we'd order lobster bisque and a glass of cool, local white wine—those were the two "foods" she could swallow when she had throat cancer. Then we'd stay at a local hotel and watch a marathon of Pride and Prejudice and swoon over Mr. Darcy, as played by Colin Firth.*

The day I took Mum in her velvet bag down to the wild Atlantic shore, a raging blizzard with a biting gale whipped up, rising up from the direction of the old but refurbished (in horrid modern vinyl, Arborite, mirrors, and cheap home décor) Algonquin Hotel on the hill, pelting my cheeks with sharp snowflakes and freezing my fingers as I released the ashes (and little bits of bone) into the murky reddish-brown waves.

The Ladysmith Harbour Tour

On a glorious summer day in August at the Ladysmith Marina, Mikki and I decided to take a tour of the Ladysmith Harbour; our boat, the *Maritimer*, its dark green awning flapping in the breeze, waited at the dock in the lapping surf while Captain Dan handed out life jackets.

The history of life jackets was depicted in the boat shed on a faded poster covered in cloudy, yellowed Plexiglass. Barely making out the graphics, I learned that life jackets, or personal flotation devices, were invented three thousand years ago and were first constructed from inflated animal skins. Cork was used later, and then a cork jacket was devised. The inflatable vest that we know today had its roots in the Second World War when the American Air Force used a CO_2 cartridge to inflate a vest—needed in case an aircraft crashed into the sea—which they dubbed the Mae West, no doubt in tribute to the actress's breasts. (The night after our boat tour of Ladysmith, I had a dream that I had enormous breasts as large as tractor tires, busting out in front of me in a blue plaid shirt!)

I heard a moving story once about Mae West, which involves the gifted Canadian comedian, drag queen, and female impersonator Craig Russell. He reached the peak of his career way back in the seventies with a wonderful film called Outrageous! *and is known to this day for his groundbreaking work that presents drag as a true art form.*

Russell was a melancholy sort of fellow, one of those raw, vulnerable people whose suffering is painfully clear to see through his jokes. When he was a teenager, he formed a Mae West fan club in Toronto, and the story is that Mae West, by then a fading star, took Craig Russell under her wing in Los Angeles. He became her assistant, and they became great and tender friends until West died in 1980. Craig Russell passed away in October of 1990.

Our little group boarded the *Maritimer* slowly and carefully and, wearing our Mae Wests, sat on narrow, green vinyl benches. One especially burly man had to balance the boat—he sat alone on one side, wearing a T-shirt stretched disturbingly tight across his massive girth, the message on his shirt declaring, for all to see, IF IT SCRATCHES I'M ITCHIN' IT. (He can't be Canadian, I remember thinking.)

We set off at a leisurely speed, the motor putt-putting over the small, dark green waves and passed a few half-sunken, derelict vessels—submerged and abandoned, a situation that has been garnering more attention in recent years as a serious environmental hazard.

In March 2018, the federal government spent a million dollars to dismantle and haul away a dangerous amount of fuel, asbestos, and other chemicals from the "Dog Patch" in Ladysmith Harbour—and this funding was for only one abandoned vessel, the *Viki Lyne* II, which had been slowly disintegrating for four years. (In 2011, Nova Scotia spent a whopping twenty million dollars to have the MV Miner removed and towed to Turkey for scrap!)

Our current federal government has introduced the Wrecked, Abandoned or Hazardous Vessels Act (Bill C-64), which imposes very heavy fines and penalties, including jail time, on those who abandon their boats in our marine waterways, either in fresh water or salt water areas. It is estimated that there are over six hundred neglected vessels in the country, which to me seems very low. The New Democrat MP for Nanaimo-Ladysmith estimates that there are thousands more, which sounds about right when you look at a map and realize that's there a vast number of harbours, inlets, isolated islands, and urban watercourses throughout and around Vancouver Island.

We passed a point of land composed of coal tailings from the industry of many years ago, before lumber became a new profitable resource. Captain Dan pointed out the property of Canadian model, buxom blonde *Baywatch* actress, and PETA activist Pamela Anderson—an empty, decaying little house nestled among towering trees on the shore. We crossed the harbour and travelled between quaint, sun-drenched islands surrounded by the carved sandstone shoreline; one island was for sale for eight hundred thousand dollars; it's been deemed unfit, by law, to build upon, but camping is still allowed.

Dan steered between the numerous log booms waiting to be sorted and towed to the local mills—and then the engine quit, right on the 49th parallel. We sputtered back to the marina, and though the group was offered a refund, we refused it as the tour had been so delightful. The beefy man in the revolting T-shirt gave us a disgruntled look as he lumbered off the boat and down the wharf, cranky that he did not get a free tour.

We had a delicious cup of seafood chowder at the charming Oyster Bay Café on the wharf, which regularly holds book readings and musical events. The café had just held a reading by a local author, the late Dr. Brian Bornhold, who had written *Early Music in Ladysmith British Columbia 1902–1912* for the Ladysmith and District Historical Society. It was a lovely little book, well-researched and with photographs. I admire writers who have a passionate interest in a very specific, local-interest topic, and who, with great discipline, create a book from their curiosity and persistence, looking through archival material and old books.

As we left the café, purple martins filled the air with their chirping, busily and happily coming and going, swooping and diving back and forth from their perches and nesting boxes high above the masts and sails bobbing below on the dark water. This marina is a treat, a delight, a community gem. It radiates a genuine affability, which even the dear little birds know.

Shortly after leaving Ladysmith, on your way to Nanaimo, you may choose to detour and take a relaxing country drive through Yellow Point or Cedar (or both); neither location is far from the Nanaimo airport area, and both make lovely rural side excursions.

Yellow Point Lodge

A popular destination for visitors, Yellow Point Lodge provides a rather rustic experience in the woods by the sea; it is not the Hilton. Mum and her best friend Barbara worked there as teenagers, cleaning the outhouses and plucking chickens after Barbara's sister Bunty wrung their necks. (This sounds horrid, but wringing a chicken's neck is quick and painless—that was how things were done in the thirties.)

Mum once told me a story about a dark summer night at Yellow Point Lodge:

A man arrived with his wife and other adults in his car one afternoon. As the afternoon gave way to evening, the man became very drunk, and by nightfall, he was so inebriated that he could barely walk. For some reason, he and his friends decided to go for a nighttime drive but ended up putting the car in reverse too close to the high bank above the high tide and drove, at quite a speed, straight into the ocean!

Fortunately, the intoxicated men were rescued, but Mum's memory of the event was vivid—the black night with only the watery glow of the headlights in the dark water below. Poor Mum and Barbara had to clean up the mess the impaired visitors made on the bedsheets and in the latrines following the rescue.

Morden Colliery Historic Provincial Park

If you want a little detour between Yellow Point Lodge and Cedar, take a trip along Yellow Point Road until it becomes Cedar Road, and then turn right onto Highway 1. Drive for about fifteen minutes north of Ladysmith along the highway, then take the Morden Road exit on the right, which will bring you to Morden Colliery Historic Provincial Park.

The drive down to the park gives a sense of going back in time—the road becomes a country lane lined with hedgerows and small homesteads. The park itself is the site of an old coal mine, as proclaimed by the sign that says WHEN COAL WAS KING.

I learned from the park's informative plaques that the mine is unique in that it includes the only remaining above-ground mining infrastructure, which (in this case) was constructed in 1913. The old decaying, weather-bleached, lichen-covered frame still stands in a small grassy clearing, and the captivating forest path circles among other industrial mining remnants such as old boilers, smokestacks, shafts, and vents, all rusting and crumbling into the damp wooded underbrush.

The towering wooden frame is aptly named the tipple, which tipped the coal as it travelled up the conveyor, cascading it into the train to be transported away. Of course, the word *tipple* also means "to drink liquor," and given the numerous successful wineries on Vancouver Island, we could say that one tipple has been replaced by another.

I love the informational plaques and signs found scattered all through BC's attractions. They offer historical information, often including photos or drawings, identification of local flora and fauna, and, my favourite, illustrated depictions of scenery both near and far while pointing out locations of interest in specific directions.

Informational plaques provide you an opportunity to think about either what stands before you or what previously occupied that spot, which in my experience, offers a refreshing pause, a sense of calm, and some satisfaction in gaining just a little more substance, knowledge, and perspective than you arrived with.

With technology today, we are relentlessly bombarded with data from everywhere and everyone through video, social networking, advertising, the Internet, e-mails, a million satellite television stations, documentaries on every single topic, and so forth. I find it refreshing to simply read an articulate plaque in the forest; it gives me just enough of a taste of information that I can calmly digest before strolling along the forest path.

Cedar

A fifteen-minute drive from Yellow Point Lodge, Cedar is a quaint tiny community with a most fascinating historical and dramatic event to its name. An Englishman named Edward Arthur Wilson (born in 1878) arrived in the Cedar area and established an isolated cult community on nearby De Courcy Island. Edward claimed, and many were persuaded, that he had visions of angels and spiritual connections to other realms. He believed he had been reincarnated from the Egyptian God Osiris, and his mystic charms convinced many wealthy people to donate to his cause. He changed his name to Brother xii, and all was well in his little self-sufficient establishment until he began to misuse funds and, worse to some, had an adulterous affair with a woman who was known as Madam Z. His downfall began and ended in a volatile and theatrical spectacle when he and Madam Z ransacked and set their village ablaze, then escaped—with much gold—in their tugboat, the *Kheunaten,* thus avoiding a trial that was to be held in the Nanaimo courthouse. They eventually they made it back to Europe. There is wide speculation that Brother xii even faked his own death.

Petroglyph Provincial Park

As you approach Nanaimo on the main highway, if you'd like to visit this wooded gem and see the petroglyph, remain on the highway leading into the city of Nanaimo (stay in the left lane and do not go over the overpass). Very shortly you will see Petroglyph Provincial Park on your right, where you will discover a small but significant forest glade in the cool woods on a rocky knoll. Though the park is relatively tiny, it's worth the stop. Here you can see and learn about the Snuneymuxw First Nation's traditional and spiritual symbols that were carved into the sandstone rocks; you may even glimpse the symbols on boulders among the cedars, firs and hemlocks, salal, huckleberries, and mossy lichens—all part of their earthly and marine culture. The petroglyph subjects often took the form of flat fish, perhaps flounders, and wolf creatures.

Above the parking area and up a shady path is a clearing where there is an outdoor interpretive centre; here you'll discover an abundance of information and replica casts of the original petroglyph designs. Beyond the clearing is another short trail leading to an original petroglyph, but it is difficult to see after years of erosion and sea storms. The trail itself makes a nice loop back to the parking lot.

When visiting the interpretive centre, take a crayon, charcoal, or pencil lay a piece of paper on the petroglyph replica cast—not the original, which we are not meant to touch—and make a rubbing. With very little effort, even the artistically challenged can come away with an impressive piece of art. Dad used to make rubbings of all sorts of things; the textures and patterns that arise can be fascinating and have provided many creative people with unique design ideas, especially in textile production. I remember Dad doing a rubbing of a Swedish manhole cover in downtown Stockholm; he was almost run over by a vegetable truck.

Nanaimo to Nanoose

Nanaimo, Protection Island, Gabriola Island, and Nanoose

Nanaimo

IF NANAIMO WERE A PERSON, THEY WOULD HAVE MANY FACES, and you'd have a hard time pinning down exactly what this person was like. Quirky and quaint? Rough and tumble? Unassuming and suburban? Or an elusive combination of all this and more? Without a doubt, this town has a complicated, ever-changing personality, and it takes patience, exploration, and careful observation to get to know it. The effort is worthwhile.

Nanaimo (whose name is derived from the anglicized version of the word *Snuneymuxw*, which translates to "great and mighty people") was established as a trading post in the early nineteenth century and soon became known for its extensive coal deposits. It has had a tough history, as have many mining towns, and this is reflected in many of the small, modest houses that you will pass while driving into town (going north) on the old road. Every May, the city still flies its flags at half-mast to recognize the tragic mining explosion of 1887 that occurred in Number One Coal Mine, where 150 miners died. Nanaimo is extremely loyal to its mining history, and there's a museum to commemorate the industry.

There's something deeply mournful about a flag at half mast, perhaps because a flag is so public, so symbolic. It is a sad announcement to all the town's citizens—especially when the flag is blowing in the wind. Even more moving is the "missing man" aerial formation and the riderless horse seen in a procession to honour a police officer who has perished on the job. These are powerful tributes to loss and despair that help us to collectively share grief and commemorate the fallen (to use a military term).

I like to stroll along downtown Nanaimo's gritty, winding streets filled with little gift shops (stores offering local, unique crafts, books, kitchen supplies) and cafés. Among these shops, here and there, are beautiful heritage structures of sandstone or red brick—classically decorated, featuring columns and ornate ironwork. Two outstanding examples are the Bank of Commerce on Church Street, built in 1914 and now referred to as the Great National Land Building, and the old stone courthouse atop the hill on nearby Front Street, designed by Francis Rattenbury, the architect who designed Victoria's elegant but stolid Parliament Building (known as the Birdcages) with its green copper domes, balconies, and turrets.

Many small towns have some version of a central square, perhaps anchored by a city clock or some other type of distinct landmark. But Nanaimo does not appear to have this. Rather than holding to the belief that the charm of a town must be found in its old-town feel, and that growth must be built on its historical roots, Nanaimo has focused its growth on its lovely waterfront. This makes me wonder: How necessary is it to maintain a connection to our past to create a vibrant town? Most cities do have a quaint and charming "old town" with narrow alleyways, perhaps underground tunnels, and pokey little shops, all squeezed together with elegant homemade signage and lace curtains on the windows. But, perhaps, apart from being a tourist attraction, a city does not necessarily need to focus on its history but rather, in the case of Nanaimo, can focus on developing what it has to offer.

The Nanaimo seafront showcases gleaming buildings of shining turquoise glass, clean concrete walkways, and pristine white enamelled railings; there's much action and many things to see down on the wharves and along the waterfront paths: little ferries and shining yachts, fishing vessels, cafés on the dock, gift shops, sea planes, pretty pocket gardens and sitting areas.

The city has extended the seawall beyond this hub, and it is well worth a stroll as it takes you through Maffeo Sutton Park, a spacious green area at the centre on the Harbourfront Walkway. This spot is filled with public art (which changes regularly)—some clever, some amusing, some symbolic, and some representative of local themes. The accompanying signage explains the meanings of many of the pieces; among them is a huge carved Dungeness crab near the water, and an intricate sculpture appropriately named *Breaching Orca*, composed from hundreds of metal gizmos—kitchen utensils, gadgets, and scrap metal, a horseshoe, a gate latch, a wrench, a spatula, a multitude of machine parts, and more. Another compelling piece is titled *Embedded*, consisting of various sections of a red canoe—*deconstructed*, to use a fairly recent buzzword—embedded into the ground in various positions. The embedding of the canoe parts into the earth symbolize the embeddedness of the Indigenous people.

Other public art includes murals, glass etchings, carvings, and sculptures, some in quite obscure locations within the park.

 Public art adds culture, reflection, and ambience to a town. I highly support it, but at times, I have observed that public art very nearly

crosses the line between art and advertising. We need to realize the piece's intention, its purpose, which is to culturally and thoughtfully enhance the town's character and entice us to have a Little Think about what the art piece is trying to communicate.

During my visit to Nanaimo, I headed north along the Harbourfront Walkway beyond the sculpture park and soon came upon the Millstone River and estuary, where there was a pretty trail under the bridge; this trail is connected to a variety of other walkways and green spaces throughout the city. The particular trail that went under the bridge, as a sign described, was part of the Great Canadian Trail.

When I looked up the hill at the old town from the fresh and gleaming seafront, the two significant sides of Nanaimo were obvious: a town in transition, the grassy unkempt bank and the derelict, crumbling warehouses and abandoned factories, their windows broken, blackberries and morning glories crawling up the rain-stained yellow stucco and rotting wood—demolition by neglect. The sight was beautiful in an austere and lonely kind of way, and it held a certain dignity beneath the overcast sky. Such beauty can be found in scenes that are crumbling with abandonment; it is a beauty that surpasses that of sleek newness. The bleached and worn colours, the various slopes and heights, the silence and memory of what once was.

Protection Island

An entertaining way to spend some time in Nanaimo is to take the little ferry with the blue painted wooden seats from the public wharf on the waterfront over to Protection Island for lunch at the Dinghy Dock Pub. There is a floating waiting room usually filled with locals who are carrying home bags of groceries, boat parts, fuel, soil and seeds, a gizmo for their septic tank, or an obscure gadget for their broken fridge. I was utterly charmed when the tubby little vessel pulled up to the wharf and the locals disembarked with their dogs—so many dogs of all types, and so mannerly, one by one stepping up on the gangplank and trotting along the bleached dock as if it were second nature, their owners

with empty, baggy backpacks ready to fill on their weekly shopping excursion. And the dogs had to pay a dollar each way! The boat leaves Nanaimo hourly at ten past the hour; it's a short trip across, and the jovial captain usually chats about the tides and the storms and the several times he could not transport anyone to and fro—oh, those ferocious winter ocean tempests! But most of the time, he will drop you off at the pub and pick you up at regular intervals.

Upon our arrival, and before we entered the pub, we took a brief stroll up through a wooded trail; the residents who had been shopping traipsed up with their heavy baggage loaded into painted wheelbarrows, and proceeded to push their cargo down the various lanes lined with very nice homes, from what I could tell; it was a delightful sight. (Many residents, I noticed, had golf carts, parked in a neat row under the trees awaiting their owners' return, rather than wheelbarrows and other homemade wheeled contraptions.) One pub regular told me that there are approximately 350 full-time residents, and many of them commute to and from Nanaimo with their own vessels.

The day we visited Protection Island, the pub was full of excitement. Among the hanging sea relics and chimes (made locally from unused or recycled utensils, pulleys, nets, brass portholes, maritime flags, rusted anchors, diving bells, lanterns, and green glass floats, all of which adorned the wooden walls and draped across the windowsills) and the scattered laminated menus that proudly displayed the main drink (Sex in a Dinghy) was a collection of older men talking up a storm, most of them grey-bearded, moustached, or goateed, all wearing yellow rubber boots; some sported woollen sailor caps as they sat drinking beer in one section of the room. They were embarking on a boat race around the island, not in their boats but with remote-controlled vessels! I noticed a large, prominent golden cup on the bar that I can only assume was a trophy of some sort.

Though the race was imminent, contestants were in no rush; they sat and chatted and tinkered with their minuscule sails and keels for what seemed like an entire afternoon. The serious competitors, however, were the wives. With their long greying hair in pigtails, they wore red fleece vests and were out on the pub deck measuring the tides, taking notes on the direction of the wind, and checking their enormous black digital computer watches on their wrists. I do not recall when the great race commenced, but as we were leaving the pub, a few of the competitors were at long last climbing into little aluminum boats and gently placing their miniature vessels into the choppy blue-grey surf, their wives anxiously beside them, ready and alert with the stopwatches.

I'm not even sure that all the competitors left their affable social gatherings to participate; when we left, many were still drinking and telling old mariner stories of when they were boys, the wives still on the decks, fingers in the air, analyzing the breezes that were churning up the grey surf.

Later in the afternoon we attended a performance by the Nanaimo Concert Band at the contemporary, tasteful, and artistic Port Theatre, a large, airy performance facility which, to me, has that federally funded look about it, with a vast carpeted, glass lobby lined with comfortable wooden benches, spotless washrooms with spacious stalls, huge, high beams embedded with demure pot lamps, and art positioned on clean white walls that curve in grand swaths away from the main entrance and lobby area.

The Nanaimo Concert Band is the oldest in Canada, established in 1872. There's something endearing about a musical society that has been operating for so many years, and the band has won numerous awards throughout its long history, including national gold medals for concert music. And it has an immense fan base—the concert at the huge Port Theatre was completely sold out! The group consists of all ages and genders, and they play a diverse selection of tunes, everything from the Star Trek theme song to hymns to even Mexican folk songs. My favourite of the program that evening was a sweet Maritime song called "She's Like the Swallow."

In keeping with the elaborate, tasteful new architecture that has revitalized the waterfront area, the Nanaimo Museum (just behind the theatre above the conference centre) is definitely worth a visit. Be sure to see the beautiful wall mural of a diverse and uniquely designed arrangement of stone on the lower level.

Jingle Pot Road

Jingle Pot Road is one of the main arteries of Nanaimo, crossing not only through town, but across the main highway. But how did this road come by its unusual name? A brief article by author Joy Murray in the local magazine *Chronicles of Nanaimo* suggests a few theories:

First, a "jingle in the pot" used to mean loose change, spare coins in the weekly household pot, no doubt from the hard work performed in the mines, though that doesn't entirely explain *how* it became the name of a major road in Nanaimo. Next, a common jingling sound was called a jingle pot in the mining communities in Yorkshire, England, caused by dripping water or pebbles between rock crevices and potholes;

many labourers immigrated to Canada and most likely brought their unique and eclectic expressions with them. Then there's the theory that the miners' lunch buckets made a jingling sound on their way to and from work.

The name remains a mystery, but it is definitely more original than streets named for a view or after a developer's wife or an obscure historical pioneer. Jingle Pot Road, as far as I'm concerned, is playful and enchanting.

Gabriola Island

A voyage to charming Gabriola Island, just across from the Nanaimo waterfront, makes a stimulating day trip, although there is enough to see, visit, stroll, sip, and do to extend your visit to two or three days. I ventured over with my friend Yumi on a late-summer day; it had rained the night before, and I was ambling around the BC Ferries parking lot (in Nanaimo Harbour) in the cool damp of early morning with Archie, who needed to relieve himself. It was gentle and serene in the pale dawn light; the air was fresh, a stark contrast to the previous weeks without rain and the lingering, smoky haze that had drifted over from the enormous forest fires on the mainland. The coming autumn's fresh but musty aroma of wild fennel and blackberries, dampened from the downpour, wafted over the parking lot: only my car and a rusted red pickup were in the lineup. The skinny jeaned legs of two sleepy male passengers were sprawled across the truck's dashboard, possibly after a hard night in the big city (the casino is just beyond the chain-link fence). A slick, modern, concrete condominium with curved glassed balconies towered above the little blue and white huts in the ferry compound; one hut was a waiting room (which was absolutely gleaming—I've noticed that all ferry terminal employees are excellent cleaners), and in the other hut sat two ferry employees sipping coffee.

One ferry worker gave Archie a liver-flavoured milk bone. A patch or two of blue sky emerged as Archie and I continued our amble, passing banners and signage that reminded us that it was crucial to conserve Gabriola's groundwater, to be aware of wildlife on the roads, and that the salmon barbecue was on the coming weekend.

There was a painted map of Gabriola with some fascinating facts: Its size is fifty-eight square kilometres, whereas Manhattan's is fifty-nine, and Bermuda's is fifty-seven. Gabriola has 225 frost-free gardening days, but Saskatoon has only 115 days. The departing terminal, with all its interesting and informative facts, served as a primer to the island we were about to visit.

The ferry crossing was brief across the choppy, dark-green sea, taking only about twenty minutes. On arrival, you have a choice of direction, to the right, or to the left—either way, heed the signage that warns you to watch for the wild turkeys.

We turned onto South Road, which did indeed head south along the west side of the island (facing Nanaimo); this side of Gabriola is much sunnier and agricultural than the eastern side, accessed by North Road, which is much more heavily treed. We drove as if we were an elderly couple on a Sunday drive. A dear little church sat on a hill, and since it was in fact a Sunday, Yumi suggested we attend! I think the last time I attended church was on Mayne Island at the Blessing of the Animals when we had to leave due to my five senior dogs soiling the clean red carpet. (Although my dogs have all been rescues, we just are not churchgoers.)

So, Yumi and I went to church! We sat in the back, and a friendly woman gave us a brochure that described the exquisite, albeit modern, stained glass windows designed (and installed) by a local glass artist. The wonderful windows were a highlight of our visit; each one was dedicated to the memory of a Gabriola resident, or celebrated a Gabriola event, and the designs were of trees. Within this design was a dogwood, a fruit tree, an arbutus, and a Douglas fir; all were within a shimmering blue cross. One of the most striking windows depicted Moses's burning bush.

The hymn that was sung in the church was "Morning Has Broken," one of my favourite songs. I always thought it was a folk song written by Cat Stevens—but no, it's a hymn first performed in 1931 and later popularized by Stevens in his 1971 recording.

After church, we drove a little farther and took a spectacular stroll through Drumbeg Provincial Park, located in the far eastern corner of the island a short distance down a gravel road; it is well marked. This park is truly a gem, with a gentle forest path through arbutus and moss and the sweet summer fragrances of pine trees and salt air. The path winds down along the shore and back to the little parking lot where there is a cove of smooth sandstone rock, typical of Gulf Island topography and geology. Starfish clung to the dark crevices, little beach crabs scurried through the tidal pools, and the crystal-clear water invited us to take a dip (having no towel, we used Archie's pungent, threadbare blanket off the back seat). If I had to select a hidden treasure on the islands, this park would be at the top of the list.

A little farther on we arrived at Silva Bay, a small community that has a motel and a marina, and to our pleasant surprise, the Sunday market was in full swing—unique vendors were set up in a circle under canopies, and a man was playing guitar on the grassy rock mound nearby. People were selling tie-dyed skirts, homemade licorice, and "huggable rocks," great round woollen "stones" that were soft (hugging seems to be a major occupation on the islands, especially at the weekly markets; people are always hugging or stroking another person's arm—not so much the old-timers, though; it is mainly the younger generation (of all genders) constantly expressing this outward affection. I notice this behaviour in yoga studios as well.

I am not a hugger, and when I do hug, I am told I do not do it well. Patrick Lane (the poet) used to give me a hug and then chuckle and say something about me being stiff from the waist up. I then began practising, as uncomfortable as I was, to sort of lean into the hug, and noticed that my legs were stiff. My friend Betty, long deceased, was even a worse hugger than I am—she could only manage to slightly bend her neck into the other person, and her arms remained rigid. I don't know what makes a good hugger, but some seem to do it effortlessly. There are even people who give free hugs on the street! Why? The more I think about it, the more baffling it is; perhaps it is my suspicious nature, but I am baffled as to why a person might want to hug a stranger, especially for free!

Yumi and I bought soap from The Happy Hippy Soap Company; hundreds of colourful blocks of soaps were stacked in wooden boxes with all sorts of names and ingredients, from seaweed to charcoal to tangerine. My soap was called Margaritaville, and one of the ingredients was lime; it came in a little brown bag with a large pink peace symbol.

In the sixties and seventies, the safe and relatively untouched Gulf Islands attracted American draft dodgers, wanderers, and other free spirits looking for peace and calm and sensibility in a world that was becoming consumerist, violent, chaotic—a world under threat of nuclear war. (Of course, today there are new, serious issues, such as climate change and the threats to the health and existence of our resident orcas.)

Back in the original hippie days, I felt the tension of the times, even though I was an elementary school student in the small university town of Fredericton in the quiet Maritimes. I recall when Martin Luther King was shot; Mum came down from her studio in our attic and, in tears, put her thick, paint-covered apron on a chair and lit a cigarette. She also grieved when Bobby Kennedy was shot—he had visited Fredericton. "Oh, that dear Bobby," she said, "walking with such charisma down University Avenue under those elm trees in the sun, waving to the cheering crowds. All the women in Fredericton swooned!"

Not so long ago, when I lived on Galiano Island, I often saw evidence of the hippie lifestyle that still lingered from the Vietnam War and Cold War years. Women gave birth in the forest and, using new technology, video-taped the event—from the front! Then there would be a big potluck among the cedars, and the child would no doubt be named after some specimen of local flora.

Many of the hippies who arrived on the islands in the seventies were highly educated and set up profitable little businesses, such as kayak rentals and woodworking or ceramic studios. The hippie movement was very influential in the region—so much so that the Gabriola Museum has a large display and exhibit called "Free Spirits, Changing Times." But even though the movement was birthed almost sixty years ago, its influence isn't confined to museums and history books: It's carried over today, albeit with a little less excitement, with generations of West Coasters—Baby Boomers, Gen-Xers, Millennials—and lives on to this day in its own eco-conscious, socially aware version.

Yumi and I ate enormous muffins, purchased from a little blue shack on the wharf; one muffin was beet and chocolate, a fabulous blend! But the best part of the day was yet to come: a head massage by a woman completely dressed in pink—SharmaRay Goldman, whose Pink Pampering Palace was next to the hippy soap lady. SharmaRay had a pink fuzzy chair on a pink carpet with a pink awning and a pink umbrella. Her lipstick was pink. Her hair was pink. Everything was pink!

As I yielded to the massage of this pink lady, Yumi, chuckling, took my photograph. I was completely slack-mouthed and oblivious as SharmaRay ran her oiled hands gently through my hair, tugging every follicle and massaging every inch of my scalp. I felt tingles all the way down to my toes!

She told me that I was unusual; many people do not like their heads to be touched. After a few minutes she put a blindfold on me (she said it was to enable me to go deeper into myself, to relax more, I think) and went down my neck and shoulders, but not before ringing some little bells and making blowing, whooshing sounds (I think there was a bit of moaning as well), whispering wonderful, empowering phrases as she brushed past my ears—things like, "You are a miracle," and "You are perfect." When it was finished, I seemed to be in a temporary trance, and I stumbled around the meadow with my spiked, greased hairdo smelling like geraniums.

Once I regained my senses, Yumi and I had lunch in town, back near the ferry terminal, at a delightful café in a small mall. We had a delicious, slightly spicy bean soup as we sat contentedly in a corner piled with green cushions.

There's something about being on a small island for the day among island residents who all love and support their community that brings on a very blissful state—it's like a little departure from life's stresses, and the ferry journey home provides a gentle and gradual transition back to reality.

Although Gabriola frequently portrays itself as an island of artists and art events, it offers much more. Next time I visit I plan to go kayaking and learn how to "Make Cheese with Paula," as seen on the website of the same name.

Here you can arrange a variety of cheese-making courses that include easy-to-make cheeses such as ricotta and burrata, to a more intense class that includes hard-pressed cheeses like Gouda and Havarti—and, for the advanced and adventurous, blue cheeses and those with rinds, such as Stilton.

I once bought a rather robust round of Stilton in England for Mum and put it in Air Canada's overhead bin on the long transatlantic flight. Somewhere over Greenland, it began to give off quite a rank pong. These days, the plane would have made an emergency landing in Gander "due to a suspicious odour," if in fact it had even made it past the pat-down—the rind alone would have set off the alarms, I'm sure. Still, as far as I am concerned, there's nothing like a slice of Stilton with some fresh pear and an espresso.

If you want to stay overnight or longer on Gabriola, there's a grand choice of accommodation on the island—cottages, bed and breakfasts, lodges, guesthouses, and lovely campsites. Many of the offerings are five-star, and the variety is spaced throughout the island. Some even have hot tubs, a luxury I am afraid I would never indulge in, unless it was my own—I am squeamish about hot water that's already had (unknown) bodies soaking and rolling around in it.

Nanoose

Nanoose is so serene and pastoral that it could be too easily dismissed as an out-of-the way neighbourhood with not much more than a golf course and a marina on a pretty bay. But Nanoose has more to it, which you'll discover if you're willing to do some leisurely exploring. It has, in fact, a history of brick-making, logging, and milling, and its location and beauty makes the area well worth a drive about.

My friend Pam, who lives in Nanoose, took me on the grand circle tour on a glorious late-summer morning—the type of morning when the ocean looks like a mass of sparkling jewels. Her lovely contemporary home sits on a rock bluff set among arbutus trees and her deck overlooks the Fairwinds Golf Club. Before we set out, we chatted as we admired, from the comfort of her deck, the dusky blue coastal mountains in the distance across the sea, which was dotted with tiny, quaint islands and little white sails in the morning breeze.

From the Fairwinds area—with its luxurious amenities such as a golf course, a marina, and a wellness centre—we made our first stop at Brickyard Community Park. There we took a pleasant wooded path through what was at one time the site of a brick factory (established circa 1911, shut down during the thirties, and bulldozed after the site was designated in the seventies as Crown land). The path leads to the shore and a little beach replete with slivered remnants of the old red bricks of days gone by; there is even a stack of bricks within an old decaying tree stump, a quiet tribute to the restorative, encompassing power of nature when left to her own rhythms.

Our journey took us around the sprawling, scenic golf course where, apparently, to control the Canada goose invasion, a falconer with an eagle named Eddy appears several times a week to deter the birds; he doesn't kill them but simply scares them off the extensive greens, ponds, and marshes.

Nanoose proudly boasts a beautiful recreation centre, an architectural marvel of glass and beams, its light and freshness blending with the rocky forested landscape that surrounds it; the interior is a wonderful combination of an upscale club and a contemporary gym with a pool facility. In one room there are deep plush leather chairs, newspapers, books, a fireplace, and a billiard table; the scene looks straight out an era when tweed-clad men could be found smoking cigars and sipping brandy while discussing the latest *Guardian* editorial. Directly across the hall, in contrast to the elegance of the club, is a room full of treadmills.

Leaving the golf club behind, we drove past forested hiking trails, closed due to the fire hazard of the dry, scorching summer, and passed a large rustic-looking log cabin. This is the community library, which is not-for-profit and volunteer-run. The Nanoose Library Centre and Event Hall also acts as an event hall that accommodates about a hundred people, and offers space for workshops, plant sales, and Christmas craft fairs.

Almost every small community on the Island has, I have discovered, a small library—or at least some access to one not too far away. Libraries in small communities may be situated in the woods or in a meadow, or—as I've seen on

Mayne Island—on a slope with the sea as a backdrop. These little gems are often the result of a community effort generated by months of bake sales, barn dances, and pie-eating contests, with construction materials and labour donated by local carpenters and builders, craftspeople, and shop owners. I have done many a book reading in such charming and enchanting places, which is always a delight.

Everyone is welcome—single parents, seniors, the local eccentrics. Volunteers stack the shelves and attend the desks. If there's Wi-Fi reception, there may be a donated computer, and if anyone needs help using the computer or printer, there's someone there who would love to assist, even if they need to be interrupted and temporarily diverted from their pickling, peach preserving, wood chopping, boat cleaning, egg collecting, chimney sweeping, or other island chores.

Sometimes the libraries may even have a unique, custom-made door, crafted from an unused slab of cedar discarded at the local mill. A stained glass crafts-man may donate a colourful window that depicts the local land and seascape; cheerful geraniums may welcome you from recycled ceramic pots and watering cans collected at the thrift shop over the hill or from the recycling depot down the road.

Art and community go hand-in-hand in these little gathering places; there is an organic, earthy feel that you cannot acquire from flat-screen technology, rows of clean white tables, databases, buzzing anti-theft security devices, and impersonal corridors found in our beautiful, modern, urban, government-funded libraries.

In the centre of Nanoose are several lakes—in fact, this area is known as the Lakes District.

One lake in this area, as well as a large central farm, is named after the first pioneer who settled in Nanoose in 1862. John Enos, like many other arrivals, came looking for gold and found none; he then took up farming, which was much more productive.

Nanoose was also the site of the Great Powder Company, founded in 1911 (around the same time as the founding of the brick-making plant in Brickyard Bay). The Great Powder Company sounds like a pleasant, fragrant, and soothing endeavour. It was, in fact, a profitable dynamite (not talcum) industry that thrived due to the mining industry and the demands of the First World War.

Logging and milling also played a part in the development of Nanoose: The lumbering community was known as the Red Gap, a strange name for a site (now a rest stop); it's said that the name was inspired by the novel *Ruggles of Red Gap* by the American novelist Harry Leon Wilson in the late 1800s.

Japan was the mill's major customer, purchasing custom-sized wood required for Japanese architecture, until the Second World War when our two countries became enemies.

So it seems the mighty military can contribute, even in a small way, to the community's economic growth in an unassuming place like Nanoose. If you're so inclined, you can always play some golf to take your mind off the unthinkable horrors of war.

From the main Trans-Canada Highway, looking across to Nanoose Bay, you can see the cold, austere grey Canadian naval ships clustered at their wharf, apparently ready to spring into action by launching missiles and torpedoes. But as it turns out, this in not where they practice deploying their armaments. The ships go around the corner to the open sea (well, it's not really "open," as it faces Vancouver, but it is more open than the bay) to where the little islands are scattered along the shore below my friend Pam's home; they launch missiles from there—dummy missiles, of course.

This spot is also, according to Pam's map, a highly desirable place to kayak—so attractive, in fact, that my friend Judy, an avid kayaker, accidentally paddled into the restricted military waters and was immediately surrounded by what she thought looked like warships, one of which sent a stern, important navy man, in white pants and gold braid, onto the deck. In a booming voice, he strongly advised her to vacate the area—and he even fined her for being in restricted Federal Department of Defence territory!

Nanoose Bay CatSpan Society

Nanoose is home to a wonderful non-profit group called Nanoose Bay CatSpan Society. For many years they have been capturing abandoned and feral cats and spaying or neutering them—more than 150 per year—then releasing the wild little creatures back into the wooded areas where they chose to reside among the stumps and forest undergrowth. The volunteers feed the cats and also supply a support system for feral barn cats. Ideally, there should be far fewer cats roaming our parks, neighbourhoods, and backyards, but the work that CatSpan has embarked upon is a grand start to eliminating the problem.

CatSpan raises money by collecting bottles, holding book sales, participating in point systems and smile cards, and donations (they will take your books, bottles, and cans). For that reason alone, it's worth a trip to Nanoose.

Driving Up-Island

AS WE MAKE THE TRANSITION FROM MORE POPULATED AREAS to the wilder parts of Vancouver Island, I would be remiss if I didn't mention a couple of quintessential Island features of driving up-island: rest stops and roadkill.

Rest stops

Whether you take the scenic route on your island journey, or the major highway, you will pass numerous rest stops, many of which look as weary and dreary as the travellers who stop there; they often look as though they need a good cleaning or freshening up (the travellers as well as the facilities). Rest stops are small, off-highway pull-outs that enable drivers to park, toss out their orange peels or bits of trash, and stretch their legs for a short while. You can linger at a sun-bleached picnic table in need of a fresh coat of paint while watching the highway traffic pass at a high-speed blur, or you can read a mildewed plaque under a weather-beaten kiosk, often erected by the local Lions or Rotary Clubs. But the *main* reason for this and other rest stops is, of course, to use the toilet. The toilets are in little cedar or fibreglass cubicles or dome-like structures, bolted to a cement pad, and are usually of the composting type as a sewer system is not always installed in many rural or roadside spots. A lonely hand sanitizer dispenser—a recent addition—sits among spindly alders nearby.

There is a rest stop on the highway in the Nanoose area, on the west side of the highway, and directly opposite from the Canadian Forces Maritime Experimental and Test Ranges. Last time I was there "resting," I noticed a surveillance camera pointed towards the three little potty shacks (and, on the rest stop's informative plaque, we are warned of the very same detail). I couldn't help but wonder: How can one sufficiently relax in a toilet cubicle on a busy stretch of road with not only a surveillance camera above you, but also a group of torpedo warships in front of you (albeit at a distance), while worrying that a gust of wind might tear open the swinging door, exposing you to the highway traffic? It's bad enough wondering who sat on the potty seat before you or whether there's a creepy-crawly lurking under the seat, having made a little nest (or worse, waiting for a succulent little meal). I'm not convinced that this rest stop is much of a rest. I would think that rest stops such as these—that is, equipped with so much surveillance and in such close proximity to weaponry—may cause a backup in one's personal plumbing.

At any rate, rest stops are different from lookouts, the major difference being that at rest stops there is usually no spectacular view; there's a fabulous lookout on the summit of the Malahat, for example.

BC Parks, which falls under the Ministry of Environment and Climate Change, does a fair job in providing us with both rest stops and views, but I believe that to *combine* them as some sort of attraction would be a most efficient use of our tax dollars as well as rewarding for the user. Imagine sitting on the toilet while watching the natural comings and goings of activities on our beautiful island. Picture yourself "resting" in the little cubicle while watching the salmon spawn in the Cowichan River. Think of how nice it could be to relieve yourself while enjoying the awesome view of a great blue heron gliding over Ladysmith Harbour as a tugboat hums along, slowly pulling its booms.

I once owned a composting toilet. It was not inexpensive—the cost was approximately twelve hundred dollars, and the toilet itself was enormous! I followed the directions thoroughly, dutifully applying peat after each visit and turning the crank which turned and blended the "material" below. (This always reminded me of Mum and her pasta machine in her kitchen, churning out great strings of homemade spaghetti.) The main instruction was to not allow the material to become too wet (as with home-made pasta); the secret of a successful composting toilet is ventilation.

The toilet was a delight, not like an outhouse at all, and neither acrid nor pungent. The most off-putting feature was that it was so silent, lacking the flushing sound that indicates completion, which meant there was no closure to the ablution. It was eerie, just a silent, dark space where no result can be seen. How very Zen—you simply do your business and then 'let it go' without looking back.

In the autumn, I applied the fertile peat mixture onto a raised bed as fertilizer, and in the spring, I planted beets. By August the dark crimson beets with their thick crusted tops were so enormous that they were beginning to split. They won the heaviest beets contest at the Saanich Fair that year, and I ate borscht all winter. I suppose you could say that they ended up back where they came from—the circle of life.

Roadkill

A report found on the website of the Wildlife Collision Prevention Program tells us that in an average year in British Columbia, seven hundred thousand dollars is spent annually on highway cleanup from wildlife collisions, an estimated five people die per year, 6,100 animals are reported as killed, and approximately 18,300 wildlife deaths go unrecorded when the injured creatures stagger away to die.

Early one morning, as I was driving along the oceanfront just past Parksville, the darkness fading with the glow of dawn just beginning to glint over the sea, I saw a mother deer on the side of the road with her fawn. They were enjoying a feast of small yellow apples; a few feet away, on the shoulder of the road, lay her other little fawn, a trickle of blood from its delicate nose pooling in the gravel. It was a sight I shall never forget. It reminded me of the Russian proverb, "Half the world weeps and the other half leaps."

And a long time ago, I saw two wild geese on a muddy driveway which led into the Sandown Raceway in North Saanich; one goose had been hit and killed and was lying in a mud puddle, her feathers dishevelled and her neck loose like a piece of rope. Her mate was bending over her, obviously grieving, sadly prodding her, making sounds and trying to get her to wake up. Impatient people in cars drove around them, some of them even cussing at these "annoying birds."

Feeling helpless and sad for the grieving goose, I watched and waited from a distance until the surviving goose flew away. Retrieving his perished mate in a burlap feed sack before someone in a car carelessly flattened her body, I carried her up the road to my farm where I placed her under my quince tree to return to nature peacefully.

The giant gnome

Just beyond the turnoff to Nanoose, off the main highway going north, is one of the most iconic features on Vancouver Island: the gigantic garden gnome, towering beside a gas station (formerly Esso, now Chevron) and a drive-thru restaurant, all set in front of a magnificent backdrop of rolling meadows, grazing horses, and those distant deep mauve mountains.

This giant gnome has been standing in this location for years—at almost eight metres tall, he's featured in *Guinness World Records 2012*.

Driving past is always a light-hearted, momentary treat, but if you pull over and get up close to him, you'll see it's a melancholic state of affairs. The gnome, according to the affable teenager who sold me a bag of chips in the gas station, was abandoned by the previous owner of the property, despite the fact that a condition of its sale to the new owners was that they were to protect and maintain the giant gnome while he remains on the property as a permanent fixture. But this all seems a bit vague—what exactly is involved with this maintenance? The gnome's pants are falling off, great folds of blue vinyl slowly slipping towards the rotting pallet he stands on. There is a thin sheet of green mould on his red pointed hat, and his enormous beige hands are badly cracked. But still he remains tall, happy, and jovial, giving a thumbs-up on the most bleak and drizzly winter's day to the speeding drivers careening over the hill.

At the time of this writing, the gnome's future is uncertain; perhaps one day his long white beard, a thumb, and his pants will finally drop to the ground and crumble into the soil like the ending of a sad fairy tale.

Central Island Heading Towards Pacific Rim

Errington, Coombs, and the road to Port Alberni

Errington

TRAVELLING NORTH FROM NANOOSE ON THE WAY TO PORT Alberni you will head along Highway 19 (also known as the Inland Island Highway). As you skirt Parksville to the right, if you get off at Highway 4A (also known as the old road), you can then take a quick detour south and find Errington, a rural community about seven kilometres to the south and east of Coombs.

"Errington?" a friend asked when I told her of a recent visit. "Isn't that the place in the woods?" Not quite, but the community does have a distinctly woodland-mystic feeling. Errington has a quaint general store and post office with posters advertising the next event at the volunteer-run community hall across the road. Unless you're paying attention or specifically looking for Errington, you may have the misfortune of missing it—in fact, I had never heard of this diminutive and unique community until I began researching the Nanaimo area and came across numerous local flyers, posters, community newspapers, and magazines advertising a concert, a memorial, a literary reading, a fundraiser, a potluck, a craft exhibit, dance, and a festival or fair held at the Errington War Memorial Hall.

Another friend (who admits her attraction to the unusual) related to me a particularly mystical, late-autumn night in 2003, when she witnessed, at Errington's Veteran's Memorial Hall, a performance that included two undulating belly dancers covered in gold paint and wearing lit candelabras on their heads; the show also featured a shirtless man wildly dancing in black leather pants, his face covered in a pagan-style mask. My friend described it as "groovy and a little freaky."

If you prefer to experience Errington in the relative safety and comfort of daylight, this enchanting community also has a farmers' market where, in addition to other treasures, you can purchase the beautiful chanterelle mushrooms gathered in the nearby woods from a very secret patch—I think hobbit and goblin fans would be impressed. If dropping by the market appeals to you check online at erringtonfarmersmarket.ca to be sure of the market's location, season, and hours.

While in Errington, nature lovers will want to visit the North Island Wildlife Recovery Centre on Leffler Road. This wonderful facility is home to birds and other animals who, in many cases, have narrowly escaped death and cannot be released back into the wild due to permanent injuries. You can get a good look at the creatures in spacious, spotless, and creative areas with informative signage that tells not just the history of the injuries that brought them there but interesting facts about their species. The injured wild animals that you *cannot* see are cared for at the back of the property in a separate facility to be released once they heal.

The most common injury to the birds at the centre seemed to be shotgun wounds to their wings and eyes, causing permanent damage and rendering them unable to fly, hunt, or even mate. One shy little snowy owl named Elsa had been found starving and weak, close to death, in the forests near Tofino. Her exquisite, perfectly white, symmetrical little face was serene as she peered through the shadows of stems and stalks, thoughtfully placed to create a safe and private nest from which she could survey the activities taking place below. There were also two barred owls high on their branch perches: one was named One Eye, the other Eye Gone—for obvious reasons.

Years ago, I had a spiritual and intimate encounter with an owl on my farm in Saanich. Back then I kept a hen house, which I locked at night to protect the hens from raccoons (there's nothing more heart-wrenching than going to see your dear hens in the morning and finding nothing but a pile of feathers and a pair of little pale-yellow chicken feet carelessly tossed aside). Their run was covered in netting to prevent eagles, hawks, and ravens from attacking the hapless, oblivious hens (though, I must say, I have known a few hens that were surprisingly astute).

One cool, grey morning, I approached the chicken barn and found a great owl with his sharp yellow talons and scaly grey legs entwined in the netting, his wings spread for balance and his eyes wide with fear. Dismayed at the plight of this majestic creature, I rushed back to the house to retrieve Gran's tattered, old Hudson's Bay blanket, some sharp scissors, and leather gloves, expecting a struggle and perhaps the bloody tearing of my flesh; if the owl lashed out, I speculated, my nose or lip could be taken off.

But when I approached the helpless owl, now lying in the netting as if in a hammock, his eyes wide as saucers, he remained calm. Wrapping him in the blanket, I left his head uncovered and held his massive body tucked under one arm as I cut the netting from his legs, all the while talking to him—apologizing, mostly. As I gingerly freed each talon, our eyes met, and, for a moment, he and I connected. I believe he knew I was there to help him, and with his head resting in the crease of my elbow, I felt a special connection I have rarely experienced with a wild animal. When my ministrations were complete, I opened the blanket. Elegantly and gently, the owl glided out of my arms and flew towards the dim alder woods across the road. I then understood, if only for a brief moment, the profound bond that a falconer can establish with a raptor.

Falconry, an ancient sport that endures to this day, is used by busy airports as a wildlife control strategy to deter flocks of birds such as geese, crows, and robins from interfering with the aircraft landings and takeoffs. While this method is not used on any of the island airports, it is used at the Vancouver International Airport.

If you would like to learn more about falconry, meet the various skilled raptors, and watch them work with their human colleagues, visit the Pacific Northwest Raptors Centre, just north of Duncan, on Herd Road. The experience is not only fascinating, but profoundly moving as one witnesses the bond that can be formed between human and animal. (In a humorous contrast, there were two young, saucy owls at the centre when I visited who refused to follow instruction from the falconers. Instead, they chose to sit on people's heads, ignoring the alluring meat bait used to persuade them to behave.)

The self-guided tour of the North Island Wildlife Centre in Errington is superb, and there is much to see, learn, and think about. Besides the array of lovely animals who have been rescued, there is the Secret Garden, the Magical Field of Stones, Turtle Town, and the Eagle Flight Cage, as well as several museum displays, a gift shop, and videos and booklets.

One of the star attractions at the wildlife centre is Knut, a chubby black bear who was born in captivity and is therefore non-releasable. During my visit, this affable fellow took a delightful snooze in the sunshine, lying on his back in the leafy shrubbery, his mouth slightly open, pink gums gleaming in the bright, warm rays. He occasionally raised a paw to flick away an annoying fly and to scratch his warm belly.

There is also the treatment centre, which you cannot enter, but you may look through its windows. It resembles a hospital emergency room, with a gurney covered in a flannel sheet, an incubator-type device, numerous tubes and tanks, and white cabinets along the white walls.

One of the most moving stories shared at the recovery centre is about Brian, a bald eagle. Brian arrived at the centre injured from a gunshot wound and was missing most of his upper beak. The only way to repair the beak (and thus rehabilitate the bird) was to construct a prosthesis. According to the centre, this had never been done before, but a clever Nanaimo dentist named Dr. Brian Andrews (who the bird was named after) and a dental technician from Victoria by the name of Fred Leak volunteered to rebuild the eagle's beak. Their combined skills and collaboration was a success! Brian (the eagle) lived a long and healthy life.

If you would like to contribute to the good work the centre does, there are a handful of options, including symbolic adoption; I adopted three turkey vultures: Boris, Vladimir, and Igor. The turkey vulture, one of my favourite species of birds, stands with a stoop and has a red and wrinkled bald head. In the United States they are often referred to as buzzards—the kind we've all seen in those old Westerns, in which someone at some point says something like, "Geez, Clem, look up at dem buzzards circlin' yonder. That's the last place we seen ol' Frank!" But more valuable than their status as movie icons are their skills in scavenging: They rarely kill prey, preferring instead to eat carrion, the meat of creatures freshly perished. When an animal in the wild dies, it releases a distinct gas that turkey vultures can smell as they fly low over the meadows and woods.

Another creature that captivated me was Petra, a red-tailed hawk. She had not been injured, but according to her informative sign at the centre, she DID NOT PERFORM WELL AS A WORKING BIRD. (*Working*, in this context, refers to falconry, and I suspect that since she had so much close interactions with humans, it might have been a hazard to let her go into the wild.) Certain birds—the chosen, intelligent, elite few—are trained to dive, retrieve, and return on command. Unfortunately, little Petra did not have the right stuff.

When I read the words DID NOT PERFORM WELL AS A WORKING BIRD, I felt an affinity for Petra. She may not have been the skilled and academic type, but alas, maybe she was, instead, an artist; there are, after all, numerous types of intelligence. I equated Petra's lack of falconry skill with my own lack of skill in mathematics or linear logic. Most of the time, I live in a dream world, a whimsical, pondering, drifting daydream, as does Petra, I'm sure. People such as Petra and myself can't figure out what others want us to do, nor do we have a good sense for how to meet and maintain the status quo.

Gazing at Petra's elegant face, I pondered the words on her sign that said she did not perform well. It reminded of me of how, when I was in Grade 4, I was placed in what was called the *opportunity class*. At the time, I thought it was a class for dreamers (which I was), or for those who just couldn't learn as quickly as others. Now, at over sixty years old, I have learned that in Australia, the opportunity class is in fact for bored but gifted children. I believe "opportunity" could be interpreted both ways, but considering my report cards averaged a strong D, or at best, a C minus, my guess is that in Canada, opportunity class referred to slowness or inability—*challenged* as they say today—rather than giftedness.

I also recalled the time when, as an adult, I took a flying lesson in North Saanich. The dials in the plane confused me; I was unable to distinguish the speed dial from the elevation dial (they all look relatively similar), so we never left the tarmac. The instructor commented that perhaps I was not cut out to be airborne (unless someone else was flying the plane).

In any case, Petra was lucky that her confidence was not shaken by the knowledge that she was "slow."

Also at the wildlife centre were turkeys donated by a local farmer. I was delighted to see them—turkeys are fascinating! Often the object of unfair ridicule, these creatures have an affectionate and sensitive nature that is usually overlooked and underappreciated.

At one time, on my farm, I had three turkeys: Fred, Wilma, and Nancy. They escaped the slaughterhouse because they had grown so large, and we had become the best of friends. Every day, at cocktail hour, Fred would waddle down to the house and sit on the porch and drink martinis with me—yes, he did, albeit a minute amount: He'd just dip his beak at the rim of the glass and then sit quietly at my feet as if listening to an interesting conversation at a social occasion. He was an excellent listener. Fred loved people, and, when in close proximity, his head would flush into a mass of flaming colours of maroon, coral, and ruby, with streaks of fuchsia, lilac, and teal. Because I loved Fred, I'd sometimes give him a little kiss on his colourful head, and it was surprisingly warm; maybe it was the alcohol.

Wilma and Nancy were more reserved; they sat under the honeysuckle waiting for Fred to lumber off the steps and join them at dusk on their stroll up to their hut, where they had deep hay beds in which to retire after a busy day ambling around the farm (and, in Fred's case, drinking). Despite Fred's cocktail routine, I never once witnessed him exhibiting impairment, bad judgment, or lack of coordination—he held his liquor quite well.

On one particular occasion, the Red Hat Society ladies came to visit the farm; the Red Hat Society is a club of women who wear large red hats, fedoras, and purple scarves and dresses, and some carry red purses and accessories of plumage, boas, and elaborate jewellery, stockings, and gloves.

As I led the ladies through the freshly mowed, grassy pathways of the edible garden, stopping to taste a bit of miner's lettuce or French sorrel, or to point out numerous edible flowers, Fred followed closely at the rear of our colourful little troupe; he was a very sociable turkey and thrived on human companionship and interaction.

The ladies thought Fred's presence was wonderfully amusing and asked to be photographed with him. We set up the photo shoot carefully, the group of ladies huddled together with the great red barns in the background and Fred in the front among swaths of purple, cobalt, and scarlet scarves, draped and billowing in the breeze. Fred's huge, flaming, burgundy and crimson wattles and loose folds of indigo and sky-blue skin perfectly matched the Red Hatters' vibrant attire. The only hint that one of the group's members was a turkey was the glimpse of a few white feathers barely visible against the colourful stockings at knee level.

The ladies were so flattered by Fred's adoration that, by the end of their excursion, they verbally deemed Fred an honorary member of their society.

> The Red Hat Society is a social organization, which began in California in 1998, started by a lady who had purchased a red hat at a thrift store. The society's aim is to seek out fun and friendship, and many do an extensive amount of community work as well. Originally, the age requirement was fifty, but currently all ages are welcome (Fred was ten).
>
> At the time of this writing, the group had over fifty thousand members worldwide; there are over a hundred chapters in British Columbia, including a goodly number on Vancouver Island.

Coombs

Ask anyone about Coombs, and you'll hear right away how it's known and loved for the famous goats on the roof. For many years we visited the Old Country Market in Coombs, a small rural community on the way to the Pacific Rim, and sure enough, there were always a couple of happy goats grazing on the market's lush grassy roof.

But there's more to Coombs than the goats on the market roof. As you approach Coombs by Highway 4A, you will pass a scattering of light industrial facilities; one of the most fun is an enormous demolition yard where you can poke around between clawfoot bathtubs and antique windows taken from abandoned barns, stacks of fisherman's rope, brass gadgets from sailboats, outdoor garden ornaments, plumbing gizmos, iron tools, and porcelain taps from demolished hotels—there's nearly everything you can think of there.

Just before you arrive at the famous Coombs market is the now-defunct World Parrot Refuge. The place used to house over one hundred rescued parrots, or other birds that were taken in due to neglect or simply given up by their owners. The refuge was run by the late Wendy Huntbatch, who worked tirelessly for them; she became quite famous in her own right for her work. After she passed away in 2016, her parrot refuge became impossible to maintain, and there was a widespread effort on Vancouver Island and beyond to help find homes for the birds.

Parrots are fascinating! I once knew a couple who had a parrot that imitated both of them. The couple had been married for many years, so the parrot was very familiar with their daily routines. After the wife passed away, the man was lonely, but he carried on. Every time he went down to his cellar, he told me, he'd hear his wife's voice from the kitchen upstairs, screeching, "Jack! Bring up the pickles!"

The parrot refuge centre in Coombs now sits devoid of its erstwhile, rescued inhabitants, and the last time I drove past, its rotting pink plywood sign was lying sadly in a field.

The Coombs Old Country Market itself is an ecosystem of funky and quirky shops and services. Many of them have what some would call a shabby-chic appearance, with the buildings slowly being enveloped in moss and lichen. Still, activity seems to carry on all around the sense of abandonment, with a curious mixture of turquoise towers and turrets, cotton candy and shaved ice kiosks, surf and flip-flop shops, a creamery, garden patios, racks of flowery dresses and scarves flapping in the breeze, hot tub outlets, hot dog stands, a Mexican restaurant, a trattoria and pizzeria, an army surplus store, a hemp shop, and more.

Down the road is a sausage smokehouse and a beach store sporting an enormous inflated pink flamingo. I purchased a tie-dyed T-shirt—I'd always wanted one!—from a little yellow stucco hut just over the bridge. You can't miss it because the vibrant, colourful shirts are hanging outdoors on a long rack. The fellow at the till was extremely friendly as he stood under a wide display of T-shirts displaying crude and ridiculous phrases such as SHOW US YOUR KITTIES, ZOMBIE OUTBREAK, and something about Girl Guides and their cookies (which I felt was extremely crude). My tie-dyed shirt is fabulous and hasn't faded in the wash.

A long time ago, when Mum came out west to visit me in North Saanich, she remarked that Dad had begun to prefer nightdresses rather than pyjamas. So we went to the local thrift shop and searched through the musty rows of nighties for a nightdress that met Dad's very particular specifications: below the knees, cotton, long sleeves with no lace. Happily, we found the one: It was pink with a small stain on the back and had a cartoon chicken on the front, emblazoned with the words I GOT LAID IN ALASKA. For all of fifty cents it was well worth it. Mum and I had a laugh, and when she went back home and delivered the nightdress, she reported to me that Dad loved it. "It has the right sleeve length," he said.

Towns have personalities, and if Coombs were a friend of mine, we'd have a grand laugh. This is a village with a fabulous sense of humour. While on the surface it shows signs of fatigue, it is alive with positive energy, like an eccentric old lady who dresses herself in vivid, mismatched colours and patterns and talks to everyone about everything.

If you visit a village, town, or city, pause a moment to absorb the personality, the emotion of the place. Take a stroll through the streets; check out the local bakery; rest under a tree and watch the comings and goings. Can you feel the soul of a location? Some locations are sad, austere, or lonely; others are confident and warm; some may be aloof or arrogant. In any case, when you feel the emotion and soul of the place you choose to visit, your journey will be greatly enhanced. You may remember the feeling and personality of a place far more than what you saw or tasted or did. Your connection to location comes down to what stirs you inside. (Of course, sometimes nothing will stir you—you can't be stirred *all* the time. It's okay to give your mind a rest.)

When Mum and I visited Prague, we were struck by its old European elegance, with its pastel buildings and gold leaf balconies teeming with geraniums and the music of Mozart wafting from every small concert hall on almost every corner. But even with all the beauty and elegance, Mum said, "I cannot find Prague's soul."

I agreed. It was a stunning place to behold, but with little discernible emotion—at least, that was my impression at that time. Perhaps it was simply that the city was in transition and experiencing change, for this was soon after Prague had broken away from its dim, grey Communist days. It could be that the stress of such transition can distort how residents and visitors alike perceive the core identity of a place.

From Coombs to Port Alberni

The road from Coombs to Port Alberni passes two enchanting places to stop and commune with nature at its finest. The first is Cameron Lake, a sweet, cool little pebble beach under a grove of evergreens, where you can dip your toes into the crystal clear water and gaze at the surrounding mountains, many of them topped with snow throughout much of the year. Some will say that if you look closely, you may glimpse the lake's fabled monster—known locally as Cammie—rising from the lake's dark lapping waves, rippling under a brisk mountain breeze.

Cryptozoology is the study of cryptids—creatures rumoured to exist. It is said they often lurk in deep, dark bodies of water or thick forests and are seen by only a few.

A helpful representative of the British Columbia Scientific Cryptozoology Club informed me of possible creatures detected by sonar—and as far as I'm concerned, this makes rumours of sightings more believable. So be careful when you dip your toes into the cool water of Cameron Lake—that sparkle of silver may be more than a sunlit wave.

The most frightening creatures of all, at least to me, inhabit Dundas Island, north of Prince Rupert: the gigantic Dundas Island blackflies, viciously attack flesh in great swarms, taking mere moments to chew out your eyes. They're also said to be venomous enough to kill a cow!

Shortly beyond Cameron Lake, along the winding mountain road, you will come to Cathedral Grove, located in MacMillan Provincial Park. This is a popular place to rest and stroll among some of our province's oldest and most serene forests; some of the trees here are over eight hundred years old, consisting of Douglas fir, hemlock, and western redcedar, our provincial tree. The tidy woodland trails and boardwalks take you through glades of sword ferns, mossy paths, and trillium groves; one path even leads to the shore of Cameron Lake.

A massive forest fire 350 years ago did great damage to the forest, but as nature would have it, the ecosystem recovered, only to be hit with Typhoon Freda in 1962, which toppled many of the grand old trees; remnants of those fallen trees can be seen today, slowly rotting into the forest floor.

As you amble through Cathedral Grove, keep an eye out for "the living stump" and the Big Tree. The Big Tree is the largest of the grove, a Douglas fir standing at an impressive height of over seventy-six metres. It is taller than the Tower of Pisa, and as the sign says, it was already three hundred years old when Columbus first arrived in the

Americas. Also significant is the grove's existence for thousands of years before settlers arrived; the stewardship of this treasure by the Indigenous people of the area is unfortunately not given attention in standard official histories.

> The native western hemlock has shallow roots and, therefore, is vulnerable to storms and fires. It is recognized by its slightly drooping top, and although a relatively nondescript tree, it's widely preferred today by millworkers. The Saanich, Nisga'a, and Gitksan peoples used numerous parts of the tree for various applications, such as hide tanning and making dye; interestingly, this dye was also used for facial hair removal.

> There are countless traditional medicinal uses of many different trees from all their various parts: tea from the roots, poultice from the sap, salve from the leaves, laxative from the flowers, and so forth. I would say, in these modern, harried times, the tree's most potent medicinal quality is its cool, canopied presence casting a green shade with a dignity that calms the mind. So if you're having a stressful day, commune with a tree, if even for a short while. Just sit and have a quiet Little Think under one of these gentle beings. You'll find that life is not as stressful as you believed it was only a few moments earlier.

The beauty of go-through towns

There are a few places on Vancouver Island that I call the "go-throughs." These are the places we all know about but know nothing about—we usually rush straight through, focused on a destination farther down the road. When we hurry through these unassuming places, the ones we disregard as we focus on the next turn-off, we miss the chance to discover many hidden gems. These go-through places are, in my experience, home to intelligent and interesting residents who initiate a diversity of unique ventures. Sometimes I wonder if the citizens of these towns know they are living in a place that most people consider unworthy of attention. I suspect they know that their little community is a well-kept secret, and they prefer to keep it that way.

Culturally, we see the middle of something as, well, middle-of-the-road. Mundane. Inferior, somehow. Think of the plight of the often-invisible middle child. Consider the expression: "I am in the middle of nowhere," which, if you think about it, is slightly derogatory in its implication that nowhere is a nothing place, with nothing to see and nothing to offer. And then we have the child's game Piggy in the Middle, with the "piggy" trapped between two bigger, taller, stronger players as the piggy desperately tries to intercept the ball being tossed over its head, the piggy's feelings of helplessness and inferiority increasing with every aching minute.

Here are some examples of in-between locations on the Island: Duncan, which travellers drive through to either shop at the Nanaimo malls, go bungee jumping, or ziplining at WildPlay Elements Park, or taste delectable wines between Cowichan and Nanaimo, along with any number of other activities; Denman Island, so often treated like a stepping stone to Hornby Island, which is known for its swimmable beaches (including a nude beach) and a funky village with a "free store"; Port Alberni, which, for some people is almost in the way of the Pacific Rim, where surfing, beachcombing, and walking the wilderness trails are paramount. More often than not, if people stop in Port Alberni, it's for the Tim Hortons at the strip mall on the main drag, or to fill up with gas on the other side of town. (The Clam Bucket in Port Alberni is a delicious, quirky place to stop for lunch. Robin Williams once ate there, as the photograph on the wall reveals. To get there, just turn left at the bottom of the hill, at the canal, and drive a block or two.)

Thinking of Port Alberni as nothing more than a place to rush through is a huge mistake! The main road that takes you through to the other side of this town, on your way to the wild, gorgeous Pacific Rim National Park, is *not* the real Port Alberni. Do not let the sight of auto junkyards and big box malls deter you from paying this town a worthwhile visit, if only for a few hours or perhaps an evening. Again—yes, it bears repeating—the section of town that you drive through to get to the magnificent west coast is not all there is to the town of Port Alberni. The true town is south, to the left, and from there, if you turn on any street, you will soon find yourself in the real Port Alberni.

Pacific Rim

Port Alberni, the Alberni Inlet, Bamfield,
Tofino, and Ucluelet

Port Alberni

AT FIRST GLANCE, PORT ALBERNI IS A MILL TOWN, ONE WHOSE boundary lies within the traditional territories of the Hupačasath and Tseshaht First Nations. The white smoke and steam from the working mill on shore can be seen from almost any location, at almost any time; it's a significant industrial facility, a complex, sprawling, yellow-and-grey metal structure set back from a wide, gritty street dotted with nondescript business ventures—smudges of beige and grey stucco, with an occasional splash of red signage here and there, all tucked within the surrounding pristine mountain peaks which form the Alberni Valley. There's an interesting juxtaposition of industry and nature—a quietly intriguing marriage of traditional blue-collar labour and the beauty of the towering majestic, mountainous scenery that envelops and imbues the spirit of the place.

Farther along this wide, main road is the town centre; it is small, with shops and services on the hill, and the marina businesses and

lovely little quay and artisan shops down on the wharves, where the
MV *Frances Barkley* prepares to chug down the long, beautiful, remote
inlet on her daily mail run and to deliver passengers and a bit of cargo
to Bamfield, a tiny village on the great Pacific Ocean, on the edge of
the world.

In my estimation, the real treasure of Port Alberni is Char's Landing,
a restored church, originally built in 1912, up the hill on Argyle
Street. It's been called the heart of the community, and I would agree.
Charlene Patterson (a.k.a. Char), the establishment's namesake, has
created this special social gathering place where diverse arts activities
regularly take place—concerts, literary readings, open mics, potlucks,
and on Friday evenings, the Creative Options Craft Circle. When I
visited on a Friday night, I spent twenty dollars for the following: a
drink of choice ("Surprise me," I told the lady behind the counter, who
served me a blue-and-yellow beverage in a glass the size of a punch
bowl), a bottomless bowl of popcorn, vegetables and dip, and admission
to the Friday night craft circle led by local artist Charli Chaisson. What
a deal!

Despite being raised by artists, I have never been one for crafts. (I
am totally intimidated by clever, dexterous people who practice the
creative endeavour of scrapbooking—oh, the patience and precision
required!) This was a new experience for me, and it couldn't have happened in a better place. The old, musty facility was full of character;
the stained glass windows and wood floors were original; there were
no pews, but there were soft, fake leather couches and chairs randomly
placed around the large, dim room; one wall was mirrored. The little
bar was in a corner, and floating from the ceiling, was a huge gold-and-
pink silk mermaid. "A community effort," Charli told me as I took a
seat at the craft table in the centre of the room. From head to toe, she
was festooned in multiple layers of fabrics and textures: a racoon fur
hat, scarves, blouses, shawls, and old leather boots—a living, breathing,

walking work of art. She was very sweet, and I instantly felt connected to her, as if we shared something deep and familiar and unspoken.

The craft of the night was rock painting. Thank God, I thought. I can do that. So I chose a smooth, round stone, picked up a brush, and began to paint it blue and silver. Charli explained that she had picked up the rocks from a beach near Halifax and a river in the interior. I sensed she was a bit of a drifter, a loner, a gentle, serene soul in her fur cap, someone who could be happy painting the same rock for over an hour. She showed me some little clay trolls and gnome-like dolls she'd made. "It's hard being an artist" she said softly, almost in a whisper.

Soon I noticed that I was the only person who had attended the craft circle that night, except for my mate Mikki, who sat at the bar so as not to disturb my artistic concentration. After a while, Mikki offered to take our picture (I had also painted a mussel shell), so Charli and I stood in front of the mirror and awkwardly posed, not really knowing what to do.

"What should I do?" she asked shyly.

"Let's show off our rocks!" I said.

We self-consciously squirmed closer together and lifted our little painted rocks with pride before returning with relief to the table to resume our project. The resulting photograph looks like Munch's *The Scream*, except there are two of us, not just one, and we are not quite screaming. But while we do have ridiculous grins, there's an almost-desperate "take the darn picture already" feel to the image.

And so there we sat, just Charli and me, in this old church with the rain beating on the tall, peaked roof, the streets empty outside. Mikki sat at the bar, having excused herself after she had attempted to paint one rock. Now, as if in a sad scene depicted in a Hopper painting, she sat alone, leaning over the counter under a single dim light, drinking her gin and soda. I kept painting rock after rock until closing time, so as not to hurt Charli's feelings. I must have painted ten rocks, each with multiple coats of paint. Though there wasn't a big turnout for the craft circle, Charli's feelings were not hurt; she had a gentle dignity about her and just the slightest edge of melancholy, as if she glimpsed sadness but did not succumb to it.

The edge of emotion, that brief pause before the potential unleashing of a storm, is far more interesting than allowing oneself to be immersed in a personal tempest. It is the edge where one could easily tip one way or the other; it is a vulnerable yet powerful place to be. When a child is about to cry, when his lower lip quivers, there is the moment of emotional choice, of all or nothing, or of restraint and calm. I find this fleeting, in-between moment to be more subtle and fascinating than a full-blown meltdown. It is where the energy is at its greatest. I am intrigued by those who pause in that moment where they can choose whether to let go or hold it in.

Years ago, before I attended the Creative Options Craft Circle, I was invited to do a book reading at Char's Landing. It was a minor little book tour with several other Island writers, and we were all reading animal stories. One woman read a story about a frog who may have (we never knew for certain) recognized the woman who had rescued it from a puddle one spring; it returned to her porch window a year later.

My story was about Boris, the dear old boar I had raised from a tiny piglet and had eventually sold, only to have him returned to me years later by a woman in Cowichan who contacted me after she had read one of my books about Boris.

"I think I own Boris!" she had breathed with excitement over the phone. She could no longer keep him, she said; she suspected he was now infertile—no small wonder, I thought (he was elderly and had spent his life impregnating an abundance of Island sows). Soon she returned him to my farm, where good old Boris quietly lived out his life with my two huge, barren sows. It remains a mystery to me why most animals I acquired were unable to conceive. I seem to have attracted neuters (as Mum called those who were not interested in sex), eunuchs, and all things barren to my farm over the years—at least when it comes to animals.

On the night of the book reading at Char's Landing, I read a passage of the Boris story—but first there was an open mic session. Open mics give members of the community the chance to read their stories and poetry in public. Many residents read their poems to enthusiastic applause and warm support from rowdy, friendly locals. I will always remember one young poet from that night: a tall, wiry fellow with pale blond hair who was obviously well-loved by the crowd. He wore skin-tight silver pants (yes, silver) that showed every sinew on his slender thighs and every other bump, bulge, and knobbly body part. He was the life of the party, and everyone loved him. His pants, pulled up so tightly, were not rude nor embarrassing in any way; he wore them with great style and aplomb. He and his outfit were highly amusing, and he oozed a wonderful, positive joy all around him with a dazzling aura that radiated through the room.

And yet I sensed within this vibrant, lanky-legged poet an edge of suffering and his deliberate choice to not succumb to its depths. It was as if he skilfully floated just above the pain that life can bring. Years later I would sense this same quality within Charli while at the Creative Options Craft Circle in the very location I'd encountered the young poet.

And now I think, after experiencing Char's Landing once again after all this time and meeting Charli, that perhaps this in-between town, Port Alberni, allows people to simply and freely be themselves. It encourages them and enables them to float between worlds, between emotions; to not fall, but to survive with oneself; to not be intimidated by others when it comes to how or what to think, or what others think; to write poetry, paint rocks, to ponder whether frogs have feelings or memories without any sentimental interference. It has quite a powerful spirit for a town that most people drive right through.

> Della Falls, in the Alberni Valley, is Canada's highest waterfall at 1,450 feet. You can visit the falls, but be prepared: It is a substantial journey that requires overnight camping, as you need to cross Central Lake and then embark upon a steep fifteen-kilometre trek to the base of the falls; from there it is a winding, challenging three-kilometre hike to the high viewpoint. According to advice found on the Trails BC website, the best time of year to see the falls is in mid-July, when the glacial run-off is at its peak.

The Alberni Inlet

A day trip on the MV *Frances Barkley* from the Port Alberni Quay will have you meandering down the Alberni Inlet to the historic seaside settlement of Bamfield, which is an absolutely delightful experience. This charming voyage of approximately sixty kilometres (thirty-five nautical miles) includes brief stops to deliver mail, food, and supplies to the few scattered inhabitants who reside in the hidden coves and bays tucked in the narrow, deep fjords of the green inlet. Wispy plumes of smoke rise from the chimneys of cozy homesteads huddled together on the remote, rugged shores; other abodes are perched on the black rock ridges among the thick, dripping, drooping forests under a low, charcoal sky. During the voyage, the friendly captain points out working mills and abandoned sites along the inlet, perching eagles, and remote fishing camps along the shady coniferous shores.

The MV *Frances Barkley* is a tough old lady. She not only takes passengers, residents, and tourists for a stunning scenic journey but also has a full schedule of important tasks to perform. According to her glossy little brochure, she is a working packet freighter, and can carry two hundred passengers and a hundred tons of cargo. When I peered down into the wet, dim hold from the deck above, it seemed to me that the "cargo" on this particular day was mostly cases of beer.

Built in 1958, the *Frances Barkley* worked in Norway for a time, and despite signs of aging—rust seeping through the chipped, white enamel paint on her hand rails, noisy but steady vibrating engines below deck, grey linoleum floors, and aged blue vinyl seats with dated chrome arms—she does the job. There's a galley below that serves breakfast, burgers, homemade soup, and even wine; the chef is a jovial lady who will entertain you with stories about Port Alberni's tsunami in 1964 when the water came up the inlet and into her bedroom.

I met a friendly fellow on the journey, an elderly Dane who had lived in Bamfield for many years. In his youth, he worked on the coal ships between England and Poland, and in Port Alberni he had worked at the mill. He told me that when he first moved to Bamfield, he had planted a row of tomato plants in front of his little house. There was a new, young policeman stationed in Ucluelet, a community down the coast; the new and exceptionally conscientious officer was assigned to visit Bamfield once a week. One day the young officer strolled up the shore on his weekly duty and saw the tomato plants, lush and about to ripen, but mistakenly thought they were marijuana plants and ripped them all out.

The only other passenger on the vessel, on the day I travelled, was a resident who had taken her old tabby cat to the veterinarian in Port Alberni; she was on her way home with the ancient feline, who was in a dirty beige plastic cage on the seat beside her. The elderly, confused cat let out nervous howls as its owner stared blankly ahead, drinking tea from her thermos. The low, threatening black clouds finally burst and pelted the salt-stained windows with a torrent; the little boat, tossed in the surf of the jade sea, chugged ahead into the mist with determination.

Along our journey down the inlet and in and out of these little remote coves and settlements, the captain of our vessel slowly and carefully manoeuvred the boat close to the weathered wooden floats and rickety docks serving the few residents who live in the tiny communities without most modern conveniences and pretty much anything except wood to burn, fish to catch, breathtaking views of eagles in their towering nests, seagulls pecking at the rockweed, and the white sea mists rolling in over the surface of the dark green water.

We briefly stopped at one such community along the way to deliver the weekly mail at Kildonan, tucked away in a secluded channel off the inlet. The dark water from our gentle wake lapped up against the rotting sun-and-sea-bleached remnants of an old salmon canning plant as we sidled up to the little Canada Post floating wharf. Two scruffy, old dogs waited, staring at us with quiet anticipation, ready for their biscuits to be thrown to them by a crew member while a propane tank was lowered from a large hook and pulley, by a quiet young man in blue overalls and big yellow rubber boots. Looking around, I noticed that one enterprising resident had made little wooden birdhouses that were for sale under a sign reading HABITATS. There are entrepreneurs everywhere!

I am still in awe that you can send a letter by Canada Post, up an obscure channel in the middle of the rainforest, to a tin shack with a faded and torn maple leaf flag proudly piercing the low pearl mist on a floating dock with loose boards that look barely able to withstand the next turbulent ocean tempest whipping in from the Pacific.

> The highest rainfall in North America is recorded at Henderson Lake, just slightly north of Kildonan.

The Kildonan Cannery represents a unique span in our province's history. Established in 1903, it employed four to five hundred workers. The Wallace brothers, from the Scottish town of Kildonan, named this site after they purchased the cannery in 1910; they operated the business until 1928, and the plant closed in 1960.

> The North Pacific Cannery near Prince Rupert was one of the province's oldest salmon canneries. It began operating in 1889 and continued for almost ninety years. The last cannery to close, it is now a national historic site and recalls a vast

and significant industry in Canadian West Coast history, employing hundreds of workers who performed a variety of skills and tasks.

The usual practice of the industry at that time took a somewhat multicultural approach, with specific duties relegated to individual cultural groups: the First Nations and the Japanese peoples would bring in the catch, the Chinese workers processed the fish and performed the canning tasks and supplied the cans, having developed excellent tinsmithing skills, and Europeans most often held the management positions.

Reasons for the decline of the West Coast salmon canning industry appear to be twofold: steadily declining salmon stocks, no doubt from overfishing, and changing consumer preferences for fresh and frozen seafood, due to the development of sophisticated refrigeration on the fishing vessels.

At one time there were eighty West Coast canneries, but only one remains today: St. Jean's Cannery and Smokehouse. Though St Jean's is operated out of Nanaimo, since 2015 it has been owned by NCN Cannery LP, which comprise five of the Nuu-chah-nulth First Nations.

Bamfield

Bamfield is a popular destination famous for sea kayaking among the nearby Broken Islands, as well as for world-class fishing, diving, and camping. It is also the northern end of the West Coast Trail, a seven-day hike linking Bamfield to Port Renfrew.

Bamfield hosts Music by the Sea, an annual summer music festival in its lovely cultural centre, perched high on a granite cliff among the arbutuses and firs and set against the stunning backdrop of the ocean sunset. In 2018, Music by the Sea and the Huu-ay-aht First Nation presented a joint event in the House of Huu-ay-aht, which opened in 2000.

There is an old logging road into Bamfield from Port Alberni, but it is rough; when the village invited a doctor to visit in the hopes of having him stay permanently, he drove the road and apparently vowed to never again embark on the journey having lost his muffler and two hubcaps.

When we pulled into the little wharf in Bamfield, the rain was coming down upon us in sheets. The crew gave us umbrellas as we had one hour to walk and explore—just enough time for the cargo to be unloaded and other supplies loaded. Despite the rain, we strolled along the boardwalk, a wooden sidewalk that wound along the shore. Above the boardwalk were little lanes and cozy shake-and-shingle cabins with gardens of wildflowers and apple trees.

Tucked along the boardwalk, on a grassy enclave just beyond the store, is the Bamfield Cat House. This is somewhat of an attraction—a colourful collection of little painted houses and shelters and shanties, all with blankets and beds of straw, for the feral cats who lived in Bamfield. At one time there were many feral cats, but thankfully, the good community members managed to capture the wild little creatures and had them spayed and neutered; eventually there were very few feral cats. But the haven remains, overgrown with wildflowers, grasses, and brambles of all sorts.

Many years ago, when we resided on Glamorgan Farm in North Saanich, I felt compelled to take in and care for any abandoned or homeless animals that chose to make the farm their home. This, by the way, is not the same as hoarding rescued or abused creatures—I did not seek out these dear animals; they either arrived on my doorstep or were discovered huddling in a dim corner of the barn. Sometimes kind citizens brought a sad little orphan to me, not knowing what else to do. Such was the case one wet, raw December, just before Christmas.

It was a typical grey day, and I made the rounds in my rubber boots among the eleven log structures spaced like a small historic village around the property. I lugged tubs of hot mash (with cooked yams, their favour-ite) to the sows Mabel and Matilda and to Boris, the elderly, infertile boar. They all grunted in eager anticipation as they rose from their deep straw beds.

I let the hens outside to peck at the mixture of grains that I tossed onto the wet soil; then I threw hay to the horses in their paddocks and filled the little duck pond with fresh water. It was a happy and satisfying routine that I embarked upon every morning and evening; while I did this, I was often followed around by a half-dozen grizzled, old dogs.

At night we'd sit by the fire and make to-do lists of farm chores—some-thing always needed repairing, weeding, mowing, piling, digging, filling in, nailing, cleaning, painting, tying down, picking, pruning, boiling, freezing and, sometimes, sadly, burying.

One blustery dark evening, after all the animals were put to bed and locked safely up for the night, and the long row of little white lights strung and looped between the swaying poplar trees down the driveway were blinking in the gusts, I had a phone call. It was a woman from a rescue organization. She had captured sixteen feral cats from a barn that had burned down in a Victoria suburb.

"I have them all in cages in my kitchen!" said breathlessly. "Can you take them in—couldn't they live in the stables?" She went on to explain that they were all completely feral, untouchable, born in the wild, terrified of people.

When I owned my farm in North Saanich, I did have a small empty barn. It was beautiful, and I rented it to a lovely group of skilled boat builders who renovated it to resemble the inside of a ship. It had a wood-stove and polished handrails, lovely old glass panes and windowsills; it was dry, safe, serene, and silent.

Later that evening, sixteen frightened little cats arrived in sixteen cream-coloured crates. They soon became part of my daily routine, with me taking them kibble and scraps. They'd peer at me from the shadows of the loft beams or from behind the cupboards when I brought them their tiny morsels,

and they crept out nervously when I moved back towards the door to leave.
I christened the cat facility the Pussy Barn.

On the old furniture and carpets I'd placed throughout the spacious room,
they lounged comfortably throughout the cold, raw, rainy winter days when
the Garry oaks were bare, and the gravel driveway was a wet, grey soup.

That Christmas Eve, a bleak, freezing rain fell and turned to a soft
snowfall by dawn. My friend Jo came over (with chains on her car tires)
for a warm cider by the fire and some turkey. After dinner, we visited all
the animals as we made the nightly rounds. Our final stop was to the Pussy
Barn, carrying a tray full of little turkey pieces, which we placed on the
floor. We lit the woodstove; I had placed two old stuffed chairs in front of the
fire, and Jo and I sat there drinking our wine in the warm glow of the fire
with the ice rain pelting the tin roof. We had placed the tray of turkey quite
a distance from us, and, after a while, all the little occupants of the Pussy
Barn appeared and devoured their dinner.

When the spring warmed the meadows of the farm, several pussies chose
to move on. Some decided that the Sandown racetrack across the road was
a preferable abode; perhaps there were more mice in the run-down, damp
wooden stables. There were certainly many old grooms who fed the cats who
lived in dented and rusted trailers that were wedged into the alders, with
blackberry bushes enveloping the sides and mossy roofs of the corrugated tin.

But several of the little creatures were ill, so with great effort, and thick
gloves, I managed to capture them and have them humanely euthanized.

By the time I left the farm, many years later, there were four pussies
remaining. Two were elegant calicos and were given a home by a neighbour;
the other two were elderly, thin, and toothless and had breathing problems.
I could not abandon them, so they came to town.

Initially, I placed them in the basement of our lovely heritage house,
where it was warm and safe. One, despite being with the other and sur-
rounded by soft beds and food, gnawed her way out of the window in panic,
the poor thing, and was never seen again.

*So one pussy remained, a toothless, timid tabby with a severe wheeze.
I named him Toby, and there he hid in the basement, buried in a box of
letters that Mum had written to me all my life (she'd written to me once a
week since I left home at seventeen).*

*Every day I took food down to Toby, and eventually he moved closer to
the steps leading up to the kitchen. The other cats were very kind to him,
and one old boy, Jimmy, befriended Toby and slept with him, this time in a
box of old photographs of my ex-husband on Galiano Island. Finally, Toby
made it to the kitchen, wheezing and coughing. He won't last the year, poor
old thing, I thought. That was seven years ago, and today, Toby lives in the
bathroom, lounging on the heated floor during the cold days, and on the
cushioned deck chair under the umbrella on warm days. He is served warm
cat food all day, whenever he squeaks for it, staring at the counter and baring
his worn-down, black gums. To this day, we still are unable to touch him.
And yet he runs the household!*

"Don't step on Toby," we say to each other.

"Don't raise your voice—Toby is sensitive."

"Did you buy that soft liver cat food for Toby?"

"I can't have my bath because Toby is sleeping by the tub."

*I seem to be at his beck and call. How did this happen? How did a feral,
skittish, scrawny cat who appeared on the farm almost fifteen years ago after
escaping a burning barn, as part of a group of sixteen other cats, end up
running a household and living in luxury, eating special vittles called Party
Mix that come in colourful and convenient little packages, delicately lapping
half-and-half cream, and sleeping on heated slate or lounging on a wicker
patio chair in Victoria, overlooking the Parliament Buildings?*

*I believe Toby succeeded due to his timidity, his caution, and his fears.
Herein we are reminded that to succeed in life, bravery, boldness, aggression,
and assertiveness are not always the way to rise above. Sometimes, even when
living in a state of outright petrification, we can prevail and attain a life of
luxury, perhaps even like Toby, with great comfort and loyal domestic help.*

Are our destinies fate? Are our destinies luck? Or do we simply make the correct choices and reap the resulting rewards? How do the events that shape our lives occur? To me it remains a mystery, something no scientist, no academic study, no survey, no computer program or consultant, nor expert in anything from sociology to zoology will ever be able to explain. I like that—the mystery of how we end up as we do.

So, perhaps the feral cats in Bamfield who took up residence at the Cat Haven, sheltered in their little shingled purple and yellow cottages, have met with similar good fortunes as Toby. Maybe they are lying by a warm stove at this very moment, with stomachs full of warm liver, or tuna treats, or Toby's favourite, Party Mix.

When we popped into Bamfield's village store for coffee and a fresh apple fritter, the six people that came into the store all knew what each was doing that evening: There was a community potluck and dance, and a party to launch a new cookbook; somebody else was having a meeting about tsunami emergencies. On the notice board, other meetings were posted: a village cleanup and renovation of the public outhouses, painting of the boardwalk, and planting of the flower boxes. One resident informed me that, by law, the boardwalk is considered a highway, and its regular upkeep is paid for by the government, which sends representatives to visit and occasionally replace a few loose boards.

Although I found Bamfield exquisitely whimsical, safe, and friendly, I could not live in a place where everyone knows my business, especially my evening plans. I'd always feel guilty because the entire population of the village would know if I did not contribute to the enhancement of the flower boxes. Come to think of it, I did not see a church, so not only would I live in a state of anxiety and guilt, I'd have no way and nowhere to confess!

Bamfield's marine history

On board the MV *Frances Barkley*, you can read a publication titled the *Ship's Log*, a very interesting little newspaper full of facts and articles about the journey down the inlet and mariner knowledge. For example, I learned that a fathom is six feet and that the word *scuttlebutt* once referred to the cask that held a ship's fresh drinking water for sailors. (Today scuttlebutt is understood to mean gossip and rumour and thus not unlike the idiom *water cooler talk*.)

I also learned that Captain Richards, who arrived in 1861, named the site after the first white settler who had explored the area a few years earlier—a Mr. Banfield. (It is commonly thought that the M was either a spelling mistake or was repeated verbally by locals; in any case, it stuck as Bamfield.)

When Mr. Banfield recognized the area's bounty of resources and proximity to shipping routes, he established and encouraged several industrial and business pursuits in the area, including lumber exports, whaling, and fishing (in particular, herring and halibut, which he sent down to Mexico and South America). He was correct in his estimation of opportunities, and was indeed an astute businessman, but as we know today, these ventures were overly exploited—especially the whaling—and took a severe toll on our natural environment.

Until whaling became a lucrative business—in our case, at the turn of the twentieth century—Indigenous peoples hunted whales for oil, meat, bone, baleen, and other parts of the creature for a variety of traditional purposes; even so, whales and humans maintained a natural balance. But as soon as non-Indigenous people realized that whaling was a profitable industry, the natural marine ecosystem, especially where whales were concerned, was rapidly thrown out of balance.

The first whaling station to open in the Bamfield area was the Pacific Whaling Company, in 1905. The station was set up at Sechart, a minuscule settlement between Bamfield and Ucluelet. It closed in 1917, and today it is a popular lodge and famous for its spectacular kayaking adventures.

> In 1911, 474 whales were caught and processed, as compared to only 90 whales in 1917.

> Commercial whaling in Canada was halted in 1972. At the time of this writing, Fisheries and Oceans Canada reports that the number of western North Pacific grey whales who migrate between the waters near southern China to the waters in the Sea of Okhotsk is extremely low, critically endangered at only a hundred whales.

> As of 2019, our resident orca population, pods J, K and L of the Salish Sea, is on the endangered list with less than seventy-five members who face three major threats to their survival: declining food sources (chinook salmon); chemical contamination and pollution; and marine noise. Sonar from military vessels is so intense that it can cause hemorrhaging—even death—in a whale.

The rain was still pouring when it was time to leave Bamfield for our journey back up the inlet to Port Alberni. Drenched from our stroll, we headed back along the boardwalk towards the dock, with its red painted rails and our little white ship bobbing patiently in the mist.

For a short distance, there was a tunnel of sorts, from the huge dark cedars arching towards the shore; the damp soil, the salal bushes, and the mossy bank gave off that lovely, pungent, woody scent. And there we saw, slowly lumbering through the trees, the lady with her old cat, heading home to her little cottage. She had stopped at the store for a few supplies, which she carried in a bulging shoulder bag. Her hair was soaked to her scalp, her shoes were wet, brown leather, and she stopped to rest on the boardwalk rail to catch her breath. I briefly slowed my step, and, for a fleeting second, looked her way, then out to the cold, grey sea. After a moment of hesitation, I continued along the glistening wooden slats towards the *Frances Barkley*.

Suddenly, a surprising wave of compassion and empathy flowed through me with a pang. I felt this not because the woman was wet, or alone, or because her shoes were soggy and worn; it was something else, something unexplainable. It was a penetrating, unexpected glimpse into a deeper part of the human condition, something wordless that came from deep inside me. And yet this intangible glimmer was clear while the woman and I were both in the rain on the Bamfield boardwalk. Although this fleeting connection dissipated within seconds, the memory of it remains.

Sometimes I worry that I am too cynical, perhaps too jaded or hardened to the rapid and frustrating world that has developed around me, a world that seems to relentlessly push me forward. But then, to my relief, I experience these brief, profound, unplanned moments of . . . well, not kindness, not love, not even like, but rather a sort of understanding of human vulnerability, a recognition of the universal loneliness we all share. And though cynicism creeps up on me at times, it has no ground in these rare moments.

If I were a filmmaker, I'd make a short, silent film of this woman with her old cat, trudging home in the rain. I'd try to capture a sliver of a little life on the edge of the Pacific Ocean.

Tofino and Ucluelet

If you would like to experience being as close to heaven as you could be while remaining alive and still on this earth, a visit to Tofino and Ucluelet, specifically to the breathtaking beaches, is essential.

From Port Alberni, the drive is spectacular. I divide the drive into three sections: Sproat Lake, the summit, and the remainder that winds its way down through the coastal rainforest past the immense Kennedy Lake—the largest lake on Vancouver Island.

An especially beautiful time to take the drive is in May when the snow only remains on the mountain peaks, not the roads, and the hardy Pacific dogwoods are in full bloom, abundant with their creamy, emerald-tinted pearl petals on spindly branches resiliently jutting out from the black basalt rock crevices and crags. Small waterfalls gush between the boulders and slabs of mountain stone that line the road. Summer cabins dot the edge of Sproat Lake, and at the campsite, you can have a dip at a small sandy beach. The lake used to be home to the famous Mars Water Bombers, great hulking aircrafts which could scoop massive amounts of water delivered to fight our all-too-common and volatile summer forest fires.

Sproat Lake is fed by many mountain streams; at the end of this lake, on the way up to the summit, is a wide river bedded with white stones and shallow sandbars. On more than one occasion, I have seen a voracious group of bald eagles feasting on the riverbank, ripping apart salmon with their great talons.

After the summit, the journey down to the ocean becomes an exercise in careful driving. I cannot emphasize this enough: *Go slowly and do not rush, even if someone is on your tail.* There are many places to pull over to allow the fast traffic to pass, if you need to. If anyone is rushing you, remember that these drivers probably either know the road well, or they are young, crazy, obsessive surfers in their parents' jeeps or pickups, dying to get to the beach so they can party for the weekend. Just let them go by! Continue to carefully gauge the narrow hairpin turns and steep drops that, with one false move, could mean a plunge to your demise. Believe me, you do not want to expire before you see the amazing beach that awaits. I recall a tragedy that occurred in 2010, when two paramedics perished as their ambulance swerved off the road and plunged into Kennedy Lake.

If you need a break from the white-knuckled driving, there is a stunning spot where you can stop along a rushing river that cascades and spills over huge blocks of granite. It's easy to find: The road widens, and there are usually others who have stopped to take in the wild and spectacular scene; its beauty makes for a natural invitation to pull over.

Without much trouble at all, you can climb down from the road and walk across the rushing flow on the great, smooth, grey slabs. Some people even lie down and sunbathe; others take a break and have a little refreshment before continuing on their journey to the great Pacific shores.

Pacific Rim National Park Reserve

Finally, the road brings you to the Pacific Rim National Park Reserve, which stretches along the ocean shore. To borrow those brilliant three words from Wordsworth, "my heart leaps" when I drive around the wide bend in the road heading towards Tofino and behold, through a break in the trees, the sea mist rising above the endless stretch of silver sand and hear the deep roar of the surf.

For me, Long Beach, the Pacific Rim, Tofino—however one wishes to refer to this stunning and uplifting landscape—is all about the beach. The Pacific Rim beaches are among the few places that have me at a true loss for words; in fact, I am not sure we even have words in our English vocabulary to capture the sense of space, light, or fragrance of the place.

And oh, the *sound!* The perpetual, thunderous crashing of the powerful Pacific surf continues unabated, all day, all night. The enormous, throbbing energy of the ocean is magical and pacifying, and though it is commonly said that silence is golden, I would say, when compared to the ocean's deep, living sound, complete silence can be somewhat unsettling. The constant rhythmic roar of waves is far superior, in my estimation, for quieting the mind and body.

The sunsets and first light of dawn are spectacular on the beaches, but the wild wet storms are thrilling as well. Mum used to paint huge oil paintings of the grey sands enveloped in the white sea mists; she'd dab a couple of tiny figures in as well, strolling in the golden light under the infinite mauve sky.

The most popular pastime on the beaches is surfing; regardless of the weather, little black figures in wetsuits are seen on every beach, dashing into the surf and paddling out to sea as they hope to catch that perfect wave back to the shallow sands.

At the resort where I stay, there is a large turquoise sign on the beach that explains proper surf etiquette in bold text, qualifying it as the SURFERS CODE OF CONDUCT FOR SAFETY:

- RIGHT OF WAY: ONE SURFER PER WAVE; THE PERSON CLOSEST TO THE PEAK HAS THE RIGHT OF WAY.

- DO NOT DROP IN OR SNAKE.

- PADDLING OUT: AWAY FROM OTHER SURFERS. AIM FOR THE WHITEWASH.

- DANGER! DO NOT THROW BOARD IN DANGER OF OTHERS.

At the bottom of the sign, the reader is reminded TO RESPECT THE BEACH, OCEAN, AND OTHERS.

One would think that most of these rules are impossible to obey given that every surfer out there spends most of their time tumbling head over heels as soon as a wave hits them, grasping for their boards, trying in vain to remain upright.

Surfing lessons are available from many facilities. I was tempted to try it out, but I found the wetsuit something of a challenge. Not only is the clinging neoprene unflattering, but countless people have already perspired, probably quite profusely, within the snug, foamy folds—and God knows what else has gone on inside that wetsuit when the first big wave slammed the suit's wearer onto the sea floor.

When I was at Long Beach recently (I usually make one visit a year), another event took place on the vast beach: a protest against oil tankers along our coast. I watched from afar as a long chain of people linked arms along the edge of the shore, where the water washes up on the sand. They had a banner, and they seemed upbeat; it was not a negative rebellion. Suddenly I felt the urge to approach and join the line. This was my first protest—and I even linked arms with a stranger!

So stunning is this sliver of paradise that many couples arrange to be married on the beach, especially at sunset. I witnessed a photo shoot of a new bride and her bridesmaids at the end of the beach, where sharp, jagged black rock, scratched from a million years of glacial activity, formed a backdrop to the lovely nuptial celebration.

The bride, in a billowing white train and veil, holding a large bouquet of white lilies with one hand, and her huge, swirling bustle with the other, tried with great difficulty to keep her balance in a brewing storm, under a dark purple sky that threatened to burst at any moment. Surrounding her was a gaggle of voluptuous bridesmaids in snug, turquoise, low-cut, sleeveless gowns, their upper arms blotchy and pink in the raw, chilly sea spray.

Suddenly, a strong, blustery squall thundered across the sand, tossing the entire entourage right into the swirling, murky, emerald brine, like detritus from a shipwreck. When the waves retreated, the wet, sandy cluster scrambled to their feet. Buffeted by another incoming wave, some toppled over yet again. Grasping one another and howling in gales of shrill, joyous hilarity, the wedding party finally managed to stagger to land, leaving the scattered lilies to churn in the tempestuous surf.

Long Beach

The Long Beach area of Pacific Rim National Park is classified as a protected biosphere reserve by UNESCO; there are 686 biosphere reserves in the world, in 122 countries. A potential biosphere protected area must be submitted by the federal government to the UNESCO organization for approval.

Parks Canada lists species that need to be protected in the Pacific Rim, including the dromedary jumping slug, the pink sand verbena (a delicate, small pink seashore flower), the northern goshawk (a medium-large raptor), and the seaside centipede lichen.

The entire stretch of this coastline, along with its forests and islands, holds a rich cultural history for the Nuu-chah-nulth (formerly referred to as "Nootka") peoples, today composed of fourteen individual nations. These are the true first North Americans that Captain Cook interacted with upon his arrival. Many of their signs and exhibits are displayed in their language throughout Pacific Rim National Park Reserve.

The Kʷisitis Visitor Centre

When you enter Pacific Rim National Park Reserve from the south end (heading towards Tofino), you will pass Wick Road. At the end of this road, right on the ocean's shore, is the beautifully built Kʷisitis Visitor Centre (formerly known as the Wickaninnish Interpretive Centre). Here you will find displays, brochures, and a gift shop. Parks employees are extremely helpful and pleasant. Outside is the beginning of Long Beach, which stretches far into the distance to the north, the great waves beating against the black basalt and the stunted, windblown, gnarled trees bent from the ocean wind. Towards the south is a lovely walking trail along the shore and through the woods, with many interesting plaques to read about Nuu-chah-nulth traditions, skills, and language on the Pacific coast.

While the website says that pets are allowed on the beach and trails by the centre, the park ranger was quite stern when telling me that I must not walk the various wooded trails and paths with my old hound Archie, even if leashed—wolves and cougars have been sighted at various times and in increasing numbers, and they consider dogs prey. There is a pamphlet that instructs visitors on what to do if one encounters a wolf, bear, or cougar; the two main pieces of advice are, "Do not play dead," and "maintain eye contact." Come to think of it, this could also work well in other threatening situations, not just with wildlife.

> It is commonly believed that a wolf's brain is somewhere around twenty to thirty percent larger than that of a dog.
>
> Black bears on Vancouver Island do not exactly hibernate (due to the warmer climate); instead, they enter into more of a state of torpor, napping and waking up to forage on berries, roots, flowers, and campsite treats.
>
> The scientific name for cougar is *Puma concolor* which means "cat of one colour."

There are numerous trails through the forests and shoreline in the park; all are unique, focusing on various themes such as life in the rainforest or the famous shipwreck of the *Valencia*, the latter of which leads you down some steep steps onto a beautifully sheltered, discreet pebbled cove. However, one of the most delightful walks is the Shorepine Bog Trail; much of this trail is on a well-constructed boardwalk over a forest bog of two-metre-thick sphagnum moss. The walk is short, around eight hundred metres, and the boardwalk is both wheelchair accessible and safe for small children. The brevity of the walk, which can be completed inside of thirty minutes, is more than compensated by the abundant atmosphere, with its compelling miniature landscape scattered with stunted, twisted, bonsai-like shore pines (also known as the *Pinus contorta*, the contorted pine). Their presence is especially unique due to their preference for the acidic and fertile brackish water moss in which they grow.

The Willowbrae Trail includes a corduroy road—the settlers' early mode of transportation along the route from Tofino to Ucluelet. Cut logs were placed snugly across the path to avoid the mud of the rainy season, but what a bumpy ride it would have been!

Years ago, I took Mum to Long Beach, and we walked the corduroy road. We got a bit lost somehow (which is to say I got us a bit lost). Mum was growing feeble, so rather than have her walk with me to discover the trail back to the parking lot, I had her sit down on a dry, crumbling stump in the sun to await my return—which, all told, took about twenty minutes. Eventually I managed to get us back to our car without incident. Still, for Mum, it was a bit of an adventure.

At that time, there was a restaurant at the Visitor Centre; it was spacious and open-beamed, with white linen napkins and a stunning view of the ocean. Upon our escape from the corduroy road, we found our way to this restaurant and decided to soothe the stress we felt from our misadventure. Relieved to be back in civilization, we sipped white wine and enjoyed a soup that Mum subsequently talked about right up until she died: a squash and nutmeg creation with an elegant yogourt swirl. When coming in and out of her morphine sleep, she'd say, "Oh Anny, remember that soup at Long Beach!"

That restaurant has since closed and is today an empty, grey shell, its windows smudged and hazy from the pounding winter saltwater surges and bracing gusts. I have heard talk of the First Nations people bringing it back to life, which would be wonderful; if that happens, I would hope that their new, signature soup might be a traditional Indigenous recipe.

Outside of the Visitor Centre (and the now-empty restaurant) is the coastal Wickaninnish Trail (now called the Nuu-chah-nulth Trail), but at the time of Mum's and my visit the informative plaques did not describe the First Nations culture. Back then, the First Nations were rarely acknowledged. Instead there was a path describing the art of the famous Group of Seven artist Arthur Lismer; this was where he loved to sit and sketch the ocean landscapes behind the bare, scrambling, and tangled limbs of the windswept trees.

Lismer, famous for not only landscapes, loved to paint harbours and boats, which also garnered him fame via his paintings of the so-called dazzle warships of the First World War. These ships were camouflaged with black and white geometric patterns meant to visually confuse the enemy. The patterns and reflections cast from a cluster of these mod-looking ships made it difficult to tell where the bow and stern were, and on which boat.

> Though attributed to the British marine artist Norman Wilkinson, it is said that the idea for the use of dazzle design in warfare was first proposed to Britain's Admiralty by zoologist John Graham Kerr, based on his observations of how stripes confuse predators in the animal kingdom.
>
> After the war, the dramatic black stripes and patterns became popular in British swimsuit design, further confirming my conviction that the English have a wonderful, deep sense of humour. Imagine using military disguise designs on swimsuits—it's so English to have a swimsuit design that disguises you in the water, especially if you are drowning!

Hazards and safety tips

Every year, people die in the area's turbulent waters, which are prone to powerful, surging waves that can rise up quickly and overwhelm you, tides that can catch you unaware, and rip currents that can pull you helplessly out to sea, so use caution when being awed by this magnificent landscape.

There are unsettling but important and interesting brochures published by CoastSmart, a "public safety pilot project [led by Parks Canada] in the Pacific Rim . . . designed to enhance coastal safety along the shoreline and in the surf zone." These brochures warn of the very real danger of being knocked off the tidal rocks where you may choose to stand. Reading these warnings, I was struck by the descriptions of how "fighting surf is like being in a washing machine" and "swimming in wet clothes is like wearing concrete." So do not venture far out on tidal rocks, despite how calm the sea looks—it is so deceiving.

Another brochure warns against rip currents and instructs you on how to escape their power. The rip is the centre of two currents moving away from the shore, so the pull is extremely powerful, accelerated by the two currents. The instructions tell us to stay calm and swim parallel to the shore; if this fails, signal for help (I'm sure I'd be signalling for help much sooner).

Tides, also covered in CoastSmart's hazard brochures, are important to keep in mind, too; it's wise to inform yourself of the tidal schedule, as well as its height!

Dressing for the Oyster Festival

Tofino and Ucluelet hold numerous annual festivals: the Tofino Food & Wine Festival, the Pacific Rim Whale Festival, and the Tofino Shorebird Festival, to name just a few. Several years ago, Mikki and I went up to Long Beach to stay at a one of those lovely beach resorts (the kind that gives you chocolate sand dollars and natural lavender shampoos) with our friend Patsy, who rose to all occasions with hilarity and enthusiasm. The Oyster Festival was in full swing and included an oyster-tasting extravaganza, paired with cocktails at a fancy hotel next door, just down the beach.

Of course, we decided to attend, especially when we heard that patrons should come dressed as oysters. Patsy and Mikki and I found this extremely amusing, but we had no costumes. Not to be dissuaded, we fashioned the resort's bedsheets into togas; Patsy had some grey scarves, which we entwined around our breasts; we used pillowcases on our heads, like turbans—and Patsy even had a string of pearls! Duly swathed in our makeshift costumes, we traipsed to the chic and elite glass-and-varnished dining room of the swanky place down the beach.

When we arrived, we had to climb over the security gate—an unexpected challenge, but we managed—and entered a door behind a thicket. Soon we found ourselves in the basement in the boiler room, and, by pure luck, we discovered and opened a door with a huge red handle. This led us to a dark hall, which led to some grey cement stairs, which took us up to the lobby behind the coat rack. We'd already had a little champagne in our lowly suites next door, and Patsy got the giggles as we proceeded, windswept and draped in our now-dishevelled finery.

Tracking sand over the polished marble corridor that finally led us to the sparkling dining hall, we took in the scene before us. Crystal glassware clinked, and busy, efficient servers in black tuxedos and tight ponytails strode energetically around the great, glowing room with silver trays of delicacies. From time to time the servers stopped to offer exquisite morsels to slim, tanned ladies with gold hoop earrings and wispy highlighted hairstyles; camel-coloured cashmere dresses clung to the ladies' small frames, and tasteful beige high heels accentuated their slender calves. The men were slightly less formal in their grey tweeds with their polished bald heads and pink cheeks as they held their spotless glasses of amber whiskys.

As we surveyed the room, we realized to our horror that nobody was dressed as an oyster! In reality, the official poster which I had seen at the Visitor Centre had in fact instructed the guests to *attend dressed in oyster colours*. (I rarely read the details when I anticipate a good time.)

We had a grand time anyway. Mikki and Patsy headed straight for the oyster buffet, and I settled down in a corner in a plush, oversized brown leather beanbag, and embarked on a deep and lengthy conversation about Jimmy Carter's peanut empire with an American couple from Carmel, California (where Clint Eastwood was the mayor). I think I told them a stupid Canadian joke: "What city is named after our prime minister, Brian Mulroney?" The answer was "Moose Jaw," to which the lady hooted with laughter as she twirled her array of gold necklaces around her thin fingers. I think we even exchanged addresses in a moment of pure love and mutual understanding, as I often do on an intimate river cruise or yoga retreat, but alas, the shared "love" of the moment gently floated away and only warm memories remain with the scrawled address probably still in an old address book in the bottom of my desk drawer. It was quite late when the party ended; in fact, we may have been the last guests to leave.

"Which way to the boiler room?" I slurred to the tired, confused girl in a black blazer at the lobby's front desk. We left through the front door and had to walk back to our resort along the highway in all those bedsheets because we could not find our way to the beach from the front door. We tried, but Mikki's leg became tangled in the irrigation hoses, and Patsy's toga was entwined in a huge rose bush.

Tofino's Botanical Gardens

Another attraction in Tofino is the Botanical Gardens. It's absolutely enchanting, and, of course, offers a special West Coast flair. The gardens begin with Darwin's Café, a quaint little wooden building with tons of books on the shelves, art on the walls, homemade cookies on the counter, delicious espresso, and a lovely patio with freshly painted picnic tables surrounded by lawns, herbs, lush hanging shrubs, ponds, and trickling streams. And then there's the whimsical outdoor art: huge wooden sculptures of figures, all against a backdrop of woodland paths and quirky surprises along the way. When you're sitting at a picnic table, you'll notice a wooden hut in the shape of a Cossack's cap; perhaps it is a fairy house or a friendly troll's abode.

There's an intimate little children's garden that resembles a jungle gym in the forest, a concoction of platforms and ladders and all sorts of little hiding spots among stumps and low-hanging boughs. Farther along on the walk through the forest garden, you can see a Nuu-chah-nulth cedar canoe, an original homestead of the area dating back to the 1800s, and Tofino Man, the humorous, fictional archaeological artifact that is crafted as if it were preserved for millennia and dug up from the Tofino mudflats.

Then there are the Three Elders (the largest trees in the gardens—a western hemlock, and two western redcedars), the Skunk Cabbage Walk, and boardwalks that take you through the difficult parts of the forest, allowing you to rise into the foliage of the West Coast rainforest canopies.

Now, I was not planning to mention it, but there are what some would call hippie elements to this garden (the brochure uses the word *hippie*, so I am guilt-free). I hesitate to use the word in description because, for some people, it conjures up images of drugs, muddy music festivals, and saturated porta-potties, bean sprouts and protests, and perhaps civil disobedience. Sometimes I attempt to convince right-wing skeptics who resent environmentalism to at least consider the importance of nature and good environmental practices, and I fear that if and when I mention the word *hippie* in a positive context, they will cease to listen as I plead my case. So if you're the kind of person who is generally put off by hippies, please bear with me.

The Tofino Botanical Gardens folk who envisioned, constructed, and today nurture and maintain the facility may be hippies, but they are modern, educated, clean-shaven, Gore-Tex-wearing hippies. They are full of innovative ideas, energy, and knowledge. They're disciplined and skilled, and they positively radiate a joy that comes from being immersed in nature. Their combined creativity, collaboration, and dedication make this garden remarkably fabulous.

Noteworthy is that the climate on Vancouver Island is similar to southern Chile, so there is much research happening in this garden with many plant species. The staff have an active interest in Chilean plants as well as the Giant Himalayan Lilies—great, voluptuous white trumpet-shaped blossoms, one of many impressive accomplishments in this peaceful and fascinating garden. Two other plants that thrive in the Tofino gardens are fuchsia and gunnera, a gigantic plant which produces five-foot-diameter leaves. Their mission, as declared on their website, is "the cultivation and display of plants native to the world's coastal temperate rainforests, and to research and education programs to improve knowledge and understanding of the ecosystems of the UNESCO Clayoquot Sound Biosphere Reserve. We believe in the preservation of the last remaining Old Growth Forests of Clayoquot Sound."

Ucluelet Aquarium

The town of Ucluelet lies thirty kilometres southeast of Tofino, at the other end of the Pacific Rim National Park Reserve.

Down on the wharf is the spectacular Ucluelet Aquarium, a relatively new addition to town (the aquarium's new building opened in 2012). Full of touch tanks and interesting information, it also has a charming, cozy reading corner filled with books on marine life and large comfy chairs to settle into as you overlook the fishing boats outside.

For a reasonable annual donation, you can sponsor a tank of aquatic life. Two sponsorship opportunities caught my eye: the tiny pink strawberry anemones, gorgeous in their massive, crowded magenta clusters, and who reproduce asexually by cloning themselves. (For all of us asexual people, this may be a great alternative to actual childbirth.) Despite their floral appearance, sea anemones are not plants; they are animals.

In another tank, there was the bay pipefish, related to the seahorse. This small, slender, emerald-green creature often swims vertically, concealing itself coyly in blades of eelgrass, a vital component of ocean life that provides a rich source of food and habitat for countless species of sea creatures. The female pipefish courts the male, and then the male carries and nourishes the eggs until they hatch. The pipefish do not have teeth; they slurp their food.

When Mikki and I want to get away, we sometimes go to Waikiki in Hawaii. We always stay in a large pink hotel, right on the beach; the warm air is filled with the odours of charcoal barbecues and coconut-scented sunscreen. The grass is fake, the drinks are yellow and frothy with cherries and little paper umbrellas, and the sinewy pool boys in baggy pink shorts are tanned the colour of milk chocolate.

Jets relentlessly stream across the deep blue cloudless sky above the white beach dotted with pink umbrellas, surfboard rental shacks, and beach bars serving pineapple-rum beverages, drawing tourists from all around the world. Behind the hotel are shaved-ice kiosks, gleaming windows of pearl necklaces, T-shirt shops, sushi outlets, and grubby little shops in dirty alleyways selling plastic flip-flops and cheap turquoise trinkets. There are also Sicilian eateries and steak restaurants, and high-end shops—Gucci, Hermès, and Chanel. The azure waters are warm, inviting, tropical, and everything is tailored for convenience, relaxation, and indulgence, and a bit of debauchery.

One afternoon, as I floated in the teal surf under a scorching southern sun, I noticed a little seahorse, delicate and elegant, bobbing vertically just under the surface. I was taken aback. Why, I wondered, would this little creature be attracted to an area of the ocean that was covered with a thin film of sunscreen and devoid of any ocean vegetation? Yet there he was, about the size of my index finger, just bobbing in the water among the masses of pink plastic air mattresses, animal-shaped life rings, and oily, pudgy thighs.

In one corner of the aquarium, something caught my eye: At first glance I thought it was a colourful piece of art, but then I realized it was a large display of plastic and beach debris retrieved from the local shores.

I recall a horrific yet eye-opening photography exhibit on seabirds at the Honolulu art gallery (one of loveliest art galleries I have ever visited; it was a cool, tasteful oasis set in an open plan with water, stone, and tropical garden features throughout, offering a reprieve from the hot greasy beach). The birds in the photographs had perished from ingesting a diverse array of plastic debris; the images revealed the contents of the stomachs of the birds, filled with things like bottle caps and cigarette lighters. And so I am one of the converted when it comes to beach litter, especially plastic, and I spend hours picking it up (along with cigarette butts) on the beaches in Victoria. (Did you know that plastics started to be mass produced in the forties and fifties? Seems like it's been longer, doesn't it?)

When I was very young, as Mum and I were walking along the Saint John River in Fredericton, she stopped, bent over, and picked up something that was lying on the shore among the reeds: plastic rings from a six-pack. She put it in her pocket, mumbling to herself something about how it would choke the river creatures. That moment has stayed with me for my whole life—Mum stooping on the riverbank, her thin red hand dipping into the lapping brown water, the enormous white Irving oil tanks in the distance behind the black railway bridge. Mum rarely taught me anything deliberately; I gained knowledge by observing her.

Protecting endangered species

While at the Ucluelet Aquarium, I picked up four brochures. (I love brochures and pamphlets and read them in great detail.) All four had dire warnings conveyed by Fisheries and Oceans Canada.

First, on abalone poaching: I had no idea that this existed, this notion of gathering abalone from our coastal waters stretching from Mexico to Alaska and depleting this endangered mollusc. Fines for gathering abalone are extremely high: up to $500,000, and/or $1000 per abalone, plus two years in jail. How are the poachers caught? The inspectors not only monitor fishing vessels, they also visit restaurants and warehouses. In 2016, a retailer on the mainland was fined $77,500 for possession of abalone.

In 1990, the entire coast of British Columbia was closed to wild abalone harvesting, but stocks have been unable to recover due to continued illegal gathering, according to Fisheries and Oceans. So, the next time you eat at a seafood restaurant, check the menu for abalone; if it's listed, ask where it came from.

> The abalone export industry boomed between 1975 and 1978. The glittering shell was frequently sold as inlay, not only for jewellery but also for guitars. Constructed of layers of calcium, stacked like tiles, separated by protein, the shells, when ground down, released a very potent, hazardous dust—especially problematic for asthma sufferers.

> I am not one for squealing and tattle-telling, but when it comes to nature, I am compelled to protect it. There is a reporting hotline called Report All Poachers and Polluters (RAPP) which can be reached twenty-four hours a day, seven days a week, at 1-877-952-7277.

Another ocean creature that is being monitored and protected is the rockfish. Thirty-seven species swim in our waters; they are mostly recognized by their spiky spine and intriguing, colourful patterns.

When I was young and spent my summers on Galiano Island with Gran, the rockfish were plentiful—I could see them swimming among the seaweeds and dark water on the rocky shores when I floated around on my air mattress. A child could simply drop a line and catch one, but currently these fish have seriously decreased in numbers. The situation today is not as drastic as that of the poor abalone, but closures and daily limits are enforced in several areas. An additional factor that threatens the rockfish numbers is their slow rate of maturity, much slower than salmon; many rockfish do not even start reproducing until they're five years old; some may not reproduce until they're somewhere between fifteen and twenty-five years old!

An additional brochure warns us of the dangers regarding releasing home aquarium species of fish and other species into natural ponds, streams, or the ocean; this is akin to releasing pet rabbits into the countryside (or, in the case of Victoria, onto the pretty university grounds, grassy highway boulevards, hospital gardens, and public parks). The reasons for the warnings should be obvious: The former pets—abandoned and now feral—overtake the natural ecosystems, interrupt the food chain (or eradicate it altogether), and pass on disease. Consequently, the cost to mitigate the damage is massive, if it can be rectified at all. The two most common creatures released into water are turtles and carp. The brochure suggests donating or returning unwanted aquarium pets, and there's always the SPCA.

When I was a municipal councillor a few years ago, a problem arose with the American bullfrog (I truly hesitate to say it, but numerous invasive species in Canada are American). This huge, plump, aggressive frog invaded Vancouver Island and could eat several ducklings just as a snack. In the case of this greedy fellow, he apparently made his way across America from New York after being introduced from France in the early 1900s as a food source delicacy—his legs, mainly.

Ironically, it was his legs that resulted in his continental destruction, hopping from lake to lake, gorging and stuffing his big, soft, wet mouth for the entire journey, crossing the border illegally and probably hitching a ride on a BC ferry.

The final pamphlet also warns against transporting invasive species on recreational vessels; all along the highway on Vancouver Island there are signs posted to wash off your boat bottoms. The signs remind me of visits with Mum so many years ago during her visits at my cozy Vancouver apartment; she'd gaze out the window at the idle tankers anchored in the blue haze of English Bay and remark, "When their little red bottoms are showing, they are empty."

Now, whenever I see a tanker anchored anywhere, I think of Mum and her red bottom comment.

When considering this warning to wash boat bottoms, I would say that this is an example of the effects of globalization. The pamphlet illustrates a variety of these invaders, mostly from Asia: the snakehead, which eats everything in its path and can live on land for three days, and the Chinese mitten crab which, so far, has only been seen in California; it loves to consume salmon eggs.

The Wild Pacific Trail

Ucluelet not only has a beautiful aquarium, but also a gorgeous walk known as the Wild Pacific Trail, which consists of a delightful stroll called The Lighthouse Loop and various other sections that run the length of the town. The loop is at the end of the town—at the Rocky Headlands, overlooking Barkley Sound—and takes approximately one hour to navigate. The highlight of the loop trail, apart from the spectacular scenery and numerous rest stops, is the famous Amphitrite Lighthouse.

The longer trail that runs the length of Ucluelet is diverse, with several sections such as the Artist Loop, the Ancient Cedars Loop, and the Bog Woodland Interpretive Loop. Here you will come across enormous vegetative growth, storm-watching decks, and the "painters' perches," where artists set up their easels and photographers their tripods.

Jim Martin, known as Oyster Jim, emigrated from the United States and settled in Ucluelet in 1979. He had an ambitious plan to establish trail networks here, and he succeeded. Hailed as a Ucluelet hero, Oyster Jim was awarded the Canadian Meritorious Service Medal as well as the BC Community Achievement Award.

The trails are not difficult to walk, and some are wheelchair accessible. They are all impeccably kept and overseen by volunteers—along with trail manager Oyster Jim—with the Wild Pacific Trail Society.

The Amphitrite Point Lighthouse

What could be more iconic than a lighthouse? The architecture of the Amphitrite Point Lighthouse isn't unique or spectacular, but its purpose, its history, and the keepers who kept her stoked with coal to save the souls at sea are all remarkable.

The lighthouse had to be built to withstand extreme ocean storms, so she is not built as a slender tower (as many lighthouses are) but rather on two solid square concrete blocks with a little red beacon at the top. She was built in 1915 following the wreck of the *Pass of Melfort*, a ship that had blown off course into Barkley Sound in a ferocious storm; there were no survivors.

It's sobering to think of the workers who constructed the lighthouse, through rain, sleet, sea storms, ocean hurricanes, and whipping winter hail, hauling in the vast array of heavy material on sleds through a trail with mud up to their knees.

The lighthouse keeper was equally burdened with challenging tasks: lighting the light, extinguishing the light, winding and maintaining the machinery, and stoking the coal-fired boiler that generated steam to operate the foghorn. For his services, he earned ten dollars a month. It was a job you could never leave—ever. In 1988, the lighthouse was automated; it is now unmanned, and cannot be entered. Still, there's a little thrill at first glance knowing that it saved many a seafaring life while standing stolid, strong, and stoic on the black rocks, overlooking the cold, grey sea. (From anywhere in the world, you can access a view of the lighthouse and the ocean via a live webcam at ukeelivecams.com— but it's not nearly as romantic as actually being there.)

As you approach the lighthouse, if you listen carefully with an ear bent towards your left, you will hear a bell that strikes a lovely but lonely, hollow sound with the rhythm of the waves; you may also be able to see the bell in the green buoy. To the right of the lighthouse, you will hear the sound of a horn in a red buoy. This sound is made by air pressure, also from the waves. These two buoys with their distinct sounds help guide the mariners, even today, through this volatile ocean passage.

Amphitrite was the Greek goddess of the sea; she is also known as the wife of Poseidon, the god of the sea and all other water courses, including floods, storms, droughts (yes, droughts!), and earthquakes. (I'm baffled by how one can be the god of water and the god of no water at the same time, but who am I to question the portfolio of an ancient Greek god?)

Amphitrite was pretty and gentle, and she loved to sing and dance. Captivated by her loveliness, Poseidon pursued her, and she fled. A dolphin found her and encouraged her to return to be with the god, and eventually she surrendered and became Poseidon's wife. She was known to have calmed the stormy sea (as she could no doubt calm her husband). While some literature refers to Amphitrite as the goddess of the sea, more often she is demoted to a minimal role as Poseidon's lovely wife.

In all the historic art I have seen depicting Amphitrite, she is shown as elegant and beautiful, whether she's on a mosaic, an urn, or even a modern European painting. She is frequently portrayed with a net in her hair or eyebrows shaped like crab claws.

Central Vancouver Island

Parksville, Lasqueti Island, Qualicum Beach,
Qualicum Bay, Bowser, Deep Bay, Fanny Bay,
Denman Island, Hornby Island, and Union Bay

Parksville

PARKSVILLE IS BY FAR ONE OF THE MOST ATTRACTIVE AND
amusing summertime resort locations on the Island. It has everything
a resort town should have: stretches of sandy, safe beaches, boardwalks,
campsites and spas, family restaurants, mini-golf, bumper boats, pioneer
museums, coffee shops, malls, car washes, baseball diamonds, water
parks, ice cream kiosks, and an enormous, oceanside park, sprawling
and green and lush with trees, containing tennis courts, a curling rink,
a clean and sleek skateboard facility, food trucks, and picnic areas. The
delightful Parksville Community Park is the site for two spectacular
annual activities: the kite festival and the international sand sculpting
competition held right beside the sea.

The sand sculpting is indeed something to behold! The amazing,
intricate, creative, and clever sculptures are constructed on a given
theme in a fenced area and judged on various criteria. In 2017, the

theme was Canada, in keeping with the one hundred and fiftieth anniversary of Confederation. Admission—a suggested donation of a mere three dollars—provides you with a walk among the magnificent creations and gives you a token to vote on your favourite sculpture.

The competition really is international: There are entries from the Netherlands, Russia, Italy, Florida, and even Lithuania, as well as all across Canada, including Newfoundland. The detail of the work is incredible. Every smile line, chipped tooth, and eyebrow hair is carved delicately with a fine, silty brown sand purchased locally (beach sand is too coarse and contains too many pebbles and shell pieces); these are professional carvings, and the correct sand consistency is crucial to maintain the sculptures. Glue, water, and wooden forms are used for precision and to prevent erosion and disintegration.

Solo sculptors are given ten yards of sand, and those with partners receive fifteen yards; the artists have thirty hours to complete their pieces.

The display of sculptures lasts throughout the summer (hopefully), so as many people as possible can be as awestruck as I was.

There are cash prizes for the winners; additionally, the competitors' travel costs, meals, and accommodations are paid for. They are also paid one thousand dollars just to appear and create their sandy constructions. This is serious business!

I voted for a sculpture called *Little Iron Horse* by Guy-Olivier Deveau of Quebec and Damon Langlois of Victoria. (It tied for third place with Marianne Van Den Broek and Daniel Belcher of St. Louis, Missouri, for their sculpture *Eau Canada*, and won the People's Choice Award in the doubles category.) I loved the shape and the symmetry as well as the subject matter: a tall, rearing horse with mechanical limbs and inner body parts, connected with hinges, bolts, springs, and wheels enveloped and supported in folding maple leaves. The entire sculpture resembled a wonderful towering triangle of horsepower wrapped inside Canadian foliage.

The Canadian horse depicted our own Canadian heritage breed of equine, the strong and sturdy "little iron horse," which was brought to Quebec from France in the late 1600s, descending from the stables of King Louis XIV. The Canadian horse is quite present today—in fact, several local horse lovers keep them in the Saanich area. They are dark-coloured and gentle, originally used to pull plows and carts through the tough but fertile Quebec farmland.

> In 1997, Parksville was the site of the third largest riot in Canadian history. It was referred to as the Sand Castle Riot and involved over one thousand youth who took it upon themselves to loot the liquor store, become extremely inebriated, and go on a rampage, their sole mission to destroy the sand sculptures along the shore. Police resorted to tear gas to control the mob, and the whole debacle cost the town $30,000. One police officer described the rioters as "little gangs of punks"; some local, some from afar.

Parksville's Kite Festival is a fabulous spectacle and, cleverly, it is held at the same time as the Sand Sculpture event. (I'm surprised that there are not more kite festivals on Vancouver Island, given the abundance of ocean and mountain breezes.)

The annual kite festival is held in a large meadow by the sea. With the blustery gusts, a big blue sky, and a glowing summer sun, the kites transform the sky into a fluttering, floating, spinning, soaring array of colour and movement. As I watched in awe, I noticed that the kites were of various sizes and exhibited a diversity of motion; some spun or swooped, some gently flapped, and some hung in near motionless suspension as though not tethered to the earth at all. Several included long fluttering tails that whipped and flailed. Many were animal themed, including a wonderful portly fish and three plump turtles, all hovering above the sparkling sea.

We need to gaze upward into the sky more often—perspectives change, and we see and appreciate beauty in a whole new way. Consider the Milky Way splayed across the blackness of a night sky, a dazzling celebration of fireworks, and in the case of Parksville, the spectacular kites.

It's said that the Chinese invented the kite in the fifth century. The original Chinese kites were rectangular, not diamond-shaped, and were made from silk sheets and fine thread precisely woven onto bamboo frames.

The Pie Factory

Be sure to visit this little hidden treasure tucked at the back of a strip mall (beside Amrikko's Indian Grill) off the Old Island Highway (Hwy 19A), about four minutes past Rathtrevor Beach and the Parksville Museum. When you see a great, big Lordco on the right, you're just about there, so get ready to turn right. If you have passed the Sparkle Touchless Car Wash, you've gone too far.

The Pie Factory is a pie shop that not only sells divine pies—meat, vegetarian, and fruit—but works with a wonderful organization called the Vancouver Island Workability Program, which trains, supports, and employs people with mental health issues and illnesses and other challenges. The philosophy of the group is that everyone, no matter their ability level, has something to contribute. They make the best pies ever; there are no barriers to their pie-making abilities here.

The Workability Program also partners with the Northwest Bay Nursery in nearby Nanoose, where the employees are trained in every aspect of the nursery business, from foliage identification to landscaping and irrigation methods. These busy people also run the 2nd Chance Thrift Store (located in the Heritage Mall as you approach Parksville off the main highway going north), giving participants job-ready experience in merchandising, customer service, store operations, and other marketing skills.

But oh, back to their pie! I happened to read a review by a woman who gave them five stars and commented that she had purchased two berry pies, a meat pie, and a lamb pie; she cooked them all and then raved about the taste and texture so much that she returned for more pie the very next day! I can only assume that this woman's appetite was enormous.

The Brant Wildlife Festival

The brant goose is much beloved in this part of the Island. There are four types of brants, and the type that visits our shores is the black Pacific brant. Also known as the sea goose due to its preference for eel grasses and other types of saltwater vegetation found on beaches and shallow water as the tides ebb and flow, our brant geese also eat molluscs and herring roe; the vast Parksville beach sand, teeming with sea life, is an ideal spot for the brant goose to fatten up on eel grass and herring and then rest after a long migratory flight home. And so the bird-welcoming people of Parksville celebrate this hardy, loyal seabird by holding the Brant Wildlife Festival every spring.

In March and April, thousands of these geese arrive from the warm south on their way back up north, where they will breed throughout the summer. Numerous viewing platforms in both Parksville and Qualicum Beach have been constructed along the shore to witness their return. Spectators not only love to observe the geese but seek to protect them from stress and disturbance as well. On a bit of a worrisome note: In 2013, the bird count was observed to be 2,204 geese resting at their stopover; however, in 2018, the count was less at 1,875 brants.

French Creek Harbour and Lasqueti Island

Just beyond Parksville, about ten minutes north on Highway 19A (which I refer to as "the scenic route") is the ferry to Lasqueti Island. With a population of just over four hundred permanent residents, Lasqueti is a bit on the rustic side: It's not serviced by BC Hydro, has unpaved roads, and does not have public transportation. They do have health services, a farmers' market, activities such as yoga and basket weaving, healing arts practitioners, and the Lasqueti Island Hotel & Restaurant. Many of the residents are artists, artisans, writers, musicians, or consultants who work at home; anyone who has been on Vancouver Island (or anywhere in the region) for any length of time knows that Lasqueti has, for lack of a better term, an off-the-grid ambience.

If you'd like to visit this small, remote island community, embark on a day's adventure to Lasqueti by way of French Creek Harbour. Here you will find a foot ferry—no cars allowed, so you'll have to leave your vehicle at the marina. (When the weather is volatile, the ferry stays tied to its dock.) While there, stop for a drink at the island's pub; with luck, you may see the Bolting Brassicas Marching Band and the Friends Circus show.

Vancouver Island University's Milner Gardens & Woodland

Do you believe in fairies? The late Edwardian British aristocrat, distant relative of Winston Churchill, and avid gardener Veronica Milner did. Indeed, she was well known for her assertion that she had seen "the little people" during her time in Ireland.

Mrs. Milner also loved her rhododendrons, as evidenced by the ten acres of woodland garden paths filled with rhododendrons that Mrs. Milner named after individuals: Mrs. Betty Robinson (a dark yellow flower with a splash of red at the centre); Doctor Arnold W. Endtz (a frilly, pink flower with a lilac tinge); and the Honourable Jean Marie de Montague (with blazing scarlet blossoms) to name just a few. Imagine having a rhododendron named after *your* full name, especially if you have a title! "Here we have the Anny Mary Bobak Scoones, known for its colourful blooms, which diminish after five o'clock in the afternoon."

So, if you're a fan of either fairies or rhododendrons (or both), and love gardens in general, follow in the footsteps of Queen Elizabeth,

Prince Phillip, Prince Charles, and Princess Diana, and visit the enchanting Milner Gardens & Woodland.

Most rhododendron species are originally from Southeast Asia and are related to our native salal and arbutus trees, hence their preference for acidic, damp woodland, soil, and coastal rainfall. There are close to nine hundred species, forty-five of which bloom in Milner Gardens & Woodland. The genus name *rhododendron* comes from the Greek words rhodo for "rose" and dendron for "tree."

The actual size of the Milner property is seventy acres, but much of the residence is natural forest. From the parking lot, stroll through the shady pungent woods to the Milner house, a beautiful tea room surrounded by rolling lawns bordered with little flowerbeds, fruit trees, ponds, rock gardens, and delicate, whimsical structures that all blend into the narrow, winding pathways that take you among the rhododendrons. The gardens are not difficult to locate, but you will need to keep an eye out for the signage between Parksville and Qualicum Beach going north on the sea side of the Old Island Highway.

Mrs. Milner's second husband, Horatio Milner, was born in Sackville, New Brunswick, in 1889. Sackville is a quaint farming town among lush pastures and farmsteads in southern New Brunswick. (Delicious cheddar cheese and fruit wines are produced there, and Mum and I regularly drove through on our Atlantic road trips in the final years before her death, always stopping to pet a donkey—Mum loved donkeys—that we'd see in a meadow along a country road en route to our seaside destination.) Horatio became a successful lawyer and businessman and eventually purchased his beautiful Oceanside estate.

Veronica, Horatio's second wife, dubbed the home "Long Distance" because Horatio was forever taking phone calls from far away. It was Veronica who created the gardens and established the rhododendron woodland, and the grounds have been lauded for its curious combination of a preserved wild West Coast native forest mixed with wildflowers, lawns, fruit trees, and rockeries.

Between 1996 and 1998, the Milner estate was willed to Vancouver Island University (at the time it was known as Malaspina College).

The Jane Austen–type Camelia Tea Room in the drawing room of the historic Milner House is absolutely charming, and the soup and scones are delicious. Little vases filled with real flowers adorn the crisp cotton tablecloths. Homemade jams and jellies are stacked on the sideboard as well as on the white painted windowsills. You are allowed to wander through the home to admire Veronica's flower paintings and pastels, old photographs, and original furnishings.

If you think this experience and setting couldn't possibly be more charming, you haven't yet heard about the Fairy Houses event. Every June since 2010, on International Fairy Day, children delight in discovering little fairy abodes that spring up overnight, tucked carefully and discreetly throughout the property—perhaps in a stump, among the fern fronds, at the base of an arbutus, in the reeds by the brook, or in a grove of fawn lilies tucked beneath the fallen leaves, mosses, and forest floor debris.

During one of our visits to Milner Gardens, we learned that fairies often appear among the petals of flowers, and that water lilies may also be attractive to nymphs; fairies can also be female or male. We also learned that the fairies who visit Milner Gardens bring joy, peace, and goodness to the earth, but if you do not believe in them, you will never see them. The children who romp through the forest paths and carefully seek out the fairies and their whimsical miniature homes on this special day are sure to see the nymphs and sprites, especially around the pond and little waterfalls, springs, and riffles, which these tiny magical creature enjoy immensely.

Creating a magical fairy habitat is a fine endeavour and is an especially delightful activity when shared with children. Here's how to do it:

Quietly search a natural area for materials that you think a fairy might enjoy—pine cones, shells, or sea glass from the beach, stones, acorns, feathers, leaves, or a little dried lichen (to keep the air fresh), sticks of various shapes, berries for colour, maybe a sweet-smelling herb or a sprig of rosemary or lavender. Collect these items in a container such as a basket or on a tray.

In your garden shed, you may have a clay flower pot, a little ceramic knick-knack, or a small dish in which the fairy could splash and bathe. Perhaps you can harvest some dried vines or grasses, which could be woven into a little piece of furniture, or a ladder if your fairy house has a loft or upstairs. Some fairies have even been known to curl up in a coconut shell or gourd for a little woodland sleep.

Find a suitable location for your fairy residence, such as a hidden or secretive spot, ideally out of the wind, or perhaps near water or close to a flower garden. Because fairies can fly and gracefully leap, you might place your creation off the ground, or on an old stump, or on a fork of a tree branch.

Finally, carefully construct the perfect home to attract the woodland fairies. Whimsical decoration is encouraged; a pathway may help guide your fairy guests, and perhaps they will even be drawn by a delicate musical chime hung from a branch.

Qualicum Beach

Not to be confused with Qualicum Bay, a much smaller community a little farther north, Qualicum Beach is the next quaint town on the waterfront—in fact, the promenade along the sea is one of its more delightful features. The promenade walk, with the green surf washing up over the grey sand and the seagulls gliding overhead above the dated motel and ice cream stands could be right out of a BBC television show set in a bygone era. Here is a town that loves its seaside, loves a slower pace of life, and encourages visitors to stop and enjoy it all.

If you love art and culture, I highly recommend that you head up the little hill into Qualicum Beach's downtown and visit the Old School House Arts Centre on Fern Road; it's an inviting historic, yellow wooden structure (with that old wood fragrance) that is now used to house a wide selection of art studios. This is a clever arrangement— you can amble through the building and observe various artists each working away in their own little spaces, some hunched over a small canvas, others dabbing at their easels, and a few who simply love to talk with you about their work.

I cannot imagine trying to think, trying to write, trying to get down exactly what is in my head with people continually walking around me and wanting to chat. Then again, it would not be very interesting for the public to watch writers write anyway, each one in a different room, thinking or cursing or looking up a word in their thesaurus, concentrating heavily on the best word to use, or what rhymes with Hoo-Hoo, or deleting an entire paragraph in frustration. When I try to write on an airplane, for example, or even in my diary, I simply am not able to write a single thought for fear that someone is looking over my shoulder; it is such a private experience. I'm not sure if writing is the most private of art forms, but I do wonder whether painters feel the same sense of being watched and therefore feel unable to free their thoughts.

The gallery offers art classes and exhibitions, and to round out its cultural offerings, the Old School House also hosts professional jazz and classical musical concerts via their Music on Sunday programs.

Lighthouse Country: Qualicum Bay, Bowser, Deep Bay

After you've poked around downtown Qualicum Beach's boutiques, purchased a locally made gift, had a snack at any of the town's collection of cafés or restaurants or the bakery, and browsed the cozy little Mulberry Bush Bookstore, take Highway 19A (known locally as the Oceanside Route or Old Island Highway, or, as I always call it, the scenic route) and travel north along the coast. This route is amazing for catching glimpses of the sparkling ocean, breathing in the fresh sea air, exploring the ribbon of modest, low-key seaside neighbourhoods, or simply cruising along in an unrushed, relaxed manner.

On your way, you'll pass the Shady Rest, built in 1924. It sits on the water above the long, curved beach, where sunsets and sunrises are stunning and the water shimmers silver. The food is typical West Coast casual, and the establishment's name itself beckons you to stop on your journey.

Farther along this route, closer to Bowser, is the Crown & Anchor Roadhouse pub. If you arrive at the right time, you can enjoy some casual, down-to-earth socializing with the locals while taking in a bluegrass jam session, "a Sunday-Funday jam and meat draw hosted by Big Daddy." The pub also offers karaoke.

The tiny community of Bowser is a little farther along; their main "downtown" is found at Magnolia Court, a newer, freshly painted little mall housing small local businesses. Here you'll find the Salish Sea Market, which offers local art and artisanal products, and the Lighthouse Gift Shop. If you need a coffee break, stop by the Brew Coffee House (formerly known as the Bean Counter).

This area is proudly referred to as Lighthouse Country, which includes the three communities of Qualicum Bay, Bowser, and Deep Bay. As you drive through the area, you'll see signs that read LIGHTHOUSE VETERINARIAN, LIGHTHOUSE BUSINESS ASSOCIATION, and THE LIGHTHOUSE COMMUNITY CENTRE. "Where are the lighthouses?" you may ask. Well, unless you look closely out to sea, you'll miss them, but if you face Lasqueti from Qualicum Bay, you'll see the Sisters Islets Lighthouse. When you're in Deep Bay, gaze a bit towards the south and you'll see the Chrome Island Lighthouse among a cluster of little red roofs that gleam on a sunny day.

VIU Deep Bay Marine Field Station

When you're in the area on your hunt for lighthouses, you must visit the Deep Bay Marine Field Station. From Bowser, continue north on

Highway 19A for about eight minutes until you see Gainsberg Road on the right—turn off, and you can follow the signage all the way to the public wharf. On your way there, and at the shore on a side road, there are many views of the lighthouses.

The Marine Field Station, part of Vancouver Island University, is along a narrow, wooded lane. The building resembles a huge, upside-down corrugated pipe, wedged into the ground. This facility provides visitors with a fascinating and informative hands-on experience with sea life, and the building itself is a LEED platinum certified facility, one of only a handful on Vancouver Island (another is the Parks Office in Sidney). LEED stands for Leadership in Energy and Environmental Design; the LEED standards offer architects and builders a list of environmentally sustainable, non-toxic, low carbon, energy efficient, eco-friendly, green construction options and awards them with either silver, gold, or platinum certification. Neighbourhoods and outdoor areas can also be designed by LEED standards. Native plantings, use of natural light and space, building materials, natural heat sources, location, recycling procedures, restoration of natural ecosystems, and use of natural resources such as wind, sun, rain, and the ocean are a few examples of LEED features and considerations.

In 2018, there were 3,712 certified LEED projects in Canada.

The tallest LEED certified building in the world is the Taipei 101 tower which also was, until 2010, the tallest building in the world.

The beautiful Vandusen Botanical Garden Visitor Centre in Vancouver is also a LEED certified structure, as is the University of Victoria's Technology Park.

When you enter the Marine Field Station at Deep Bay, you will immediately feel the effect of the natural light and space. Throughout the three levels of the marine centre, separated by staircases and platforms, various examples of the green building construction can be seen: the wood on the stairs is made from the dead pine trees that perished from the massive pine beetles; rather than use one hundred percent concrete on the foundation (concrete requires such an immense use of water and energy), the clean grey walls consist of only fifty percent concrete and fifty percent ash and other natural substances; the heating is produced by recycled sea water; the parking lot contains porous crushed oyster shells to prevent waste water and toxic run-off and to encourage groundwater filtering and retention.

Inside, there are tanks of sea life along one wall and a panoramic view of Baynes Sound on the opposite. You can see urchins, sea cucumbers, a variety of shellfish, and wolf eels that emerge from dark rock crevices, slowly winding their way to the surface when they know food is on the way; with their little wizened faces and tiny, sharp teeth under their domed noses, they look like wise but secretive old souls from an ancient Greek myth.

From the ceiling hangs the impressive skeleton of an excavated grey whale. In a glass case beside the large white bones (real, not replicated) is its baleen, clean and beautiful, like a fringe of delicate silk strands, taken from its mouth—such a vulnerable yet powerful display. Looking at this, I ponder what makes the whale, whether in the wild or in a glass case, so awesome, so moving. Perhaps it is the whale's gentleness combined with its power. This blend of opposites has always been attractive and fascinating to humankind, whether in art, in leaders, in weather, in nature, in philosophy. These two features—gentleness and power—are so clearly exhibited in the whale, even in death. Those two qualities combined define, to me, the essence of dignity.

The discovery and restoration of the grey whale's remains at the Marine Field Station was quite an emotional process that began after its dead carcass washed up on an East Sooke beach in 2010. Sharon Cooper from the Scia'new First Nation was strolling on this beach and noticed that people had carved their names into the body, as well as disturbing other parts of the whale. The sight of the majestic whale's remains being demeaned, disrespected, treated with such a lack of dignity was extremely upsetting to Sharon, so she was compelled to save the whale, both physically and spiritually. She arranged to have the whale towed to a safe and protected place to provide it with an honourable burial.

The whale was then left to decompose for four years. When that stage was complete, volunteers from the Marine Field Station rallied, delicately and with great respect, exhuming the now-exposed bones so they could preserve and display them at the Marine Field Station in Deep Bay. One of the volunteers was a retired radiologist, and his medical skills apparently came in handy during the lengthy and meticulous process.

I believe this project must have been a deeply moving experience for the volunteers as each bone was gently brought out from the ground, cleaned, and placed back together with the rest of the skeleton. Today, the whale's skeleton, ten metres long, is the Underwater Harvesters Association Grey Whale Exhibit, artistically and elegantly suspended from the ceiling of the field station.

Restoring dignity to the whale was almost like an apology to nature—a wonderful apology that brought the whale back to us in a new form to be generously shared with all who visit this beautiful facility.

Regarding sorrow and apologies and the restoration of dignity: I feel deep sadness when I see a cigarette butt floating in a tidal pool among the little snails and sea anemones. In moments like these, I ask myself: If we are connected to nature, how can we regard the lives and deaths of other creatures with such obscene carelessness and insensitivity? Are we born with an innate connection to nature? If so, what leads to our disconnection? How can we become more aware of it and cultivate compassion for the dignity of the animals and nature, both in their lives and in their deaths?

When I see a dead bird, rabbit, a raccoon, or frog, I am compelled to move it to a quiet, private place, perhaps under a shrub or stone, as a way to preserve its past presence on earth. Death is not the problem, but rather it is the lack of dignity in death that I think about. How do we teach ourselves and one another to have respect for all living creatures who will inevitably reach the final stage of life (as we will)? How do we help others to feel compassion for other species? How do we cultivate our own compassion?

In the summer of 2018, there were multiple opportunities to feel empathy for creatures of the ocean when whales were featured prominently in the news. First, a young male orca, alone and transient, had found his way into the waters off Comox, in the fertile, mud-based estuary where the Courtenay River empties into Comox Harbour, which in turn flows into the ocean. The whale was monitored daily in the news, alone, breaching, and feeding, seemingly content to frolic and feed among the paddleboarders, fishing charters, kayakers, and other marine activity. Soon, however, it became apparent that the whale and the public were not so compatible; furthermore, the seemingly placid whale exhibited no signs of moving on. Scientists, the government, and other ocean experts began to worry that perhaps the young whale might either be confused or abandoned or lost from his pod of relations.

The news then focused on how to guide the whale back out to open water. Those facilitating this endeavour achieved the objective with remarkable skill by attracting the youngster out of the harbour with whale whistles and other communicative sounds. Thus the Comox visitor swam off with great energy, hopefully to rejoin his waiting family.

Around this time, there were two other whale incidents that took place farther south in the waters off the Southern Gulf Islands in the Salish Sea.

A young female resident orca named Scarlet (also known to researchers as J50) became ill. She looked emaciated, and the whale experts and environmentalists were alarmed. After using a long pole to capture a sample of her breath from her blowhole, the scientists had the sample analyzed for disease and bacteria. They found a somewhat partial answer—something to do with worms and parasites—but while all this studying was taking place, her condition worsened. In an attempt to help her, they injected antibiotics into her with a dart of some sort. But Scarlet, who fought a valiant battle, disappeared, and in the middle of September, she was declared dead by the Center for Whale Research on San Juan Island in Washington state. Her fragile, emaciated body has not been found.

And then there was the heartbreaking tale—one that made global headlines—of what the press dubbed "a tour of grief." In August 2018, Tahlequah (J35) was a mother orca who had given birth in the Salish Sea, not far from Victoria. Sadly, the baby died soon after from unknown causes.

The mourning mother then carefully balanced her little baby on her nose, thus keeping her dead calf afloat. With her pod of relatives, she travelled through her territory for many days without eating, holding fast to her baby, who lay gleaming in the sun with its little mouth slightly open while its body rested on her mother's broad, graceful, sad head. The longer this tragic saga continued, the more the public grieved with her.

Her tour of grief lasted for seventeen days, a lengthy time for such a quiet yet vivid expression of pain. This demonstration of public grief caused me to reflect upon how it seems that we can feel pain and empathy more deeply if given a greater amount of time to experience or witness it. An unhurried period can provide us with the time to feel, reflect, and face our own vulnerabilities; the silence gives us the space to work through feelings that words seem to so often interrupt. The profound and moving expression of grief demonstrated by this mother whale is one to which all species can relate.

The Marine Station's resident giant Pacific octopus

Every summer, the Marine Station raises a young giant Pacific octopus, and by autumn, when she is mature, she is released. In 2017, the octopus they raised was named Octavia—their first octopus in residence.

The octopus is a fascinating being: It has nine brains, one in each arm and one in its head, along with three hearts and blue blood. These creatures are extremely intelligent and sensitive and can dismantle marine equipment, including components of the tank in which they are held captive. The octopus also solves problems by using tools and recognizes specific humans. A video on *National Geographic*'s website shows an octopus tricking a shrimp into becoming a delicious morsel by using one arm to touch the little shrimp so that it jumps forward, right into another of the octopus's arms.

But perhaps the cephalopod's most endearing feature is the female's extreme care and protection of her eggs; she can lay up to four hundred thousand eggs, which she fiercely defends. She spends hours cleaning her brood by blowing water and washing off algae; so dedicated to her maternal duties is she that she stops eating and pours all her energy into ensuring her minuscule, rice-like babies are clean and healthily hatched. Finally, exhausted, deflated, and thin, she fades away and dies, her body washed away in the surf, her lovely pale pink arms swaying with the tide, perhaps becoming dinner for a hungry seagull.

When I think of the dear octopus's devoted care of her eggs, I recall a peculiar comment Mum made a long time ago. I often agreed with most of her views, but I believe she was quite inaccurate when she said, "Having children is the most creative thing a woman can do." (The notion still makes me wince.) It was an odd comment for her to make, especially as it was clear that I had chosen to not have children. The thought that I would never be fully creative wedged itself in the back of my brain for a very long time, almost crushing me at times with self-doubt and a sense of inferiority. Perhaps that is why I turned to animals and farming and writing. The animals I have cared for and the books I have written are, in a sense, my children, and I love them as dearly as a mother octopus would.

October 8 is International Octopus day, which kicks off International Cephalopod Awareness Days, first established in 2007 by TONMO, The Octopus News Magazine Online Forum.

According to my friend Brenda, who works in a bank, the date of October 8 has something to do with the octopus having eight arms—and it turns out she's right! In the old Roman calendar, October (based on the Latin octo, meaning "eight") was the eighth month. When the calendar changed from old Roman to Julian, and subsequently Gregorian, the name of October was carried over. I wouldn't have put two and two (or four and four) together to have figured that out—and that is why I don't work in a bank.

Horne Lake Caves Provincial Park

If you are feeling adventurous after a visit to the Deep Bay Marine Field, you can go from visiting the creatures of the deep to exploring the deep caves inland. Winner of Destination BC's first Remarkable Experiences Award and Tourism Vancouver Island's Innovator of the Year Award (both bestowed in 2015), as well as TripAdvisor's Certificate of Excellence, the Horne Lake Caves are a must-see. It's fairly easy to get there from the VIU Deep Bay Marine Field Station, and the signage giving directions is excellent.

Horne Lake Road, an impeccably maintained gravel road that has no potholes or dust, is wide and scenic; it opens onto beautiful Horne Lake, which seems to have a growing, flourishing little community tucked below a stunning backdrop of mountains. This growing residential neighbourhood is made up of tasteful, nicely built homes along the lakeshore; there is even a welcome sign at the bend of the road, which soon becomes a charming, winding country lane. Continue along Horne Lake Road until you reach Horne Lake Caves Provincial Park.

After checking in at the reservation office and signing up for the one-hour, basic main cave experience, I was fitted with a red helmet with a light above my brow. Our small group traipsed across a suspension bridge and up through a forest path to the first cave (there are seven caves in total).

I wondered if I might have a spell of claustrophobia, especially when I saw the cave's entrance, a slim dark slit cut into the side of a massive, lichen-covered rock face. But the cave, although dark and enclosed, felt more like a safe and peaceful hideaway. I am much more claustrophobic in car washes (especially when purple and green soap and swirling felt strips hit the windshield and block out the light) or revolving doors (they may look slow and harmless, but they could stop or hasten at any moment and knock me flat).

> Claustrophobia is the fear of confined spaces; cleithrophobia is the fear of being trapped, which, when you think it over, is quite a different fear.

> A doctor I know suggests that when you feel overwhelmed, anxious, or panicked in a confined space, visualize a place of serenity. Ironically, this could well be a cave! In my experience, the natural, peaceful mystery of the silence and the darkness can be an antidote to anxiety.

> We are extremely close to nature when in a cave; this may be quite soothing to many. It may be why, when emerging back into the sunlight after spelunking, people often feel transformed in some way and are even momentarily speechless as they float back to everyday, above-ground, modern life.

> I suppose it is possible for a person to feel panic-stricken when placed in a completely natural setting. I know people who panic in an open meadow; some have been known to experience total anxiety in the expansive far north, where the land reveals no end in sight.

The caves are inside the mountains, within a limestone belt, carved over time from underground rivers, flowing, dripping, falling, and pooling in the direction that nature guides them, leaving stunning geological features with names such as cave pearls, soda straws, and cave glitter. In the cave we explored, there was even a small waterfall, a narrow, jagged crevice with a gushing stream of water, which we had to climb and straddle across, and then returned to the route via a special little slide.

Inside the cave, we climbed and crawled and slid through tiny narrow passages between great slabs and folds of cold, wet, butterscotch-coloured stone formed by the mineral calcite and along eroded ridges, all shaped by underground streams.

(Before we get any further with my caving adventure, I should tell you that there was a bit of climbing, gripping, and sliding within the damp cave; the rock was not smooth, and the cave was fairly chilly. Wear a jacket and comfortable pants and be prepared to get muddy and wet. I also suggest gloves—any type, really, because of the constant need to touch the cold, rough surfaces.)

Ancient sea fossils called crinoids are also in the caves, indicating that millions of years ago, these rocks were in the seabed—and, in fact, not even in a British Columbia location, but much further south. According to the brochure at the sign-in counter, the caves are 290 metres above sea level.

Are there animals in the caves? Yes! Some of them have no eyes, as is the case with the eyeless shrimp and the olm salamander. The cave has its own life force; its ecosystem includes a multitude of fungi, slimes, bacteria, and algae. There are also worm species and spiders. Many of the little creatures are not only eyeless, but colourless—colour and sight are useless in a cave.

Although there is no light in this ecosystem, it teems with nutrients carried in the running water, which is rich in minerals gathered on the stream's long journey before it reaches the darkness of this habitat.

The caves are cool at approximately eight degrees and are damp and very dark. At a certain point, we were instructed to grip the wall, and then turn out our headlamps. This was an experience like none other I have had in my life. I have never "seen" darkness like this, and the only sound was the occasional drip from a crevice high above.

There is nothing to fear from the still and silent darkness; it is a rest for the mind, for the eyes, for the body. There is plenty more to fear in our sighted world. As the cave guides said, "This is the most amazing thing you'll never see."

Perhaps one could call this a spiritual experience, if one were inclined that way; indeed, it seemed as if we were, in a very profound sense, enveloped inside of Mother Nature. I felt the rock took on a spiritual form and became more than rock, more like a part of *us*. Your experience may vary, but I am convinced that if we relax and listen and see and feel the nothingness, we may sense that rocks do have a mystical, living energy.

I felt this kind of energy once at Cox Bay in Tofino when I walked the length of the beach and reached the basalt edge. Quite unexpectedly, I felt a palpable energy from the black, scratched, barnacle-covered rock; it held me for a moment, a deep and rather moving moment. I felt as if I were attached to the rock—not like a mussel, but in a spiritual or intangible way. When I related this experience to a newspaper reporter a long time ago, she suggested that if my thoughts were published, people may think me unbalanced. But I am telling you this now, here, so make of it what you will. As far as I'm concerned, to feel nature deeply—especially from a rock—is perfectly sane.

After our small group emerged from the caves—all of us quiet, introspective, and awestruck—I reflected on how the experience was about more than the caves themselves (which are stunning and intriguing). Spending time underground, deep within the earth, our planet, our home spinning around in black space, also gave me a new appreciation of what the cave can teach us about below and above. Its many features offer a new way of seeing the earth and reveals a vast, secret world buried beneath, a world that is just as rich and full of life as the world above ground. Ever since my time at Horne Lake Caves, I have been acutely aware of how we noisily drive and stomp and tread unaware above the vast tunnels and caverns filled with exquisite silence, profound darkness, and concealed life.

Spelunking, a slang term for caving, has been in use since the 1940s; it is a term derived from the Latin *spelunca*, which means "cave." However, the term is apparently not often used by serious caving enthusiasts as within that community the term spelunking is now associated with untrained, unskilled cavers. But it's still a fun word to say!

Fanny Bay

After the intense and wondrous cave experience, you may feel the need to return to the scenic route of Highway 19A and continue your travels north up to distinctive Fanny Bay, a ten-minute drive from Deep Bay. The main landmark is the Fanny Bay Inn, a quaint old pub established in 1938. Painted white and blue and perched on a grassy meadow that overlooks Baynes Sound, the pub is a friendly little place to stop for pub grub and local oysters. If you're the kind of person that likes humorous souvenirs from obscure locations, you can purchase baseball caps and T-shirts emblazoned with FBI (for Fanny Bay Inn) and another rather naughty slogan about shucking, sucking, and eating, which my intuition is advising me not to repeat here.

Oyster farms are everywhere here in Fanny Bay, as evidenced by the many piles of white shells stacked along the seafront. The sight of them can take you by surprise if you've never seen an oyster farm; to my eyes it is a rather haunting visual, but I don't know exactly why. It's almost like a moonscape, all those empty white shell mounds against a slate-grey sea.

Phantom-like whispers of white in an open, colourless space exude an austere ambience. We tend to expect colour in the physical spaces of our lives, but the lack of it can be quite powerful, especially in a landscape; it is eerie in an interesting and beautiful way. It doesn't surprise me that Vancouver Island is world-renowned for mystical and ghostly sightings, considering the wispy, silvery apparitions in the sea mists, rolling fogs, mountain rain shadows that descend from a steely sky, drooping cedars, the breast-height salal in the old-growth rainforests, the skunk cabbage bogs, the lush moss, and the lichen-covered bluffs.

It seems to me that, in many places, our West Coast landscape is composed mostly of grey, white, and green hues, especially in winter. These washed subtle scenes are captured in the watercolour paintings of the late Toni Onley, long-time resident of British Columbia, recipient of the Order of Canada, and celebrated artist.

In contrast, Eastern Canada glows with colour. Consider its fiery autumn foliage and huge, cold, sapphire-blue winter skies; the blinding light which reflects off the swaths of fresh snow; along the frozen shores of Lake Superior, the winter's sunlight glitters over golden ice, pink granite, and silver icicles. I find our West Coast landscape lonelier, more remote, muted.

When contemplating those haunting mounds of shells in Fanny Bay, I would say that an oyster shell resembles our coastal topography with its rugged, sharp curves streaked with shades of black and charcoal, hidden glistening pockets of polished shimmering sea green.

The oysters raised on Vancouver Island are farmed, and they are either suspended in the water or beach grown. In fact, some oysters are raised in our waters and then "finished" (like a fine wine!) in the sand to harden the shell.

There are a few areas on the Island where the public may gather wild oysters, but I prefer to acquire them from a farm where the shucking is done for you. I wince a little when I pull a live oyster off a rock; it seems so intrusive to yank a wild creature from its home. A farmed oyster is just as healthy to eat, and since it is raised to be consumed, I do not feel the same pang. In addition, unlike wild salmon, oysters from "farms" are sustainable and do not consume industrially produced feed, as do farmed salmon; rather, they take their nutrition naturally from the plankton in the sea.

One of the most ominous threats to oysters and other shellfish (and to those who eat them!) is known as the red tide. Scientists prefer to call this worldwide ocean phenomenon "an algae bloom" because that is what it actually is—the red colour of the bloom has nothing to do with tidal action. In any case, it is called red tide because it is often red or rust-coloured; it takes place seasonally with the change of water temperature and current action.

> Massive toxic algae blooms occur in various forms and locations on the planet, both in salt and fresh water. Currently, an immense and expanding bloom is off the coast of Florida; Lake Erie also experienced this severe toxic invasion in 2017, caused by fertilizer run-off from rural lands close by. The causes are diverse, and they vary from place to place.

Red tide can be toxic or non-toxic, and when it occurs, signage is erected on the beaches, using great, dramatic warning language. Once you've done your due diligence and have all your safety warnings out of the way, it's time to talk about eating those oysters.

There are many types of oysters raised by British Columbia oyster farmers. Species vary greatly in taste and size—my research tells me that the most popular oyster is the delicate little Japanese kusshi. I can easily swallow a few of the larger varieties, such as the sea angel, referred to as "jumbo" at seventeen centimetres (or more), right off the shell with a squirt of lemon.

Swallowing a raw oyster is repulsive to some, perhaps due to its slippery, slimy texture as it glides down your throat. If you're hesitant to partake, I urge you to put aside any notions you have regarding slime; focus instead on this small but magnificent, nutrient-packed creation, grown in our own beautiful Pacific Ocean, lovingly hand-picked and shucked, ready to slip down your throat and provide you with enough zinc to last a lifetime.

Oysters are especially delectable followed by a fresh, crusty loaf of bread and a glass of chilled, dry white wine—crafted in the region, of course.

(If you'd love some local baking, there is a wonderful home bakery called Just Like Mom's just a few kilometres past Buckley Bay, where the ferry takes you over to Denman and Hornby Islands. Look for Mom's big sign on the hill, then turn left on the little lane. Mom's still uses the honour system of payment, and Bev (a.k.a. Mom) stocks her little cabin with delicious baked goodies six days a week. After stocking up on oysters—and Mom's bread—head back to the ferry and take a day trip to Denman or Hornby where you can get yourself some wonderful local wine.)

Oysters contain many vital minerals, especially zinc, which is said to remedy sexual dysfunction and performance. And even better—yes, far more important than sex and baguettes, as far as I'm concerned—are the (admittedly rare) pearls. Yes, even the gates to heaven, the Pearly Gates, pay tribute to the humble oyster.

The next time you are uncomfortably sipping cocktails at an opera gala or art gallery opening, surrounded by elegant women (who know precisely how hold their champagne flutes in their manicured hands) wearing little black dresses and delicate pearl earrings and necklaces, remember this:

Pearls are often the entombment of parasites that invade the mollusc. The oyster deals with the intruder by encasing it in multiple layers of a calcium-based substance called nacre, forming a little chamber which we call a pearl. In other words, the oyster does its daily ablutions and makes its pearl at the same time (though it takes approximately seven years to create the gem).

Comfort yourself with the knowledge that those lovely drop earrings and necklaces adorning the earlobes and necks of the elegant ladies are, in fact, suffocated parasites blended with oyster excrement. Still, they do look divine with little black dresses and even with a nice a pair of jeans and a crisp white blouse!

Back in the late nineties, after I travelled to Belarus, I had my own peculiar oyster experience. I had visited Minsk, the main city in Belarus, to finally satisfy my childhood curiosity about Communism and Soviet society. I had a contact there by the name of Nonna, a translator who taught at a small college in Minsk; she had come to Canada for six weeks with a group of thin, pale, undernourished children from the Chernobyl region about a year after the accident. A group of concerned Canadian citizens had formed a charity to help the children recover. The children been exposed to radiation—from which some of the children's parents had perished—and their country was short on fruit and other products. These children were in dire need of nutrients, fresh air, and rest.

I had a small farm just outside of Victoria, to which I invited Nonna's group for a day in the country. The children had a lovely time riding the horses and devouring the apples from my few trees, eating even the apple cores and seeds and stems, so desperate they were for fruit. It was during this visit that I met Nonna, and that connection led to my trip to Belarus and the country villages near Chernobyl.

I was so moved by these children, dressed in threadbare sweaters and little cracked leather shoes with broken buckles, that I decided to visit them in their villages and to deliver to the Minsk orphanage an assortment of items. Nonna and I wrote to each other as I made plans, and it was surprisingly easy to set up the whole venture. Wonderful, generous people in Victoria donated new snowsuits, school supplies, shampoo, cough drops, toys, peppermints and more, all of which I stuffed into two enormous hockey duffle bags.

When I arrived, Nonna and her husband met me at the airport. Her husband (whom she detested because he sat around all day in his undershirt) had a car. As the guest I was given the front seat, but the floor was rusted out and I had to straddle the dashboard. They took me to their apartment, where I was to stay, one of hundreds in the endless rows of gloomy grey blocks of flats.

Nonna's husband had a friend who had agreed to take me on a tour to visit the country villages. The day after my arrival was hot and humid, and this large, happy fellow in a little white van with blue curtains picked us up on a street corner. As we drove, I thought of how Minsk looked like a lovely, elegant, but tired elderly lady, with its sooty pastel buildings and wide streets, busy with rickety yellow and red tram cars sputtering along their tracks. But the Belarussian countryside was lush, a country of moistness, of watersheds, streams, and lakes full of fish; here there were fertile soils, meadows filled with wildflowers and birch and nightingales, wild lilacs and forest floors covered with mushrooms, a staple of the Russian and Slavic diet.

We were very close to the Chernobyl area the day we visited these villages, and yet there was no sign of radiation or nuclear contamination—unless you glanced at the residents' throats: One out of five had a neat little scarlet scar. Nonna explained that this was evidence of thyroid cancer caused by radiation.

These sweet, humble villagers treated me like royalty. They gave me dried fish, sour milk, and cubes of pork fat, all contaminated. The fish had large tumours in its gills; the milk came from a cow munching on poisoned grass; the pork came from a pig who had been rooting in irradiated soil. But I consumed it all as my hosts took pride in offering a guest their hospitality.

Their moonshine—every home had a still behind it—was especially smooth. After partaking of it, I fell asleep on a carpet of moss in a warm shaft of sunlight, enveloped in the subtle fragrance of lily of the valley. This was, for me, a terribly spiritual experience—I felt completely happy, albeit slightly impaired, and fell in love with Belarus and the generous people who had so little.

Shortly after my return to my little farm near Victoria, I decided to take a trip up-island to Comox to visit my godmother Barbara. It had only been a week since I had been lying in a Belarussian meadow sleeping off the moonshine made from cabbage roots or birchbark or turnip tops or a combination of all three (you can make moonshine out of anything).

I took the slower scenic route along the sea. It was a lovely late summer day, and I was looking forward to pulling into Barbara's parking lot behind her condo and sitting on her balcony full of blooming and climbing geraniums with a cup of tea and telling her all about my new and dear Belarussian friends and adventures. As I neared Fanny Bay, I spotted an oyster farm in the distance, with its distinctive mounds of white shells from years of shucking. I suddenly had an undeniable craving for oysters—never had I experienced such a craving!

I pulled into the parking space and dashed into the shop. Wet and smelling of fresh fish, the shop was busy with workers in yellow rubber aprons loading nets of oysters onto metal tables. I bought a litre of fresh oysters, sat in the car, and ate them all, right then and there. Then I went back in, purchased another litre, and consumed that entire container, too.

I've always wondered if this strong desire for oysters was linked to my visit to the irradiated villages of Belarus. After all, oysters contain iodine, zinc, and other minerals which are so important to the health of the thyroid. My dramatic consumption of those two litres of fresh oysters remains a mystery, but when I think of those neat little scarlet scars on the throats of my Belarussian friends, I suspect my body knew that Vancouver Island oysters were exactly the medicine I needed.

Buckley Bay to Denman and Hornby Islands

Four kilometres north of Fanny Bay on Highway 19A (still on the scenic route) will take you to Buckley Bay, which has a ferry terminal, should you wish to visit Denman and Hornby Islands. These islands are popular destinations as they are easy to navigate, have interesting attractions, and are well served by the ferry. Be prepared: The cost of the return trip from Buckley Bay to Hornby and back again comes to over eighty dollars—that is for a car carrying two adults. A similar visit to Denman and back (a ten-minute journey each way) is just over forty dollars. When considering a trip that includes BC Ferries, I highly recommend visiting their website to be sure of their schedules and fares.

At the Buckley Bay terminal there is a gas station and a Subway, but do be sure to visit two delightful enterprises just steps away: Weinberg's Good Food, a modest and quaint little café and gift shop, and the Fanny Bay Oysters Seafood Shop. While waiting for the ferry you can pick up some candied salmon at the seafood shop, chat with the knowledgeable staff about fresh and current seafood, and then go down to Weinberg's to peruse their delightful merchandise and organic produce. Weather permitting, it's lovely to sit at their outdoor wooden tables topped with big, beautiful dahlias in vases next to racks of colourful sarongs and little quilts. Here you can sip an organic tea or coffee, enjoy a treat, and watch the little ferry, the MV *Baynes Sound Connector*, make its way across the narrow body of water as it comes to pick you up.

> The Baynes Sound Connector is a new cable ferry, the first in BC Ferries' fleet—there's no smokestack, nor steering for that matter, as it is completely driven by cables. It uses half the fuel of a conventional ferry and is therefore considered eco-friendly. Overhauled in 2016, the cable ferry cost fifteen million dollars to build and install.

Watching this little cable ferry reminded me of the day I took Mum down to Saint John from Fredericton to see Dad at the hospital. The weather was glorious—cool, but bright and sunny, a vivid contrast to the sadness, awkwardness, and stress we felt as dad drew closer to taking his final breath. The Saint John River flowed quietly among the bright yellows and scarlets of the changing sugar maples as it meandered towards the old Saint John Harbour, surrounded by the sooty, turn-of-the-century red brick buildings, stone churches, and blocks of beige hotels along a newly constructed walkway lined with concrete planters of pink petunias.

The hospital was enormous, but eventually we found Dad's room. Asleep under a thin blue sheet, he looked tiny and shrunken. Mum knew it was the final time she would see him—we both knew. After a long, emotional chat with the lovely, kind doctor, Mum and I decided to drive back to Fredericton on a different route, through the countryside and over the marshes and rivers that make up southern New Brunswick. That day, we crossed the water by three cable ferries. We were so sad but also keenly aware of the natural beauty of the river and of the lush green, the rolling auburn hills, and the jovial ferry workers. On one of the three ferry crossings, a farmer was trying to retrieve his old brown cow who had somehow swum across the water from her pasture on the other side.

Those memories have created a special place in my heart for cable ferries.

Here, years later, back on the West Coast, the cable ferry to Denman glided through the dark sea to a little village. Denman Island is well known for its annual writers' festival, and this is no small event: Writers such as Marina Endicott and Miriam Toews have read there, so if you like reading, listening, and schmoozing with writers, this is one literary festival worth visiting.

Tucked in the village is the quaint Abraxas Books and Gift Shop. There is also a real estate office in a tiny house that seems more like a fairy cottage, with its little peaked roof and blue trimmed windows and a desk just big enough for two people to sit in small chairs while mulling over the various properties; here you can see what's available and dream about the possibilities—fixer-uppers, small farms, abandoned wineries, waterfront homes, view lots with wells and driveways already established, and cottages in the village advertised as "within walking distance of the ferry."

We dropped by an art gallery on the main road just beyond the village; among other things, it sold the famous Denman Island organic and fair-trade chocolates with flavours from raspberry to rosemary, all neatly contained in a rainbow of locally designed labels. In fact, you can take a tour of the "factory," which is nearby in a beautifully designed West Coast-style structure in the forest. And there is an artisan on Denman who creates cozy colourful felt insoles at a very reasonable price—perfect for slippers or rain boots.

Since our visit took place on a summer Saturday, we stopped by the farmers' market at the Old School Grounds and Recycling Depot on Denman Road. As with many small communities, the Denman Farmers' Market operates from May to Thanksgiving weekend, and only from nine-thirty AM to twelve-thirty PM—these farmers need to return to their chores. Here we bought delicious buns made with egg and, as the sign said, "a touch of honey," and a warm loaf of bread that made the car smell lovely, masking the ever-present wet dog odour. Vendors gathered in a circle, selling everything from flowers to heirloom tomatoes to homemade granola. Musicians were setting up, and the number of cars parked on the shady road grew; locals appeared, some carrying baskets in one hand while balancing a child, often with a boot missing, on their hip.

We decided to drive around the north end of the island but discovered it was a series of dirt roads through Denman Island Provincial Park. On our wanderings, we saw many natural areas, as well as farms, artist and artisan studios, and wineries, such as the Corlan Winery, which has an amusing logo depicting two sheep toasting with wine glasses. The chilled Sandy Island White, their estate-grown Ortega wine, could be a great accompaniment to the fresh bread from "Mom's" and the Fanny Bay oysters purchased earlier, as well as the baked goods from the market.

Denman is delightful, but many people choose to continue over to neighbouring Hornby Island, which is considered to be the star, as if it is the beautiful older sister, slightly out of reach, more remote (a quality so appealing to us humans). In fact, Hornby is known as the Hawaii of the North, and a short ten-minute ferry trip from Gravelly Bay on Denman Island will take you there.

An immense section of Hornby is devoted to natural parkland, including the famous, spectacular, white sandy beach at Tribune Bay, said by some to have the warmest swimming waters of Western Canada. Then there's Little Tribune Bay, a "clothing-optional" beach. Although I am a bit shy about stripping in public, I will admit that there's nothing like swimming naked. The worst thing with a bathing suit is taking it off after it's wet, so perhaps I'll give this little beach a try next summer—under the cover of night and a canopy of stars would suffice, I think.

If you like shopping but find you are low on cash, visit the free store at Hornby's recycling depot, where they proudly claim that seventy percent of their waste stream is either recycled or reused.

Hornby is blessed with a multitude of musicians, including the Songbirds, who play music from the sixties and beyond, as well as some of their original tunes; the Rosehips, a female folk group; and a blues society. If learning about nature is something you enjoy, there's even a little natural history museum at the school; on display is a fossil of a mosasaur's backbone, an ancient sea predator related to a lizard. The museum offers a speaker series and field trips in the summer.

Hornby is abuzz with activities, entertainment, outdoor sporting opportunities, and community activities—and is famous for being the summer destination of the large and passive bluntnose sixgill shark. Related to the dogfish, this shark migrates to the waters surrounding Hornby every summer, where they lurk among the nudibranchs, jellies, and wolf eels. And since the waters in the Salish Sea surrounding Hornby Island are considered to be one of the top diving destinations in North America, you may even be able to get up close and personal with these creatures. Diving is not for me, due to my fear of sinking like a stone, but I imagine it is breathtaking for those who practice it, seeing the world from this beautiful and quiet perspective.

> The sixgill shark is unique in that it is closely linked to its primitive relatives, detected through ancient shark fossils. Most modern species of sharks have seven gills, not six.
>
> I've often wondered why the seventh gill was needed over the time the shark developed. Aren't six enough? It certainly is for the sharks that gather off the Hornby waters.

Hornby has another unique and fascinating site: the Jeffrey Rubinoff Sculpture Park. The immense steel pieces of art, over one hundred of them, naturally lit and shadowed from all angles by the natural elements, sit with great strength on a two-hundred-acre pastoral property of the late and talented artist Jeffery Rubinoff. Tours of the sculpture park take place in the summer; the park and the art are professionally cared for, thanks to Rubinoff's generosity.

A little-known but significant fact is that Rubinoff began his career as a mall designer—a building developer—and simply took his skills and imagination further to become a sculptor. (As I've often said about strip malls: There's something to be said for viewing them from an anthropological perspective, as works of art, as installations—and, yes, as perhaps a blight on society, but a telling blight of how we humans think or don't think, for that matter.)

A series of intellectual forums called "The Company of Ideas" are also held at the park. Titles of forum topics have included: The End of the Age of Agriculture, Resurgent Tribalism, The Importance of the History of Science, and Humanism and Integration. It seems a bit intellectual, but as the park's website states, "Art provides a means to experience the sacred beyond prescriptive narrative." Rubinoff was such a remarkable individual that art historian Dr. James Fox wrote a book called *The Art of Jeffery Rubinoff* (Douglas & McIntyre, 2016).

Union Bay

Seven kilometres north of Buckley Bay (where the ferry will take you when coming back to Vancouver Island from Denman and Hornby Islands) on Highway 19A is Union Bay, a tiny, interesting, busy community. While the bay itself may appear to be small at first glance, it is very deep—the deepest in Baynes Sound, as the gaol museum curator in Union Bay informed me. This is why, back in the day, it became the only port for exporting coal, hence growing into a major community in 1888 when the Union Wharf was built to serve the shipping needs of the Cumberland mines; the first shipment went out in 1889. Union Bay was a cargo port, specifically for coal, a hive of economic, marine, and business activity.

Chinese workers established a Chinatown and worked as "trimmers" on the coal piles loaded on to the ships; when coal was loaded, it formed a peaked heap, creating an unbalanced shipping cargo; trimmers spent hours flattening the load with rakes, at times needing to crouch or lay on their stomachs to carry out their task.

Coke ovens, steam engines, machine shops, and trades of all kinds sprung up in Union Bay out of the need for repairing and building mine machinery. Alas, all things must come to an end, and by the sixties, the demand for coal had dissipated.

Union Bay's Heritage Row features a historic, now empty elementary school building, a church, a post office, and gaol (jail), all sitting steadfast on the side of the road, restored and freshly painted a tasteful red-brown brick with cream trim. The post office, built in 1913, is notable as it incorporates many of the original features, such as the oak counters, and original brass mail boxes still used by Canada Post, which rents the main floor from the Union Bay Historical Society. The church sports lovely new bevelled glass windows and is open for Sunday services.

The knowledgeable volunteer at the tiny gaol museum told me the story of Henry Wagner, the notorious smuggler and robber also known as the Flying Dutchman who raided the West Coast in his twin-engine boat *Spray*. His wanted poster described him as "bowlegged and a little stooped" with eyes of "steel grey" which may have added a slight drama to the threat—after all, steel grey is so much more terrifying than hazel or emerald green.

Wagner decided to burgle the Fraser and Bishop General Store. A gunfight ensued, and Union Bay's Constable Westaway was shot in the lung and died. His assistant, Gordon Ross captured Wagner and called for help. Wagner went to trial in Nanaimo, was found guilty, and was hanged in August 1913.

Poor Constable Westaway! I always wonder what people who are dying think, feel, and say when taking their final breath, especially when they did not expect to perish. Westaway's reported last words were not unique, but they were indeed sad and resigned: "Goodbye, Gordon. Goodbye."

Just a stone's throw from the gaol museum and Heritage Row is Union Bay's popular eatery, the Highwayman Saloon, which lured me in for a burger. I just was compelled to enter. From the outside it looked as if it was about to fall over, but that's simply its outer image; inside it has been renovated. "Your Local Rumhouse in Historical Union Bay, BC," as it describes itself, had a flashing neon sign listing the specialty: 45 RUMS AND SCHNITZEL. During my visit, there were numerous gleaming motorcycles parked in front on the gritty, cracked concrete. I looked with admiration at the glistening chrome exhaust pipes, long leather seats, and polished gold-and-scarlet, teeth-baring cougars and flaming skulls emblazoned on the front tanks. This, at first glance, gives the impression that it's a biker's bar, or perhaps the modern version of an old-time saloon where motorcycles have replaced the horses.

Above the door, almost looking as if it may fall on your head, is a glassed-in veranda with huge saloon girl cut-outs plastered in the windows, faded from the harsh sun. The dark walls inside are adorned with guitars of all sorts, traditional as well as the shiny, pointed rock-star types, as well as posters from films such as *Scarface* and *The Terminator*. The room is filled with the aroma of beer and barbecue sauce, and blues music scratches out of speakers above Arborite tables and red vinyl chairs. When I was there, the main bartender had long, beautiful grey hair, perfectly parted in the middle. Bikers of all genders strode in casually, crossing their leather-booted legs as they comfortably downed a drink or two.

The food servings are hefty and delicious; I had a pulled pork burger on top of a mountain of all-you-can-eat chips. There's the option to sit outside, just off the bar, next to the diminutive red-and-white Union Bay Fire Station garage, which sports a sign that says COMMUNITY FIREFIGHTERS NEEDED.

For all its tough biker image, Union Bay's Highwayman Saloon has a great heart. The bathrooms are spotless, the servers are friendly, and when I was there, the staff at the saloon were excited about their very first annual fundraiser, Hogfest, which included the Saloon Girl photo shoot, among other draws. The money raised was to go the Comox Valley Child Development Association, the Comox Valley SPCA, and Diabetes Canada.

Comox Valley

Cumberland, Courtenay, and Comox

Cumberland

IN THE COMOX VALLEY, WHICH IS ABOUT FIFTEEN MINUTES
past Union Bay when travelling north, is the enchanting and historic
Cumberland, a small community comfortably settled against forests,
mountain ridges, and rugged slopes. When you find yourself at the old
Waverly Hotel, you are in the heart of this very special town.

Cumberland, originally named Union in 1888 (after the Union Coal
Mining Company), and renamed Cumberland in 1891, has its roots as
a coal mining town. In the late 1800s, this lucrative venture attracted
people of diverse backgrounds—Japanese, Italian, Chinese, and Blacks,
to name a few—with each group living in segregated communities.
The Chinese were particularly ambitious, owning over one hundred
businesses, and at the end of the First World War, Cumberland was
home to one of Canada's largest Chinatowns.

The major coal baron of the time, Robert Dunsmuir—the original owner of Victoria's famous Craigdarroch Castle—was also in
the railway business, founding the E&N Railway from Esquimalt

(Victoria) to Nanaimo. Sadly, the E&N went out of service in 2011. Now dormant, languishing in public ownership, the old tracks remain, slowly being enveloped and returning to nature in a tangle of grasses, wild asters, and goldenrod. The iconic black and white signs, now faded and peeling atop rotting signposts, spell the names of each town's charming station as the neglected rusting rails curve on their approach into the little Island communities.

Cumberland and coal mining

Coal mining has a bleak history. Even today, it is unsafe, filthy, and associated with nothing but dark misery. In Eastern Canada and in Europe, children were forced to work in the mines due to their small size and ability to move through the low and narrow tunnels deep underground. Children were often replaced by small ponies, aptly named "pit ponies," who spent their miserable lives pulling carts of loaded coal throughout the mines, never seeing the light of day.

A friend of mine back east, in Saint Andrews, New Brunswick, told me of a rescued pit pony from a Cape Breton mine; his name (the pony's name, not my friend's) was Sparky. Sparky's forelegs and chest were a gnarled mass of twisted bone and knotted muscle, but he lived a grand retirement with a dear goat companion on a farm owned by a wealthy railroad heiress. (I find heiresses intriguing—many of them have demonstrated immense compassion towards animals. Perhaps, as the cliché goes, they live very lonely lives, animals being their truest companions.)

The worst coal mining disaster on Vancouver Island occurred in 1887 when there was a massive underground explosion in the No. 1 Esplanade Mine in Nanaimo; 148 miners died after the explosives had been improperly laid. At that time, the mining tunnels were under the harbour, specifically, under the Newcastle Island Channel, reaching the few smaller islands in the bay.

Approximately one-third of the miners were Chinese workers; their names were never recorded, as this was not an official practice until 1897. However, some were able to be identified by the numbers on the tags they wore around their necks. Perhaps the most pitiful (though not the most appalling) feature of this tragedy was that when the rescuers reached the perished men, they discovered that the miners had written goodbye messages in coal dust with their shovels.

It is notable today that these empty, hollow, and abandoned mining seams and tunnels are an infrastructure challenge to the municipality and developers because in several locations, the tunnels are only a metre under the road's surface, making sinkholes a major concern.

It is arguable that Cumberland's most prominent historical figure was Albert "Ginger" Goodwin, the pacifist and anti-war labour activist who led a miners' strike as they fought for a better quality of life, higher wages, and fair working conditions. This was a major event in Canadian history, and what gave it a more dramatic finish was Ginger's tragic death: He was shot by a policeman in 1918.

For over thirty years, the Cumberland Museum & Archives has put on a Miners Memorial Weekend in late June, commemorating this colourful but dirty time in coal-mining history.

Cumberland's retro architecture

There's an old-fashioned, unspoken pride and quiet dignity to this town, quite unlike other historic towns that intentionally seek to recreate the past by constructing boardwalks, saloons, and dance halls. The architecture, particularly on the main street, is a major historical and cultural feature in Cumberland. With the exception of several Chinese structural replicas at the top of the hill (one of which is now used as a cultural hall), numerous buildings have been preserved from a bygone era; in fact, some of the old buildings have simply endured, without obvious efforts at preservation, and are still in use today. They are an authentic, uncontrived part of the community.

A short stroll west from the town will take you to Coal Creek Historic Park, the forty-acre site of the original Chinatown, old mines, and the Japanese settlement. A walking tour map of significant historic landmarks is available at the museum up on the hill.

Cumberland's buildings have a retro look—a peach-coloured stucco movie theatre looks like a giant stereo from the fifties (originally an opera house in 1924); the Waverly Hotel on the corner of Dunsmuir and First Avenue has its red neon sign still glowing above the sidewalk; and the solid sandstone post office at Dunsmuir and Third, built in 1907, is now the lovely, airy Wandering Moose Café, which has many of the post office's original fixtures and wooden features still intact.

There is something very appealing about the look and feel of the retro era—and by *retro* I am referring to the time around the forties and fifties, when a pastel-green Mixmaster was a common sight on many a household's kitchen counter. It calls to mind Fred Herzog's photographs of everyday, working-class scenes on the streets of Vancouver—windows with red trim, families walking along grey sidewalks, small, everyday shops on busy streets under power lines and red neon signs.

This retro appeal, depending on who you talk to, is strong for those of us who are of a certain age. Baby boomers in particular still feel connected to an era that felt relatively simple and honest; we were not as bombarded with the massive amounts of information coming from every direction, including from the clouds. While there were, of course, unsettling events—the Red River Flood, the outbreak of the Korean War, the Trans-Canada Air Lines collision near Moose Jaw, Hurricane Hazel, rioting in Montreal and Vancouver over hockey, Nova Scotia's Springhill Mine Disaster, the FLQ crisis—it seems as if today, in our electronic age, we are even more inundated with endless, diverse reasons to fear. Take, for example, online luring of children by pedophiles, computer hacking, the constant threat of financial collapse, mosquitoes spreading the Zika virus, drones flying randomly above massive airports, defective air bags, sexting, cancer-causing UV rays and the dubious health and environmental effects of sunscreen, E-coli on your lettuce—so many fears!

I believe the mid-century modern (roughly 1945–75) architecture and industrial design of what seems like a more innocent era offers something of a warm, cozy security blanket. The buildings of this era are often plain, square, neutral-coloured stucco boxes with bits of brightly hued wood trim and plain signage; perhaps the clean, uncomplicated design is soothing to the mind and our emotions.

Such are many of the preserved buildings in Cumberland—there's a winsome simplicity and gentleness about Cumberland, despite its rugged and tumultuous history.

Cumberland has experienced a couple of tragic fires; the oldest surviving hotel, built in 1884, is the Waverly, originally a temperance boarding house—so says the little brass plaque stuck onto the beige stucco under the green awning. Here, the locals sit at a massive oak bar, surrounded by antlers on the wall, and have a pint after a busy day.

The building that draws the most attention from first-time visitors is the Ilo Ilo Theatre across the street. In 1914, this stolid, peach, orange-painted movie theatre was an opera house; it was also a dance hall known for its suspended, maple sprung dance floor downstairs. The last film shown there (so says the little brass plaque on the street) was *These Wilder Years* with James Cagney and Barbara Stanwyk.

The Foggy Mountain Fall Fair

In 2016, I attended Cumberland's annual Foggy Mountain Fall Fair, held on the last weekend in September, in the heart of the village at

First and Dunsmuir. The festivities included a guided heritage walk (organized by and starting at the museum; participants pay by donation), dinner and drinks in the village, games for children, musicians and craft vendors, and the Comox Valley Arts' Fall Fair Follies.

The fair was best known for its pie-of-the-year contest. Contestants make two identical pies, one for the judges and the public to taste, and the other to be auctioned off. The money raised goes towards the Cumberland Forest Society. This contest is a major event; when I was there, it seemed the entire community took part, lining up to taste the pies in the early evening before bidding on their favourites.

I've enjoyed many food and cooking competitions at numerous Canadian fall fairs, and, as a result, I've come to the conclusion that out of all of them, pie competitions are the most elite—much more chic than the contemporary gluten-free muffins or cranberry biscotti . . . let's say that the pie competition is definitely the upper crust. The champion's flowing blue-and-gold rosette for preserves, chutneys, or muffins just doesn't seem to hold the same prestige as the grand lady of them all—the pie. My guess is that it's all about the agricultural tradition and that the pie carries the torch for symbolizing autumn bounty, especially the fruit pie. Making a good one is an all-consuming activity: In addition to often growing and harvesting the fruit, most serious pie makers have special tips on pie crust consistency, lending elements of pride, secrecy, and friendly rivalry to the process. Consider the skills, resources, labour, effort, and hands it takes to grow and harvest fruit and to gather ingredients to actually put the pie together! A truly beautiful pie is an exquisite (and edible) work of art that takes an inordinate amount of time to put together when compared to how quickly it is consumed. It reminds me of sand mandalas painstakingly and mindfully created by Tibetan Buddhist monks, grain by coloured grain; when the mandala is finally complete, the monks gently brush it aside, destroying what they worked so hard on. It illustrates that nothing is permanent, and everything is in flux—thoughts, actions, weather, everything . . . even pie. Especially pie.

Mother Nature performs the same way: Just look on the beach, observe the patterns of the rocks, the arrangement of the pebbles, the life within the tide pools. Notice the arrangement of the seaweed and shells in the sand. Then, with one tidal cycle, the entire beach is altered.

The acknowledgement of impermanence can be a difficult philosophy to live by, but even so, it's good to recognize that what we do and how we perceive our world is all about being aware of the circle of creation, of enjoyment, of completion, and of time, however brief. And that is what making a pie is all about! Pie makers no doubt have a clear idea of this peaceful and wise Buddhist philosophy.

The pie event in Cumberland was billed as "legendary" and "almost-world-famous." The community waits all day for the grand pie judging and tasting, and then they allow the competition to continue for hours.

On this particular afternoon, the rain was coming down in sheets, creating small, gritty streams down the main street; the forest mists were low, seeping down over the drooping cedars and evergreen forests on the mountains; the night before, the wind had tossed leaves and debris across the sidewalks and onto the soggy lawn in front of the cultural centre. Undaunted, the cheerful, enthusiastic residents made their way to the fair in dripping-wet raincoats and rubber boots while holding their umbrellas aloft.

The warm, glowing hall buzzed with community spirit. The pies were laid out in a horseshoe configuration, and there was a lively band playing country tunes in the middle of the room.

By the door, a woman sold T-shirts emblazoned with the words SAVE THE CUMBERLAND FOREST, and on the far wall there were hot cider and hot dogs on offer. A lady dressed as a unicorn in a shiny green dress (and with huge, black eyelashes) seemed to be busy greeting guests and mingling with high enthusiasm in the crowd.

I had planned to bid on a pie, but not the prettiest one; often, with pie, looks are deceiving. The tastiest (but not the prettiest) one may have filling oozing and dripping onto the serving dish, or it could be topped with an asymmetrical crust. There were twelve or more pies on which to bid, but after three hours, the judges—three attractive and bubbly Cumberland "celebrities" (a chef, a chocolate maker, and a baker)—had only made it to pie number four, a great concoction containing, of all things, bacon and maple syrup, complete with gingerbread forest animals clinging to thick folds of filling on its rim. It was much more than a pie: it was a project, a sculpture, an installation of sorts, depicting the nearby woodland with all its flora and fauna.

Luckily there were also cakes! On a far table against the wall were four cakes ready to be bid upon by a silent auction (cake just doesn't warrant celebrity judges). I wrote a bid for a large, solid, heavily frosted chocolate coffee cake, decorated with thick white-and-pink frosted trees, mushrooms, and a squirrel. In the centre was a lopsided, pink-wheeled mountain bike with a rider who seemed to be toppling sideways, oozing over the edge of the giant rim. The other cakes were too perfect, a lightly dusted, precisely shaped Bundt cake without a crumb out of place, a cake with (olive) green icing and orange candies—nice but too green; I just cannot bring myself to eat a green cake—and an immense cherry tart with a flakey crust and a few elegant decorations placed strategically on its rim. (I think that should have been on the pie table, but it was put with the cakes because there was only one; for the pies, there had to be two—that's the rule.)

When the bidding closed, I had won my chocolate cake! Feeling triumphant, I carried my surprisingly heavy, delicious-looking purchase towards the door of the old musty hall, leaving the legendary almost-world-famous pie auction tastings and judging to continue at the far end of the now-crowded and steamy room, which was by this time bathed in a warm orange glow as night had fallen. The peeling white hall door was slightly open, and the rain was still pouring in sheets as darkness surrounded the dripping trees on the large, soggy lawn. A lone streetlight flickered across the street in front of the fire hall in the shadowy mist, and I noticed that the fire crew were all tasting pie in the warmth of the hall.

I desired to meet my cake makers, and when I expressed this to the lady who took my cheque, I learned that her niece and her best friend had made the cake. She found them, Emma and Libby, in the crowd; they were eating a cherry pie, their faces covered in removable tattoos and face paint of cats and stars. The two girls, around ten years old, enthusiastically and proudly gave me a brief interview, and this is how it went:

Me: Wow, girls, why is this amazing cake so heavy?

Emma and Libby (in unison, very excited): It's the frosting!

Me: I love the pink and white decorations . . .

Emma and Libby (again in unison; pointing to each item on the cake; the enthusiasm continues): These are trees, and this is a mush-room, and this is a mountain biker guide riding through the trees and this . . .

Me: Is this cake made from a mix?

Emma and Libby (again in unison): Something something web something dot com . . .

Me: Wow, a cake from scratch—nobody does that anymore. That's terrific! What are your future plans? Will you stay in Cumberland and make cakes?

Emma and Libby: (vigorously nodding together)

Me: Okay girls, last question: What is your favourite tree in the forest that you are trying to save?

Libby and Emma (now both in unison and separately, extremely excited and breathless, responding in sentences as if they were questions): Well, there's this tree? And this scary squirrel? And he sits in the tree? And it's really scary . . . and when we walk under that tree? The squirrel throws nuts at us! It's really scary!

Emma (pointing to the cake, a pink squirrel on a tree): That's him there!

That night I ate a huge piece of that amazing heavy cake, and it was absolutely delicious. The decorations melted in my mouth—and I even ate the scary pink squirrel. I had an additional piece before bed, and by noon the following day, the entire cake was gone, as swiftly as the Tibetan Buddhist mandalas or a fleeting thought. The indulgence was all about the moment (of eating) with no intention of preserving Emma's and Libby's masterpiece. I ate the creation with gusto and enjoyed every bit of it!

A final point regarding my lovely encounter with the cake makers: At no time did their mother appear to check me out, even though she had been told that "a writer from Victoria wished to interview the girls about their cake." It is a sad commentary on modern times that I would even have to wonder or question if a mother might worry that I was some oddball (a writer at that) talking to her children, or that I would even have to consider asking permission to talk to these youngsters covered in cherry pie and face paint. I know people who live in urban areas (such as Vancouver) who would *never* allow their children to give a complete stranger their cake recipe, let alone talk to them. The fact that the adults at the Foggy Mountain Fall Fair were free of paranoia and so at ease in their community with strangers such as myself, and so trusting of their children, was as refreshing as the cool evening rain I was about to head into. It gave me a glimmer of hope for the world. And so the Foggy Mountain Fall Fair was well worth a day's excursion to Cumberland; this town remains one of my favourite places to visit on Vancouver Island.

> There is pie for sale up and down Vancouver Island, at markets, fairs, roadside stands, and in village shops. In addition to attending the pie competition in Cumberland, and visiting the Pie Factory in Parksville, I also purchased a meat pie from a stand in Cassidy, just south of Nanaimo. I asked the pie maker for her special pie tips. "Never make a pie in a bad mood," she said. "Always make a pie with love."

As soon as I sense autumn on the horizon, with the heavier morning dews and a bit of a nip in the air, I start looking forward to the imminent fall fairs. They are almost as exciting as Christmas, especially for adults, not only due to the peak of the harvest, but also because we anticipate a great rest, a hibernation (until we do it all over again next year).

The fall-fair tradition symbolizes the completion of a year's worth of labour, capping off a busy year with a big burst of the joyful industriousness of harvesting, canning, storing, pickling, and so on, which culminates in displays and demonstrations, awards and celebrations. I love the paradox that exists as the fall fair signifies the end of the year: It's a time of rest but also of intense labour; it is the time to preserve foods for the long, quiet, chilly winter season; we make pies and freeze them; we use bushels of spare apples to make juice and sauce and cider; we split kindling, stack fragrant woodpiles; we dig up potatoes; we end our busy days at dusk hours, which comes earlier now, filling the animal pens with extra hay and straw, our feet protected by thick, warm socks and rubber boots. It's all very cozy and comforting, a way of living and being which the Danish call *hygge* (pronounced "hoo-gah").

I have had numerous experiences at fall fairs, most of them embarrassing disasters through eliminations and insults. Once, when I was living on my farm in North Saanich, I entered the heaviest cabbage contest at the Saanich Fair, one of the grandest and oldest fairs in British Columbia. My cabbages were enormous—tight purple globes as big as basketballs, grown in the tough but fertile Saanich clay soil all summer, watered by the runoff from the chicken coop. I had to use a wheelbarrow to haul them into the truck for the journey to the grand agricultural hall!

These colossal cabbages dwarfed the competition on the long white tables in the vegetable hall at the fair; the other pitiful cabbages were half the size and shrivelled by the scorching sun of late summer. However, when the blue rosettes—the awards—were handed out, the judges had written on my tag ELIMINATED—TOO MANY OUTER LEAVES REMOVED. The shrivelled, dry little pale things next to my dear spectacular display had the rosettes proudly pinned onto their scrawny stems! My friend thought the whole thing was rigged—she said I should lodge a complaint of "cabbage elitism," but, as it turns out, there are very strict rules at fall fairs, which, of course, I did not heed. I never read the rules.

After my cabbage calamity, I found myself in a pickle with my eggs—pickled eggs, to be precise. (Again, I suspect there were rules that I didn't read up on.) I used an alias so the hundreds of people that read these tags would not know it was me if I was once again insulted. My alias name was Gracie Grey, a name chosen by taking the name of the first pet I once owned and the first street I recall living on. I'm glad I used an alias for the pickled eggs because this time the judges wrote LID NOT TIGHT, LEAKS, RUSTED RIM—COULD CAUSE BOTULISM. They hadn't even tasted them!

I admit I didn't buy a new jar, but really, why did they have to insult the competitors like that?

I ate the eggs (after I quickly smuggled them of the fairgrounds a day early; we had been strictly warned that under no circumstances were we to remove our entries until Monday evening, but I was not prepared to have Gracie Grey insulted in public like that for two more days as streams of people sauntered by and read those terribly insulting tags). My eggs were delicious, and I did not have to call 911. I have no regrets.

I have had a somewhat successful, or at least a non-embarrassing showing at the fair, though: My tallest sunflower (twelve feet) won, only because there were no other entries, but at least I was not eliminated. And one year, when Mum was visiting from Fredericton, I convinced her to enter her bread at the Salt Spring Island Fall Fair, where she placed second out of three. It was Gran's recipe, which Mum had carried on and made every week for as long as I could remember. Every Sunday, there would be huge, warm, white bowls of rising dough with the bread pans lined up on the wood stove in her kitchen. Mum's sleeves would be rolled up, her hands covered in flour as she repeatedly pushed her glasses back up the bridge of her nose while kneading the loaves and shaping and spanking the buns.

Dad disliked her wholesome, grainy bread and bought the processed, white, sliced variety—in protest, I think. He always said that Mum's bread gave him the runs. "Bruno prefers that soft, processed, 'enriched' stuff in those plastic bags," she'd whisper to me as the three of us sauntered, almost hypnotized, through the gigantic Fredericton Sobeys bread aisle.

Mum always encouraged me to carry on Gran's bread tradition, but I was simply not interested. I experienced a fair bit of guilt over the years about not walking in Gran and Mum's bread-making footsteps, but I did other things, such as pickling eggs! I don't think it's strange to feel an obligation to continue a family tradition; on the other hand, times and circumstances change, and we are very different from our ancestors. Truth be known, Gran and Mum's bread did crumble, especially when filled with devilled egg or something moist, often breaking apart and delivering a big sloppy mess on your lap (which was embarrassing in junior high school). That's probably why Mum didn't win first prize at the bread competition on Salt Spring Island; her bread was not firm.

So, sometimes, tradition is not all that it's cracked up to be, and maybe there are times when we should just let it fade away—let it go, as they say in yoga circles. Sometimes tradition is nothing more than societal or familial pressure to hold on to the past, and it may not be as crucial to cling to as you may have believed. Come to think of it, I have ten boxes of photos in my basement, all turning into damp, mouldy dust. Perhaps it's time for a bonfire on the beach (which is illegal in Victoria, but I could probably get away with it at Halloween), similar to a grand cremation as was done for the poet Percy Bysshe Shelley.

Little Thinks outside the Cumberland Museum

I cannot leave Cumberland without mentioning the museum, a sturdy historic wooden structure attached to the cultural hall at the top of the hill across from the fire station. But first, I must tell you about the benches outside, made to look like coal mining carts, a nod to the town's mining history. These benches are found along the main street.

In my estimation, if there is anything that can represent a community, it is the humble public bench. And when you sit on such a bench to simply take in the feeling of the place, it seems passersby are inclined to approach you and talk. This can lead to surprisingly candid and pleasant exchanges and gives you a deeper sense for the unique characteristics of a place.

Alternatively, if you're sitting alone with your own thoughts, you can absorb the small moments found in the passing of time, enjoying your

Little Thinks, the unexpected, unanticipated, and unplanned floating thoughts that pass by and are caught for a brief amount of time. In these seemingly unimportant moments, we can feel what it means to simply exist, to just sit and allow the mind to drift without an agenda.

In Cumberland, I sat on one of their mining-cart benches, and before long my mind drifted to the strangest place:

> *Wasn't it a miracle that Dad's sperm actually met Mum's egg, only to result in me, sixty years later, sitting on a weathered old mining-cart bench in front of the blue stucco Masonic Hall in Cumberland?*

Such is the nature of public bench-sitting and Little Thinks.

The Cumberland Museum

Almost every small town has a little museum organized by a heritage committee to showcase the area's past. Cumberland is no exception, and during my visit a few years ago, their collection contained a few surprises.

First, there was a fascinating compilation of beautiful, simply framed, austere black-and-white photographs by Japanese photographer Senjiro Hayashi, who lived in Cumberland in the early 1900s. The images depicted Cumberland's numerous residents during that era.

What makes the photographs nuanced works of art rather than simple, everyday portraits is Hayashi's keen ability to capture his subjects' authentic feelings and personalities, ostensibly without having them pose, even if they seem casually aware of the camera as they stand in the studio's parlour-like setting. There is something about Hayashi's use of shadow, the way the light falls across the creases in the skin and then fades to dark; something wordless is conveyed in the subtle placement of a wrist or the fleeting twitch of a sad mouth.

The resulting images give a haunting, moving, yet light impression of a deep sadness, a resignation to what must have been a difficult life. Perhaps these people were homesick; maybe they were weary from the rain and mud and coal dirt. Still, there is determination and dignity in their expressions. These photographs are treasures, not only because they record a specific time is history, but also as a remarkable, noteworthy art form.

Much of today's portrait photography, in my view, is somewhat egocentric; it is not meant to preserve history, or to capture the ambience of a moment, or to record the fleeting emotions of the subject. Instead, it seems to be an opportunity to create an unrealistic, overly contrived, posed (with one of those selfie sticks), excessively Photoshopped snapshot of someone who wants to be considered as conventionally attractive as possible to a great, vast, generic crowd out in cyberspace.

In my opinion, there is a huge difference between this type of photography and professional photography as an art form. When the photographer pays attention and deeply sees their subject, and when the subject drops their façade and authentically looks into the lens, vulnerability seeps through the camera and eventually reaches us, the audience; then the image, and what it conveys, resonates in our hearts and minds.

Perhaps one day, in a hundred years or so, mass-produced selfie portrait photography will offer interesting fodder for academic societal analysis on early twenty-first-century culture, right up there with strip malls and Pop-Tarts.

Another exhibit at the Cumberland Museum is the medical display. In a tall glass case, there are numerous (and what I would call gruesome) tools and devices of days gone by: a vein stripper; an abdominal spring retractor; an old iron lung, painted yellow and fading with age, a small rubber hole through which the patient would put their head.

Looking at the old, serrated, saw-like instruments, I am reminded that there is an element of pain, sometimes extreme pain, associated with this profession, even today. But I am also struck by how powerful it is that we have the desire and ability to work to save one another. Because of this, I find the medical profession intriguing. The vulnerability and trust required, the complete reliance one must have on another for the sake of well-being is, in my view, mutually intimate and quite remarkable. A physician can reach under our skin, can go deeper than muscle, even touching the place where the very pulse of our life beats. (Our heartbeat is a miracle in the first place!) This ability transcends science, as far as I'm concerned; it is almost divine.

For all these reasons, I am fascinated whenever I observe antique medical tools—not only for what they can do, but for what they represent. No other field is so personal, so intimately acquainted with our deepest fears or so aligned with our most urgent instincts to do what we can to preserve life, an impulse which is so fundamentally human. And so visceral: surgery, poking around in our bodies, especially with cold, metal, serrated tools, is almost macabre—at least it would be if these instruments did not save our lives. Perhaps this too informs my fascination: How could something be so macabre but so lifesaving?

A little while ago, I visited my doctor; not only were there cheerful, pink knit socks on the stirrups of the examination table on which I lay, there was also a small plaque on the side of the table conveying appreciation to a donor. Well, that got me thinking: What could I donate? What does my doctor need? Something unique—perhaps something for "the nether-regions" (as Mum used to call below-the-waist private parts)? I decided to gift my doctor's office with a wart remover (for the nether-regions) as this is what she said she required (thankfully not for me).

When the nether-region wart remover arrived, to my great excitement, I thought that it looked like a silver blowtorch, oddly similar to something a labourer would use for disintegrating asphalt roof shingles.

When I made my donation, the receptionist asked me if I'd like my name engraved on the blowtorch, but I politely declined, explaining that it might taint my reputation if a patient could read my name during this rather unseemly and humiliating procedure.

Today's medical utensils are still as unsettling as the antiques. I came to this conclusion a couple of years ago when I had my first alarming medical encounter. I was sent (referred is the word they used, but I was sent) to a woman's lower-regions specialist. I was completely terrified, and my anxiety level rose to abnormally high levels; yoga didn't help at all.

"Do you smoke?" my sweet, kind doctor asked. "Did your mother ever have cancer?" These were scary questions as I sat in my doctor's little green-walled office in a brown stucco building wedged in between a vacuum shop and a dog groomer.

My eyes nervously drifted to my doctor's glass cabinet. On the shelves, behind the glass, were a diverse variety of tools. Some looked to be about two feet long, with little shovels, snippy bits, and scissors on the ends; others were bent at various angles; still others had loops. I thought I saw one with a pulley, another with a lever, and one with a small wheel—the three greatest inventions! Several looked as though they belonged in Dad's fishing tackle box or from a glass-blowing studio.

I clung to my chair, refusing my doctor's request that I move onto her examination table. Sensing my terror, she tried to put me at ease, saying, "Oh, don't worry. We won't need those . . . today."

"Today" would come a month or two later, at the hospital, while I was under anesthetic.

Before my operation, I prepared according to the instructions I'd been given. These included many detailed illustrations that depicted, quite graphically, how I should wash my nether-regions as well as my belly button. I was to acquire from the pharmacy a special sponge, with which I would wash twice—once the night before the surgery, and once the morning of.

(When I described this process to my friend, who also happens to be my horse's veterinarian, she said, "I can get you that special sponge for half the price—it's the exact same kind I use for birthing mares." She was true to her word: The huge, cellophane-wrapped package she handed me read for equine use only. This helpful transaction saved me money, but the humiliation was substantial.)

And then the big day arrived. I had met with my regular doctor for the necessary pre-operation check, during which she had to list me in one of five categories, the first being "a healthy patient," and the fifth being a "patient unlikely to survive 24 hours with or without surgery." My affable, relaxed doctor quickly checked off "healthy patient." My contribution was a nervous chuckle.

The drive to the hospital along the Trans-Canada Highway was surreal; I couldn't believe that I was going to be anesthetized, completely out of touch with the world. What if they get the gas wrong and I never wake up? I worried. "Have we updated our will?" I asked Mikki; it struck me that I had never fully realized I was mortal. "Remember," I said, "to give a big cheque to the cat rescue place in Nanoose should I not regain consciousness."

As we sped past the massive, lichen-covered slabs of rock lining the roads, dotted with flecks of orange poppies just about to bloom, I wondered if this would be the final drive of my life; was this what it had all come down to, speeding down the Trans-Canada Highway on an overcast day on the cusp of spring? Housing developments were going up rapidly, sprawling over the distant hills, shrouded in mist. Cars whizzed past us, carrying people going to work. Life went on all around me, but I was heading for the unconscious world of nothingness.

I was unable to connect the two, life and nothingness; I felt separated from both. Maybe, at the end of the day, they were opposite sides of the same coin. My mind felt completely detached from my body, from the neck down: It could be probed, taken apart, dismembered, but my thoughts were so entirely separate. Maybe this is what some people mean when they say that they made friends with their cancer (which, as it turned out, I did not have). Soon the hospital appeared in the distance, a looming grey cement box, steam spewing from its flat roof into the grey sky.

When we walked into hospital, there was a longer lineup for Tim Hortons than for admissions, and that gave me hope. No matter what we're going through, there are always donuts.

The waiting room, once I arrived there, was a gritty, grim little corner that reminded me of both a livestock holding pen at an abattoir and a Minsk bus station in winter. Nervous patients, perhaps sedated by Ativan, were slumped and draped over dated, tired-looking chrome chairs. The floor was a dingy beige linoleum, and faded, dated gossip magazines were scattered on an Arborite coffee table. A smudgy plastic water cooler sat under a yellowed handwritten sign that reminded us to make sure we have arranged for pick-up following our surgeries. In the midst of the dinginess, there was a hand sanitizer dispenser fastened to the grey wall. A little late for that, I thought.

I brightened up when a friendly Polish nurse, right on time, called my name and escorted me to what I'd call the "holding pen," a bright room full of beds and gizmos on wheels, and little cupboards where we could store our clothes until we come out on the other side. A sense of calm washed over me, especially when this lovely nurse wrapped me in warm blankets and told me about a sanatorium she knew about in Poland. I'm not sure how the conversation began, but it ended with her recommending a trip to one of these facilities—she said they call it "a medical spa" nowadays. Her favourite, she told me, was in Gdańsk because it was the least crowded in winter. Winter at a sanatorium in

Gdańsk, I thought, on the Baltic Sea?

Staff wheeled patients in and out of the room with a busy precision that called to mind Heathrow Airport. Some were like little airplanes kept in holding patterns; others were pushed into curtained alcoves as if going into a hangar for maintenance; a few were being refuelled at the gate. Finally it was my turn. After donning a sterile shower cap, I was wheeled into a hallway to prepare for takeoff. I waited on the runway and watched two cleaners dusting the windowsill, causing the debris to hang and sparkle in a beam of sunlight; it reminded me of the divine golden rays so often depicted in the religious paintings of the Annunciation, when the angel Gabriel appears before Mary—often shown passively sitting on a stone slab or bench (maybe having a Little Think) in her drab drapes of cloth—to administer his heavenly act. It seems that I often think about heavenly beams of light in the Annunciation when I am either blissfully contented or terrified out of my mind.

And then my moment arrived! My dear doctor appeared, dressed in baggy green scrubs, just like in the medical television shows; to me, she looked divine in the most literal sense of the word. As I was pushed around the corner and into the operating room, the doctor walked beside me, giving my palm a few little strokes with her pale, delicate fingers. I'll never forget her tiny gesture.

While shifting my body onto the table, I noticed a nurse organizing those dreaded metal tools, lining them up on a towel at the end of the table. I had a brief glance of the pulley, the lever, the wheel, the trowel, the garden hoe, and the two-foot scissors, all in a neat order, all ready to be wielded for the maintenance of my nether-regions.

The anesthesiologist, just before she put the mask on my face, paused and asked, "Anny? Is that you? Didn't you teach me horse riding a long time ago?"

"It depends. Was I nice?" I answered nervously, thinking, I wonder if she was that kid who fell off the horse and broke her arm. If so, is this my penance? And then I thought, Wow, I taught this kid how to break in a horse—look at her now!

And then the doctor asked the most peculiar question: "Anny, can you tell me why you are here?"

What's with this doctor? I wondered. And I thought I had a bad memory! Turns out they always ask the patient this question so they don't cut off the wrong leg.

The next thing I knew, I was waking up from the best sleep ever, wearing a pair of stretchy gauze underpants that, with little effort, I could pull up right over my head, like a tent or shroud. Soon I was wheeled back across the tarmac and into the hangar where those warm towels awaited me along with a little handwritten note from my sweet doctor who said that I was not to have a bath for two weeks. I lay there in awe, and somebody gave me a red popsicle.

My hospital experience, although relatively minor, was a curious experience. Surprisingly, I remained completely in the present moment at all times, as if in a very alert, but also meditative state. I never looked back, nor looked forward, but rather experienced each second as it occurred—something I have never been able to do. This may have been out of a combination of fascination and terror, but I am inclined to believe it was out of resignation to being at the mercy of another, to have no say and no responsibility. This absolute dependency was liberating; in fact, it was almost exhilarating to have no control whatsoever, to accept that there was nothing I could do to control the outcome. How freeing it was to not have to make choices for even this brief amount of time, to give up all power to fate, to Mother Nature, or to what others may call God. No wonder people find religion so compelling—it's comforting.

Before my surgery, I had expected to be in a frail and fragile state, so I had prepared a little spinach soup at home. After my surgery, while on my way home, I thought I might lie on the couch and watch Judge Judy all afternoon. But when I got home, I was ravenously hungry, and so I walked to the grocery store and bought a rotisserie chicken and a carton of caramel ice cream. As I devoured both, I felt so grateful to be alive.

I do not know which I prefer: to give up all power and to trust in the unknown, experiencing elation and peace, the inner freedom of nothingness, or to agonize over writing or creating a work of art, trying to get it right, exactly the way I want it, despising myself when the words will not appear, feeling the terror of looming dullness that lurks, but then catching inspiration as it floats by.

Perhaps genius momentarily strikes when these two positions occur unexpectedly and at exactly the same time, when we are out of our heads but vulnerable to what is present.

Courtenay

When, after enjoying the many delights of Cumberland, you are ready to get back to exploring the Island, head to the town of Courtenay—it is well worth a visit and a stroll. Even on a rainy Saturday in the late afternoon, the charming Fifth Street, lined with quaint and interesting little shops, is vibrant. On one such visit, the rain poured down in sheets, then streamed down the hill into the murky river. Undaunted by the weather, I passed the surf shop, where huge, yellow inflated inner tubes were stacked next to rows of paddleboards and surfboards. After visiting the Laughing Oyster Bookshop, which exuded a warm, intelligent ambience, I purchased two highly entertaining novels, one based on Einstein and the other on Edison—both manipulative bastards, according to the stories.

Courtenay also has a beautiful library on Sixth Street, halfway between Cliffe and England Avenues. It is a true delight, with its high, varnished wooden beams separating wide, glass panels, spacious yet cozy sitting areas, and little nooks. Here you can sit and ponder, enjoying a private place where you can be with yourself alone, simply to read and catch up on the bestsellers, the news, the ideas of the world, maybe your own ideas. A good library should not only provide an array of books and periodicals but furnish a space for mental rest. Information should not be stressful, should not bombard us, but instead be simply offered while we decide if we wish to take a closer look. A library can be a place where such fundamentally human joys can be experienced in this way.

Visiting the Courtenay library is like walking into a spa, only without the essential oils, candles, seaside music, and teas that have the aroma of a forest after a summer rain. Rather, there are books and information waiting for you—a massage for your mind, on your own terms. There are some similarities between spas and libraries: Everyone whispers, and the toilets are spotless.

The library sits on the site of a large, historic dairy operation, the Comox Co-operative Creamery Association, which operated from 1901 to 1968. Beautifully displayed in a glass case is the elegant brass creamery whistle used in the dairy to announce the hours of labour and breaks to the workers. The whistle was blown at eight in the morning, at noon, one, and five o'clock, calling the workers to feed and milk the cows.

I sketched a picture of that whistle. I rarely sketch or draw, but perhaps when I retire I will learn. When I was very young, I sat in on a drawing class that Mum, a well-known Canadian artist, taught at the University of New Brunswick. She would enthusiastically tell her students, "Just scribble, just scribble."

Dairy Farms in the Comox Valley

The Comox Valley is known for its agricultural awareness in promoting healthy and "happy" livestock, fresh and organic food production, and a clean, sustainable environment—fine, forward-thinking, necessary ventures.

The dairy cow industry (considered a very significant part of the agricultural industry) is the subject of many conflicting views on such a variety of subjects. For example: to pasteurize milk, or not? The advantages to drinking raw milk are many, but when an individual becomes significantly ill from a batch of "dirty" milk, the debate rages on. And then there are milk allergies and lactose intolerance, artificial insemination (in cows), and the use of antibiotics and hormones on farm animals. And now there's the question of soil degradation that cattle produce, compared to, for example, the effects on a field used for lentil production.

And what about the health of cattle? A grass-fed cow in its natural surroundings should have a lifespan of approximately twenty years, but the average commercial cow's lifespan may be only four or five years. (This no doubt applies to all livestock raised in commercial facilities.) Many cows in a large dairy operation are fed corn and kept indoors most of their milking life for the sake of labour and efficiency, government regulations, milk quotas, and, of course, revenue.

Dairy facts and teat-bits:

At the time of the writing of this book, there were approximately five hundred dairy farms in British Columbia and just under twelve thousand in Canada.

There are over eight hundred breeds of cattle, the black and white Holstein being the most common due to its heavy milk production. The Holstein was originally a hybrid cross between two breeds from Holland and Germany.

The first (recorded) dairy in British Columbia was established by the Hudson's Bay Company in Fort Langley, and one of the initial dairy export operations was butter to the Russian/American territory of Alaska.

On many dairy farms in Europe and Australia, the animals lumber into the barn to relaxing classical music and are milked by automated pumps, but to calm the cows further, an intelligent cow can nudge a switch on the wall, which activates a warm shower accompanied by a series of rollers and brushes producing a serene massage; there is also a fan to deter flies. I am not one for technology, but if it can be this beneficial to the cow's constitution, I am a great supporter!

Cattle are often fed distillers' grains, the brewery solids that remain following the yeast, fermentation, and filtering process; horses are frequently given a bottle of beer! Beer is fed to horses, usually after a hard day of work, as a calorie booster; the alcohol is easily digested and is not a health concern. The horse does not become inebriated, and the brew is not revealed on drug tests.

The practice is quite common in Ireland and Britain. I give my dear old horse Valnah a can of Guinness as a treat, poured into warm bran mash, after the Saanich Fair every year.

A cow is able to eat fifty gallons of food, which is first processed in her rumen, the first chamber of her stomach.

Interestingly, one of the websites I visited when doing research on the anatomy and foods of cattle also provides information on the signs and symptoms of constipation in goldfish. (Yes, I'll admit it—the Internet can be wonderfully informative.)

Comox Valley Farmers' Market

The Comox Valley Farmers' Market is a great community gathering place as well as one of the most entertaining and diverse markets on the Island. Here, I was impressed to see locally made water buffalo yogourt. In addition to dairy, there is an immense array of unique and locally produced foods—everything from pink carrots to venison sausage and a delightful, delicate, knobby heirloom potato called a fingerling. This little potato, which does in fact resemble fingers—albeit slightly arthritic fingers—is absolutely delicious, especially baked with, as the song goes, parsley, sage, rosemary, and thyme. Especially delicious are crispy fingerlings prepared by boiling first, then slicing and baking them with a little oil, salt, and pepper.

A few years ago, the Canadian Food Inspection Agency decided to begin regulating and inspecting food items sold in markets and roadside stands; the result is that farm and homemade edibles are divided into two categories: banned, high-risk goods (such as baked beans, cabbage rolls, garlic spreads, and guacamole) and low-risk, regulated items (such as jams and jellies, honey, and baked goods). The latter list is monitored, tested, and tasted by inspectors, and the paperwork is extensive.

The farm stand is one of the great traditions alive and well on many of the Island's country lanes and rural areas. I love this system: It's based on the good old honour system, hard work, and efficient use of an abundance of produce and farm food.

I encourage you to venture out to any Vancouver Island farmers' markets and especially roadside stands, often referred to as "honesty stands," to seek out a food you have never consumed; perhaps it will have an intriguing name, or it may have an odd colour or shape. If you have any hesitation about your potential purchase, talk to the farmer and ask them for their recommendation on the best way to serve it. Then go for it! Who knows—it could introduce you to a whole new culinary world.

Courtenay train station

In the town of Courtenay, at the top of the hill, sits the little red abandoned railway station. Its bleached and weathered red paint is peeling off the old wood. The ticket counter window is broken, and paper coffee cups and other litter has blown into the long grass growing over the rusting tracks. Spindly shrubs are slowly enveloping the gravel parking area and the few rickety steps up to the waiting room. Hardy little sprouts of broom push through the railway ties.

There is something so melancholy about the disappearance of train stations. It seems the romance of rail travel has all but ended and is too time-consuming for most people. Slowness is not popular; people do not want aesthetic pleasure—they want speed and contemporary stimulation. This dawned on me when I started to notice the increasing rarity of hotel room bathtubs, hotel windows that open, and a hotel key that fits into a hole. Showers, air conditioners, and card swiping are more convenient.

We are still able however to travel across Canada by rail (albeit more as a tourist attraction rather than for utility). However, rail travel has been discontinued on the edges of both coasts, here on Vancouver Island and back east in the southern part of New Brunswick.

My friend Jane and I travelled up to Courtenay by the train a while ago, before the E&N rail line was discontinued. We had an absolutely delightful journey, drinking gin and tonics from our thermoses and reading novels as our lumbering yellow car rolled through the forests and over trestles, along the sea, and stopping briefly at the little stations all the way up the Island. I was reading *The Woman in White* (by Wilkie Collins) and felt particularly weepy, no doubt due to the gin, but also because of the romance of both the story and the rail journey.

This reminds me of a sad story that Mum told about Gran (her mother) who, as I have mentioned earlier, lived on Galiano Island here on the West Coast. Gran took the train, in winter, across Canada to visit us in New Brunswick where we lived. (Dad had a career there, as the artist in residence at the university.) I was about six or seven.

We were to pick Gran up at Fredericton Junction, in the freezing dusk, when the last golden light in the cold purple winter sky dimmed over bare black trees and meadows covered in snow. But earlier in the day, Mum had received a telephone call from a man with a French accent; he was calling from the Montreal train station.

"I have your mother here," he said. "She's having a bad day."

Then Gran took the phone. "Oh, Molly," she sobbed into the receiver. "I missed the train and I am terribly ill. It's my chilblains!"

As it turned out, the lovely stationmaster gave Gran a cup of tea and put her safely on the next train. (Can you imagine an Air Canada representative comforting you today with a cup of tea if you missed a plane? At most you would be put on standby, be given a voucher for a cold tuna sandwich wrapped in cellophane, which would be impossible to open, and told to "watch the screen" or "check your app" for the next available flight. You may or may not be offered a paltry rebate to get off the next flight due to overbooking.)

I was quite young when I knew Gran, and as a child, I did not realize that she was so emotional. Mum was emotional as well, but I am different: I have a certain objectivity, observing life from a distance. I would even call it a detachment of sorts, which in childhood I purposely cultivated. It is not something I can reverse, nor would I choose to if I could—not yet, at least. I greatly admire those who can share their feelings with their loved ones, especially their family.

As I mentioned in the introduction of this book: I left home on the train following my final day of high school, skipping my prom. I had finished high school by the skin of my teeth, earning a D in algebra with a C minus average overall. The best thing I learned in high school was how to swim. I had a wonderfully kind and patient physical education teacher who sat on the edge of the pool gently coaxing us to put our faces into the water and blow bubbles. After six weeks, I was jumping off the pool tower, and Bev Boyce, Canada's Olympic diver at the time, became my idol. I remember that she had short cropped blonde hair and she was large and muscular; she came from Pickering, Ontario.

I embarked on my train journey on a warm June evening. Dad drove his green Buick out to Fredericton Junction with Mum in the front seat and me in the back. We stood on the bare concrete platform alone, just the three of us as the sun faded (this time in early summer, not winter when Gran visited) over forests and rolling green meadows. I had one suitcase. The train hooted in the distance and then came chugging around the corner in the dusky air.

"Remember Anny," Dad said, giving me some last-minute advice, "never borrow money."

"Remember," Mum said, "you can always come home."

Later, on the train, I ate an egg sandwich that Mum had given me as I watched a gentle porter make my bed by folding down the seat. The sheets were crisp and white, and the bed was soft, like a cocoon. What a delightful way to leave home, being rocked to sleep while being carried across the country.

One of my favourite paintings is by the British artist J. M. W. Turner called *Rain, Steam, and Speed*. You can barely make out the train, but the painting evokes the romance and energy of its speed; you can almost hear the clacking of the cars racing past the Thames and smell the rain and soot in the air as it whips through the smoke of industrial London.

Comox

When I think of Comox, I can't help but think of my dear friend Lesley, who lives there. Les and I are childhood friends; our mothers were best friends who grew up together at Burnaby Lake, Vancouver.

Mum and Barbara—Lesley's mother (and my godmother)—worked together as young women at Yellow Point Lodge. It was their first summer job, and Mum told me that they "worked like slaves" doing laundry by hand, peeling carrots, and cleaning the outhouses (not always in that order), shucking oysters, and plucking chickens after Barbara's sister Bunty wrung their necks out back where the guests couldn't see.

Barbara married Ted Henderson, an Air Force pilot. When I was young, Ted called me Spitfire because of my temper, while their daughter, my good friend Lesley, was so sweet and serene. (We have not changed.)

Mum became a war artist overseas and met Dad there; they settled in New Brunswick where I was raised, but every spring I came out west and lived with the Hendersons while Mum and Dad travelled throughout Europe to paint.

When Mum and I flew from Fredericton to Vancouver, Barbara, with Les in tow, would pick us up at the airport. I was only five or six years old, and Vancouver was, to me, a magical fairyland—we'd always arrive at night to the smell of rain and sea and West Coast flora. The drive to West Vancouver sparkled with the big city lights, so unlike little Fredericton. We'd pass the fountain in Stanley Park's Lost Lagoon, all lit up as it sprayed its white mist into the night, and we'd cross Lions Gate Bridge, which looked like a palace with its lights reflected in the sea beneath. The entire drive ignited in my soul a lifelong passion for the West Coast.

Barbara smelled faintly of Pears or Allenburys soap, and she had an array of silver bangles on her tanned arms that rattled when she drove or worked in the kitchen. She and her family had a lovely cedar-scented home in West Vancouver that was of typical West Coast design: low, with a flat roof and large windows that looked out over the hazy blue harbour. There was a large grey stone fireplace in the spacious living room and a huge amber glass wine cask that had been artfully converted into a lamp. In the den were rattan stools with red vinyl seats.

Out back, beyond the hedge of rhododendrons, was a damp mossy wood of drooping cedars and salal. I spent my days playing with my trolls among the ferns, waiting for Les to come home from school—she was just a couple of years older than me. I set up elaborate tea parties on the front lawn surrounded by Barbara's rock garden in great antici-pation of her arrival, using an old decaying stump as the table. Barbara gave me a faded floral tablecloth, and the trolls and I, and a few of Les's stuffed bears, sat around the stump, pining for Les to appear, trundling up the gravel driveway with her heavy satchel from the little yellow stucco elementary school at the bottom of the hill.

In the seventies, Barbara and Ted moved from Vancouver to Comox and had a lovely, airy apartment on the main street, overlooking the marina at the end of the estuary where the Courtenay River meets the sea. They also had a cozy beach house on a sheltered bay close by. Ted used to put me on his back and swim; I vividly recall the back of his neck, which was soft and smooth, tanned and freckled. He'd also take us out to the reef in his rowboat; I was in awe of the beautiful, colourful undersea life as huge, succulent, orange and magenta sea anemones swayed their elegant tentacles in the clear current, and purple starfish clung fast, folded and squeezed on top of one another in rocky crevices.

Years later, Les and her husband, Mark, and their boy Justin moved to Comox. They lived on a pleasant residential street with a large back garden.

Ted had become very interested in health food, organics, and the environment during their time in Comox. One day, he was walking out of the grocery store with his bags of ingredients for a dinner party when, all of a sudden, he said, "Oh," and collapsed. (I hope I die that quickly when my time is up, perhaps from a fall off my horse). Mum wept heavily when I called her in Fredericton to tell her the news; he was the first of the four of them to go, and it no doubt felt like the end of their era. I think it shocked her far more than when Dad died (much later). With Ted, it was so sudden; none of us saw it coming, especially with all that health food.

Les's passion was to teach art to preschool-age children. She established an amazing little art school in her home, which she named the Roseberry Pre-School. (Roseberry was the street in West Vancouver where she grew up). It was not just any art school: Her school was spectacular, based on an Italian educational philosophy known as the

Reggio Emilia approach. Les even travelled to Italy to study the method based on the children's interests and their individual expression through art. When she returned, she transformed her spacious back garden into a magical fantasy land filled with treehouses, castles, tunnels, human-size bird nests, turrets, secret trails among the trees and ferns. Her friend from Hornby Island gave her a little house that looked like a hobbit abode, and the interior walls were made of mud; Les had her little artists embed costume jewellery and other treasures into the walls.

Inside her preschool were dazzling, colourful paintings—landscapes and portraits—as well as huge papier mâché sculptures, mobiles made from recyclables, collages, textiles, and wall hangings created by her young artists. Every space was filled with creativity, colour, and texture.

Les exhibited the work of her young students in Comox and called the show "The Group of Under Seven." Mum and I thought that was brilliant. And when the Comox municipal council planned to spray pesticides on the wild apple trees in the park, Les's devoted little students all dressed as lady bugs, bees, and garden grubs, and traipsed down to the Town Hall meeting. The little bugs and insects sat on the floor for two long hours as the parents convinced the council of the dangers of pesticides. Two years later, they won! The bylaw restricting the use of cosmetic pesticides is in effect—not only in Comox but in Courtenay and Cumberland as well. The Comox Municipal Hall distributes a detailed and informative brochure on the topic.

The Courtenay–Comox area is a curious blend of urban and rural sprawl, strip malls, old-town charm, agriculture, and development. It has become a desirable retirement area and is an environmentalist's haven. It's common to see a big box store, with its massive paved parking lot and array of orange lawn mowers, next to a restored watercourse or a meadow of wildflowers. There's a local kayak shop next to a fast-food chain, and a quaint little bookshop beside a discount furniture outlet full of vinyl recliners, giant television screens, and pressboard wine cabinets, all made offshore. (I'm pretty sure *offshore* usually means made in China, but I suppose offshore sounds so much more sophisticated.)

Comox, Courtenay, and Cumberland all share an interesting selection of second-hand shops full of knick-knacks. (I've always thought that knick-knack and bric-a-brac are perfect terms for cheap but oddly appealing junk.) It's easy to see the appeal of these stores—retired people move to new communities, shed clutter and downsize, and then take their wares to the stores to be picked over by eager bargain hunters.

There are some fabulous deals on furniture in thrift stores, but even so, I wonder: What is the universal appeal of knick-knacks? I think of my Uncle Ernie's wife, Elma, who collected souvenir spoons from everywhere, from Niagara Falls to Nashville. My friend's mother collected ceramic cats, and my friend's father collected beer mugs and shot glasses.

Perhaps it's a way to hold on to happy memories of a vacation; when you're back at home, whenever there's tension—say, you lose your job or are going through a divorce—you can look at your Miami Beach toothpick holder or your Dole Pineapple Plantation piggy bank and think, maybe things aren't so bad after all. I suspect we have an innate need not only for visual connection but also for tactile connection to our past joys and happy memories, an impulse to seek out possibility and connection and positivity through the acquiring of appealing items we can touch.

Knick-knacks bring me pleasure, a sense of security, and feelings of nostalgia; they make for a comforting, cozy home. (Mum hated knick-knacks, so every time she visited, I hid them.) A row of glass birds on the mantle or a variety of little vases on a shelf is so traditional in a retro kind of way—so evocative of the days of yore, when the living room was comfy and warm. Seeing knick-knacks makes me feel secure in the same way the aroma of the Sunday roast wafting through the home did. When I enter a thrift store, a great calm comes over me. I know for the next while I can quietly wander and search and rummage and possibly find a little treasure—an elegant lamp, or a glass fruit bowl, maybe a hooked rug, or hand-sewn quilt. (In 2016, I went through a doily phase.)

A while ago, I purchased a small summer cabin on the beach in Comox. Les, in great excitement, took me around to all the thrift shops so I could decorate the new place. With her grand sense of humour, she roared with laughter as she listed the shops' names, the most brilliant being Too Good To Be Threw, which is run by the Comox Transition Society. Another thrift store, the Treasure Shack, is run by an amusing, friendly woman named Christa, who is forever polishing the store's furniture. When we visited her establishment, she'd had a grand run of Empress Hotel desks, bar tables, and ashtrays. She told me that the strangest thing she ever sold was a bezoar, a hairball from a pig's stomach; people thought it was a petrified coconut or the ancient egg of an emu. Can you believe she sold it for forty-five dollars?

> A bezoar is an indigestible mass of high-fibre fruit and vegetables such as figs, berries, apples, coconut, corn, Brussels sprouts, and the skins of potatoes and tomatoes. So much for eating roughage! To add to the horror: bezoars don't just occur in pigs—they show up in humans, too. Oddly, Coca-Cola is known to be potent enough to dissolve the blockage.

On that grey, drizzly autumn day, when the clouds were low, Les and I drove from one knick-knack place to the other in Les's new keyless Mazda. I purchased a small coffee table at a consignment store that donates its proceeds to the Comox SPCA, and when we completed our outing in the late afternoon, Les drove me back to my cabin on the beach. There we had a glass of wine by the fire, using the newly purchased coffee table, as the fog and tide rolled in over the endless stretches of sand scattered with sea lettuce and clam shells.

The entrance to Comox and the I-Hos Gallery

When I consider the quiet, understated entrance to Comox—there are no ostentatious signs heralding your triumphant entry when you cross the bridge from Courtenay to Comox—I can't help but reflect on the different styles of entrances to cities, towns, and villages. The conventional attitude is that a town's welcome sign represents its pride and identity; it is there to make a good first impression. Some towns really go out of their way to encourage you to visit, with pretty signs on the road that say WELCOME, asking us to admire what's on offer, to drop in and have a coffee, and ultimately to say, "Wow, what a lovely place!" But Comox's entrance is, in my view, refreshingly modest.

When first entering the Comox area from Courtenay, turn right onto Dyke Road over the bridge that straddles the Courtenay River; this river flows into Comox Harbour, where the little town and its marina sit along its shores, but first it creates a wonderfully rich estuary. Just over the bridge on your right, you will see a large, abandoned paved area, the now empty and abandoned Field Sawmill, which has been purchased by Project Watershed, a volunteer organization that restores and protects watersheds and collects and maps data on the estuaries and watersheds within the Comox Valley. At the Field Sawmill lot, Project Watershed has partnered with the K'ómoks First Nation to restore the land, to "unpaved paradise" and connect it back to the nearby estuary.

In honour of the original First Nation village in this area, the K'ómoks have renamed the site Kus kus sum, which translates to "very slippery," referring specifically to the local seaweeds and algae, although the word's origin is still being researched according to Caila Holbrook of Project Watershed.

With government funding and citizens' donations, the project will rehabilitate the lands and provide stewardship and care of the river and estuary.

The word *K'òmoks* translates to "place of abundance," and through these local watershed restoration efforts and fine initiatives, abundance will surely return to the waterways throughout the Comox and Courtenay region.

A sturdy, attractive, well-maintained structure is on the right soon after the bridge. It is wheelchair accessible, has been freshly painted in a grey-green, and has a vast view over the estuary. Beyond, facing southwest, you can see the Comox Glacier, which never melts (we hope). The K'òmoks call this glacier *Queneesh*, which means "white whale," and that's exactly what it looks like with its great swath of snow that remains even on the hottest days of summer. The knowledgeable people at the I-Hos Gallery, just metres down the road, are happy to tell the tale of how Queneesh saved their people from a great flood.

This area just beyond the bridge and the lookout onto the estuary is on the traditional territory of the K'òmoks First Nation. The land is the site of an original K'òmoks village, with a unique entrance to the town that includes the beautiful I-Hos Gallery and information centre, adorned with intricately carved totem poles.

In the Coast Salish language, I-Hos translates to "sea serpent." The double headed sea serpent is known to the First Nation people as Sisiutl, one of the most powerful symbols of their culture. Sisiutl is the guardian of the supernatural world and offers protection and strength to the home. He also has great healing abilities and spiritual qualities. This is why many First Nations homes and facilities have the image of Sisiutl carved above their entrances.

In fact, the serpent has three heads—one in the middle and one on each end of its spreading appendages. The serpent is able to alter itself from an animal to a man. He is described as having sharp teeth and curled horns and resembles a mystical warrior and helper—such a lovely symbol, this blend of strength and protection.

Inside the spacious, airy building and tastefully lit rooms of the I-Hos Gallery, you can browse and enjoy numerous educational activities at specific times of the year, such as weaving a cedar hat using traditional methods and skills or crafting drums made from deer skin. During my visit to the gallery, the drum maker told me that deer skin, rather than elk skin, is used on the drums because deer skin is thinner, has fewer flaws, and is easier to work with.

While researching deer facts online, I noticed a number of advertisements for skin tightening and eye bag–reducing concoctions, right next to a picture of a moose's bulbous nose.

Strange . . . is that a coincidence? I wondered. Noting that I'd rather look like a moose than have a smooth, swollen top lip full of Botox, I casually clicked on an ad for a deer antler spray, thinking it must be something to either deter or attract the animal.

Oh, how wrong I was! It turns out that deer antler spray (and pills) are a breast and muscle enhancer used mainly by bodybuilders. If I read the ad correctly (yes, I was so disgusted that I skimmed the ad out of morbid fascination), the velvet of deer antlers contains a hormone that enhances human muscle, or skin, or energy, or something.

The side effects (this bit of information is always the most morbid part to read, so, of course, I had to) are breast growth or breast sensitivity as well as "behavioural changes"—including, perhaps, eating your neighbour's spring tulips?

Now, whenever I do an online search for any fact, I am plagued with pop-up ads for that deer antler velvet breast and muscle enhancer (and other useless products that are aimed at our private parts), which flash intermittently onto my computer screen. One of my friends, a computer expert, says that the computer probably took a photo of my face and, capturing the sagging, dark-blue skin under my eyes, catapulted the image through cyberspace, sending it to some great skin enhancement depot in "the cloud" where countless little cyber beings eagerly anticipate my inevitable purchase of a can of hormones.

The largest member of the deer family is the moose, most recognizable for its bulbous nose and huge rack of antlers. Elk and deer are ruminants, as is the moose—they all browse and graze, and their food is digested by a four-chambered stomach full of microorganisms; this helps them digest most plants, grasses, roots, and shoots. Both elk and deer mate in autumn; the off-spring of the deer are fawns, and the offspring of elk are called calves.

As members of the deer family, both elk and deer live in the forests of Vancouver Island, but they have distinct, differentiating characteristics—most prominently, they differ in size, voice, and coat.

Elk are larger, with a deep, loud, trumpeting call; deer have a delicate little bleat, with a sad, pleading, lonely tone. Elk have a thick, coarse coat; deer have a finer covering. And elk eat a variety of grasses and forest vegetation while deer (as any Island-dweller with a garden can confirm) prefer legumes, roses, and tulips.

Elk live in the Comox Valley. This is why, lining the highway, within a twenty-mile radius of the area, there are numerous signs alerting drivers to the presence of these majestic creatures.

The gallery offers an abundance of fabulous gifts created by many First Nation carvers, silversmiths, glass artisans, weavers, and blanket makers. I picked up a calendar that featured the work of Andy Everson; he's the artist who depicts those wonderful spawning salmon and hummingbird paintings that can be seen in numerous shops as cards or journal covers. There is also a variety of lotions and health products made from naturally healing ingredients such as peppermint, pine, and

nettle extract. I couldn't stop myself from purchasing a healing bracelet created by Indigenous artist Gordon White; the bracelet was made from lava (for grounding) and clear quartz (for clarity, which I seem to need more of as I head towards my golden years).

There is tea as well, hand gathered by a native Cree woman on Cormorant Island, a little further north. She picks forest flora and creates a variety of teas, which each have their own unique purposes and medicinal aids. My choice was an energy concoction although I was torn with a few—poor digestion, sore feet, dry skin, or a detoxer. My energy tea was mild and smooth with six types of clover as well as stinging nettle (nettles are extremely healthy and do not sting once cooked). After I drank it, I chopped a load of wood, cleaned the windows, and painted my office, all before the sun rose!

The Wild Harvest Native Teas pamphlet is full of testimonials, mainly from spouses!

One husband says that the tea saved his marriage because his wife drank it for her menopausal symptoms, and the wife writes that she served the husband the tea for insomnia, and he slept for ten hours straight! "What a relief" she says, "I bought ten more bags!"

With its jovial and helpful staff, a visit to this beautiful gallery and shop is the perfect activity to enjoy as you begin your visit to the town of Comox.

Estuaries

Arguably some of the most intriguing ecosystems on earth, estuaries are a mixture of fresh water from rivers and streams and saltwater from the sea; this creates the amber-brown brackish water that makes up these complex natural transition zones. The largest estuary in the world is Canada's own Saint Lawrence River, which is 1,197 kilometres long.

Estuaries in British Columbia are often the sites of rich fishing grounds due to the vast variety of food sources that attract fish to these valuable feeding sites. The estuary in the K'ómoks territory (across the road from the I-Hos Gallery and along Dyke Road) is also historically significant.

The remnants of K'ómoks fishing traps and weirs, some over one thousand years old, can be seen in the estuary—saturated, water-logged rotting posts poke their decaying, knobby heads out of the mud among the marshy grasses at low tide. These deteriorating, sodden stumps are part of a beautiful, symmetrical variety of patterns designed to lure, trap, and hold the fish in the days when the Indigenous people derived all their food from the land and the sea. The posts have been patiently mapped by archaeologist Nancy Greene (not the senator and Olympic champion) and her husband, David McGee, and their exquisitely detailed and precisely patterned maps can be seen at the Comox Archives and Museum on Comox Avenue, revealing the vast diversity of their shapes and patterns. One set of traps was constructed in a heart formation, another in an elongated funnel design; all were constructed to trap the various specific sizes and species of fish that visited the estuary.

Standing on the estuary's lookout platform in the drizzle and fog one autumn day, pondering those stumps in the white mist—once so useful, abundant with the winter's food supply for the village that was once on the shore and surrounding area—I thought of the modern-day, detailed, technical maps of the traps' patterns exhibited in the Comox museum in town. It felt good to think of how our Indigenous and non-Indigenous cultures can be appreciated together today through a shared passion for tradition, skill, and knowledge. Among other benefits, the mapping of these ancient fish traps also helps us to appreciate one another. Our mutually shared wisdom, through education, provides visual proof of how the First Nation people lived on the estuary shores.

The K'ómoks First Nation land comprises the territory between the land just after the bridge and the land just beyond the I-Hos Gallery. The road that travels along this stretch is Dyke Road, which becomes Comox Avenue as you leave the traditional lands. When Comox Road was built along the last stretch of the estuary leading to the town of Comox, a dyke was constructed along the estuary to prevent spring flooding. Alas, along with development—in this case a paved road—comes a challenge to the environment. The dyke looks like not much more than a mound of mud, but it is indeed a dyke. It can be clearly seen at low tide when it is covered in seabirds, all squawking and singing, cackling, and chirping as they peck and poke for their dinners and suck what they find from the nutritious silt of the river and tide. A sign on the platform describes the blue heron feeding times, calling to mind the mad rush of a Boxing Day sale at a big box store—though here we see birds shopping out of necessity rather than greed, and without the useless violence of pushing and shoving and sometimes trampling. Other educational signage explains the estuary's ecosystem, including the challenge of controlling our Canada goose population and their impact on this important feeding site.

Beyond the beautiful I-Hos Gallery and the estuary, the municipal signage marking the entrance to Comox gives us very little. The actual boundary of the town is halfway up a wooded hill crowned by a yellow-brick, flat-roofed hospital, which is now the site of an extended care facility and hospice. Comox has a brand-new state-of-the art hospital, a huge, gleaming green-and-white facility up by the big box stores and endless retail outlets.

Comox Road turns into the main street of the town. Here you'll find all manner of amenities, including a hair salon called Urban Hair. I wondered what I might come out with if I asked them for rural hair or a suburban style.

If you enjoy strolling around towns—as I do—to acquire a feel for the place, then picking up a walking routes brochure is a good idea, and they are fun to follow. Comox has a glossy walking-tour map that offers several options. I chose the one that began with the famous Cumberland donut at the Church Street Bakery. It was a good choice: the famous Cumberland donut was delicious, light, and doughy, not too fatty. The bakery also offers a variety of sweet and savoury baked goods, and, of course, their offering of daily bread.

I love it when a town says that a particular food is famous or, even better, world famous; it reminds me of the time I took Mum on a road trip through southern New Brunswick. One bright, brisk day, when the leaves were turning to scarlet and gold, we drove through Fundy Park and came upon a tiny seaside town which sat by the red, muddy, murky Fundy shores. Fishermen were hauling in their nets, and although Mum was losing her sight, she spotted a hand-painted sign on the road that read: STOP HERE FOR OUR WORLD-FAMOUS CLAM CHOWDER. *How could we resist? We pulled over, and the chowder was indeed divine—not too thick with starch and cream, but in a broth, chockful of seafood and thankfully free of sand, shells, and gritty crunchy bits.*

From the Church Street Bakery, I continued on my walking tour, which sends participants ambling through parks, woodland, and seascapes. A major natural feature of Comox is Goose Spit, called Pelxqikw (which means "round on point") by the K'ómoks. It gracefully curves (as spits do) into Comox Bay like a long, protective arm. (Spits are often confused with sandbars, but they're not the same thing—a sandbar joins land on both ends, often forming a lagoon).

Pelxqikw/Goose Spit is 2.5 kilometres long and is a provincial park. One of its most crucial purposes is as a migratory bird stop, heavily used by the brant goose. This plump goose is not to be confused with the Canada goose, who usually do not migrate but prefer to eat in farmers' fields and city parks for twelve months a year.

Spits, like estuaries, are extremely sensitive ecosystems due to their ever-changing transitional landscapes. The spit is always in flux, continually shifting, depending on the winds, currents, tides, and geographical features both above and below the tidal zone. The life it supports within the salty grasses, sedges, dunes, seaweeds, silt, and everything else that drifts, collides, blows, and settles there supplies countless necessities and nutrients for many birds and creatures. Goose

Spit is fed by the Willemar Bluffs, where up to six metres of debris and erosion a year can add to the spit.

> Formed by shifting winds and tides that angle the sands, land deposits, erosions, freshwater flows, and sediments, spits grow and extend vast, graceful, curving arms, the longest in the world being the Arabat Spit in the Ukraine. Formed in the Sea of Azov at 112 kilometres long and 0.270 to 8 kilometres wide, this massive spit housed, at its tip, a seventeenth-century military fortress built by the Turks. The longest freshwater spit is in Canada at Long Point in Lake Erie, forty kilometres long and a kilometre wide at its widest point.
>
> Many spits are protected wildlife and conservation areas; a good number serve as protective harbour beacons with working lighthouses. Others are military settlements, due to their strategic locations, and still others are popular tourist site, built up with boat marinas and hotels, such as La Manga in Spain.

A spit is most breathtaking at low tide when the vast, seemingly endless beach reveals how small, in every way, we actually are. The infinite sky and beach and ocean are all you can see—except, of course, at Goose Spit, the Department of National Defence property, all wind-swept and sand-beaten, looking slightly derelict among the surrounding salty grasses and the rickety, rusting chain-link fence at the far end. It's a strange sight, but it works—Mother Nature's creation blending with the sun-bleached, pockmarked cement structures meant to defend us.

The defence compound is in use as a summer cadet base. (Last time I was there, it looked as though there was some office work going on in the building. Behind the automatic gate, there was a young soldier dressed in dark green trousers; he looked as if he was wondering how close he was to his coffee break.) In the distance, you can see HMCS *Quadra*, a decommissioned naval ship patiently waiting for a new purpose.

Filberg Heritage Lodge and Park

Just down the road and up the hill from Goose Spit is Filberg Heritage Lodge and Park. This nine-acre property was once owned by a wealthy businessman, Robert Filberg, who, like many other wealthy businessmen on the Island, made his money in the logging and railway ventures. The informative brochure at the site provides an outline of Filberg's personal history and alludes to his rather amusing personality, as reflected in the décor of the various rooms in his home, which you can tour.

Originally from Sweden, Robert's parents were in the sewing business. Sadly, when Robert was only ten years old, Robert's father, Adolph, died while searching for gold up north. When Robert grew up, he played his cards right and married his boss's daughter, Florence. They started building their house in 1929 but didn't complete it until 1935. Why did it take so long? Apparently Robert was a kind man, and during the Depression he stretched out the labour to keep the locals employed.

Robert died in 1977 and generously left his beautiful property and unique home, overlooking Goose Spit and distant shores, to the public for our enjoyment. The house displays many features that are unique, amusing, creative, and even a bit eccentric. Embedded in the stone fireplace, for example, there are two smooth round stones; one is a rock and the other is a cannon ball, but I could not spot the difference between the two; that was one of Robert's fun little games. To the right of the fireplace is a petroglyph of a frog, estimated to be over one thousand years old, which Robert found washed up on the beach.

Robert constructed his staircase from repurposed Douglas fir railway ties. In his living room there is an absolutely massive sofa, but the most remarkable feature in the house, in my view, is his pink-and-gold art deco-style bathroom, designed in the same style of his stateroom on the ship, the *Queen Mary*. Imagine designing your bathroom after a room on a ship!

And then there is the gift shop upstairs, but really, it is very difficult to tell the household items and relics from the items for sale. Mrs.

Filberg loved her teacups, watercolours, and needlepoint, and there's dozens of them upstairs. Some are hers, and some are for sale, all scattered among teddy bears, old books, quilts, and elegant furniture. If you shop, you may very well go home with one of Mrs. Filberg's doilies.

Mack Laing Nature Park

Close to the Filberg property is Laing Park. Hamilton Mack Laing, whose home was built on this property in 1950, was as environmentally astute as Filberg was creatively eccentric. Laing was, among other things, an ornithologist. A naturalist of the finest type, he hailed from Ontario and settled at this lovely waterfront home which he named Shakesides. A little plaque in the tall wispy grass declares this A VERY BIRDY PLACE. Laing's meadows, glades of poplars and aspens, wild rose shrubs, pebble beaches, and a meandering brook provides a perfect sanctuary for migrating birds, spawning salmon, and a variety of wildlife who amble, paddle, quietly munch, and rest in this gentle sanctuary among the snowberries, trumpet honeysuckles, wild currants, and other flora. Another plaque tells visitors that the wildflowers are SWEET CICELY, FAIRY BELLS, and YELLOW WOOD VIOLET, all of which sprout at random in the grass, sedges, and moss and along the creek side.

Mr. Laing was born in 1883 and died in 1982. I feel that his peaceful, gentle, elegant property is very much like he himself would have been, humbly wedged between the Filberg property on one side—in such contrast to its cannonballs and giant sofa and doilies and pink art deco toilet—and MacDonald Woods on the other side, which was fought for, tooth and nail, with the neighbours mortgaging their properties and money lent by famous but very private heiresses, which I will tell you about now.

MacDonald Wood

The MacDonald Wood is a ten-acre forest that blends into Mr. Laing's pastoral property. The forest paths meander throughout the towering firs and cedars, bushy salals, and giant lush ferns. Skunk cabbages fill the low, damp hollows, and rotting stumps and logs provide the musky, pungent, woody aroma as they slowly break down to become part of the fertile forest floor as nature intended. Can you imagine the billions of microbes feasting beneath such a log? The sun sends shafts of cool, golden light between the great boughs above, just as Emily Carr would have seen and depicted in her heavenly (and earthly) paintings. But these woods were not always so serene: they were once for sale and sold to a developing company who had big plans—one hundred waterfront condominiums!

Just on the other side of the woods sits a small, rustic gathering of original homesteads blended with modest houses and cabins. Here you will find old fruit trees, chickens, wild gardens, and ancient, rescued dogs who patiently wait at the edge of the narrow lanes while their owners, in rubber boots, stop to chat about the neighbourhood woodpecker, or the approaching storm, and trade eggs for apples. The neighbours also keep a watchful eye on the lovely woods at the end of the lane—after all, they fought hard to save it.

My friend, Anne Gardner, a retired speech therapist, led the fight which began one early grey dawn in the late 1990s, when she and her neighbours awoke to the sounds of chainsaws at the end of the lane. War was declared, and there was no peace treaty for five years: The local residents blocked the road. This summoned a local police officer whose solution was to send everyone home. This set Anne to work.

Anne took me on a lovely forest stroll through these serene woods as she explained the long, arduous journey she and her neighbours embarked upon (with assistance from all levels of government) to buy the woods. The endeavour stretched over five years of bake sales, community dances, food booths, and tree adoptions, which included the privilege of having one's ashes spread beneath their adopted tree. As I listened, we wandered across little bridges and boardwalks that crossed Brooklyn Creek (the same creek that runs through what was the Laing property) and under the canopy of the damp growth above; we climbed over and around nurse logs that provide habitats and nutritious meals through mosses, lichens, and fungi to the forest floor; we stopped to chat with a man in a yellow slicker, who enthusiastically told us that the salmon were beginning to pool below. By this time, I was mentally exhausted from her tale of the efforts to obtain the woods, but was I ever impressed that they did it!

Soon we reached the shore and ambled along the pebbled beach that blended into a meadow of rust and ochre sedges on the foreshore where several deceased and decaying salmon lay after expiring from their own journey home to spawn. Like rotting forest debris, the salmon's bodies slowly merged with the soil and grasses, taking their place in the life cycle of the earth. I contemplated this cycle as I passed their limp bodies, covered in grey-yellow skin, like thin, wrinkled threadbare sheets, their little jutting mouths still open after taking their final gasps. The incredible urge of salmon to return to spawn at their exact place of birth, in the very gravel hollow that their mother created years before, is, to me, one of nature's most moving and awe-inspiring events.

As we stood in the light drizzle, Anne and I had a lively discussion about the sport of catch and release. This type of fishing requires the fisherman to, as the name suggests, not keep the fish caught; instead, after playing with it on the hook until the fish is exhausted, the fisherman releases the fish back to the water. But here is the catch, so to speak: That poor salmon is already exhausted, spent from its journey from the sea, from its escape from eagles and whales, from the transition to fresh water, from lack of food, lack of oxygen, navigating between the massive, grasping paws of hungry bears, and from summoning all its final energy to leap over rocks and waterfalls to arrive at its birthplace to spawn, desperately seeking its little gravel pocket, its final resting place in which to either lay or fertilize eggs. And now, if it has an ounce of energy left in its weakened body, it must struggle on a hook for the pleasure of man. Are we hardwired to pursue recreational pleasure by harming other creatures, all in the name of sport? I don't know the answer to that, but this was our shared rant, and Anne and I stand by it.

Middens

Along the shore at the bottom of MacDonald Woods, hidden under centuries of tidal, wind, forest, and the earth's debris, lies an untouched First Nation midden. Most of us know that middens are, in simple terms, locations, most often coastal, in which Indigenous people disposed of their food scraps. Layers of clam and other mollusc shells are the first examples that most often come to mind, and that is usually where we stop thinking about middens. But there are more to middens than the disposal of shells. Often dating back five thousand years, a midden can be a treasure trove for archaeologists as they can discover not only the traditional cultures of the Indigenous peoples, but also botanical and geographical knowledge; in this way, a midden can be a rich source of natural history.

The debris in a midden goes beyond that of shells; some definitions of middens translate to "dung heaps." While that can sound rather off-putting, dung, or human and animal waste, provides meaningful insight into human biochemistry, food sources, and flora and fauna availability at a specific time. Also found in middens are ash and burned soil, which indicates human habitation rather than a deposit from a land shift or earthquake.

A midden is the original and most wonderful system of recycling. Decomposition is a crucial part of how we live and connect with nature. What would be in your midden today?

Years ago, during the time that awareness of First Nations middens were receiving attention due to their historic and cultural value, I was an elected councillor in a rural municipality close to Victoria. Our council was somewhat divided on opinions regarding housing and business development, particularly on or close to the shore. The subject of midden protection arose. There was an elderly councillor whom I respected, but with whom I constantly disagreed. Whenever he spoke about middens, he said "mittens," which sent me into silent hysterics on my tall vinyl seat behind the wooden dais that (wrongly) gave the sense that we were elevated above those not elected. (I always felt that to govern, at any level, the system might operate better if the council or government chambers were set up more like a living room—a warm den, perhaps, with lamps, a fireplace, and ottomans.)

Our discussions on the tender, vulnerable foreshore and middens continued for days. "Is there any way we could negotiate removing the mittens?" the councillor asked. "Mr. Mayor, could we consider constructing the marina around the mittens?" And then, to my great delight: "Perhaps we could create a mitten park, a mitten historic site, with interpretive signage . . ."

Did you know it takes six months for an orange peel to decay? Or that a cigarette butt takes twelve years, and a plastic bag up to a thousand years?

In Scotland, there are signs on the hiking trails that request you take home your banana peels (it takes two years for them to break down). This fact reminds me of a visit I took to Mount Fuji in Japan, where a sign posted at the base asked all hikers to please not leave their soiled toilet paper on the trails. That struck me as odd until I realized that to hike to the peak required more than twenty-four hours.

Also—and yes, this is related—did you know there is a model referred to as the Odour Wheel?

Briefly, it is made up of "smell families" (sounds like an American reality television show), a legitimate paradigm of decomposition created by scientists as a method of categorizing odours which emit from composting facilities, often the source of complaints from citizens who are downwind from the pong. (I love the word pong— it's an old British word used to describe a pungent stench.)

There seems to be a diverse collection of smells on a variety of odour wheels, ranging from very academic and scientific, to somewhat informal and descriptive, addressing such stenches as wet dog, boar taint, and perm solution.

Here's a fun activity: Make a wheel of pongs in your home and neighbourhood. List the odours as well as the pleasant aromas and fragrances, and then describe the smells. Kids will love it, and it makes for fine conversation!

Kye Bay

A short distance away is a little-known but spectacular beach and park area close to the Comox airport. It is a lovely bike ride down Lazo Road from the town centre of Comox, but it's a bit far to walk. Comox is fairly spread out, and a car is necessary.

At Kye Bay you will find a combination of rustic beach cabins and a few higher-end homes, small resorts, and pocket parks, all overlooking an immense stretch of sand where the shallow sea breaks across a faraway reef in the distance—one which you are able to reach at low tide. Across the water in the hazy distance is Powell River; you can also see Texada Island where, on a clear day, you'll observe a swath of large, barren, sloping rock that marks the quarry. It has ceased operation but has become a popular swimming destination for the locals—and for visitors, too, if you are able travel to this abandoned limestone landscape.

Kye Bay is magical at low tide (tide tables are easy to read and are accessible in the local newspaper or on your devices). The never-ending expanse of sand will have you awestruck—you can walk out more than a kilometre, and the water will still be gently lapping at your knees. Warm, shallow tidal pools shimmer like jewels and are filled with low tidal life and glimmering little treasures—busy little flounders, flat with a lovely symmetrical body camouflaged as sand, dart among mauve and cobalt shells, pearly white stones, sand dollars, and amber, emerald, and auburn seaweeds. Tiny crabs crawl and flow sideways down the trickling streams to the sea from the pools. There is so much life teeming at low tide that, at times, I am hesitant to tread! Many times I have felt the pangs of guilt when I trod on a living creature that was minding its own business, innocently and patiently resting until the cover of water returned.

> The flounder is a fascinating fish in terms of physical growth and maturity—especially when it comes to its head. As the young flounder develops, its skull twists, and one eye actually shifts to the other side of its head. One wonders what evolutionary necessity was present for such a trait have occurred in this particular creature.

One of the most delightful aspects of Kye Bay takes place in the summer during the afternoon low tides. Young families make their way to the sand, carrying colourful kites and plastic pails, air mattresses, beach toys, towels, and canvas bags full of sandwiches, thermoses of tea, and lemonade. By lunchtime, the entire expanse of white sand is dotted with little groups of umbrellas and deck chairs and happy children building castles or squealing as the cool waters lap at their ankles. In England they refer to these happy clusters as "holiday-makers." Going to the seaside for a day at the beach (perhaps with a pink peppermint stick) is a charming, traditional pastime, free of admission fees. When I was young and we lived in England, Mum would take me to the beach; I remember carrying a little red bucket and shovel, and in the distance, on the sand there were donkeys which, for a pence, you could ride, and they wore big floppy sun hats.

One summer, at the end of the lane at Kye Bay, an enterprising teenager, a relative of one of the beach cottage owners, converted an iconic airstream trailer into a quirky ice-cream stand.

I have travelled extensively and have come to the conclusion that a little beach visit provides the best option for rest, rejuvenation, and revitalization. Beach excursions make the perfect breaks and mini-vacations that we all seem to need and desire.

> I have what I call a Three-B Vacation formula for getting away from it all on Vancouver Island: Beach, Book, and Beverage. Here's how it works:
>
> 1. Select a beach—any beach, at any location you are able to access.
>
> 2. Select a book or two or more—and I mean traditional paper books, not e-books. Going analog rather than digital adds to the aesthetic pleasure of the Three-B experience. If you are unfamiliar with books (as many busy people are), just take along anything to read, even a children's book, one of those appalling adult colouring books (there's something quite embarrassing about this trend but I just cannot pinpoint what it is), or a magazine.
>
> 3. This speaks for itself: Take your beverage of choice.

If you find it difficult to relax, try it for only an hour, like a little test. Just sit there and read as you sip your drink—maybe even close your eyes and breathe deeply now and then. Give your vision, and all the tension that occurs from seeing things, a vacation too, if even for a few moments, and allow your hearing to be receptive. You'll be amazed at the rhythms and flow of nature that you hear; there are so many diverse sounds that float around us, concealed and flooded out by visual distraction and the clamour of modern life.

Savour and treasure this feeling, this experience, and call it up again later when you are standing on a scuffed turquoise carpet in a long, hot line at immigration (usually immediately after three jumbo jets have arrived from other faraway countries), perspiring and terrified that you'll be caught with fifty more dollars in goods that you are allowed to bring home. Recall the peace you felt that day near the beach when your passport jams in one of those new machines with the flashing green lights because you inserted it backwards as other tourists stream past, looking at you with judgment and disgust for being so technically incompetent and holding up the lines. Invoke the peace of the ocean when sitting under fluorescent lights in a beige waiting room at midnight after being told your flight is three hours delayed. Close your eyes and recall what the sounds on your Three-B Vacation brought you when your eyes are too strained to read, and your stomach is too bloated due to the huge greasy burger you ate just hours ago during the first delay.

The good news is that the peaceful oceanside space you inhabited, however long ago it may have been, is still there inside you, even when you're stuck in line at security, temperature and blood pressure rising, loaded down with hand luggage, a tangled scarf around your hot, sticky neck, documents under your arms or held between your teeth, delayed behind a person who has misplaced their boarding pass, searching for that little plastic bag of toothpaste and other gels and creams, any of which could potentially explode if over a hundred milligrams. I seem to be randomly selected every single time by a bell and a red flashing light, as if I was the lucky big-money winner on *Let's Make a Deal*, chosen to enter the scanner, a device that reminds me of Dr. Who's TARDIS, cutting me off from the world while someone looks right through me. (I've always wondered why they cannot combine the security scanner with some sort of cancer detection device that we all dread—why not go through security and at the same time have a mammogram and even a test towards the lower, nether-regions? They already have the gloves on and are swabbing us anyway. Can't they just do all that business and send the results directly to the doctor?) I thought my idea was pure genius until I heard someone on the CBC radio program *This Is That* suggest the very same thing.

Still, it does seem like a very practical proposal.

Every time I am in that glass tube with my arms up and legs apart, I wonder if they can detect anything in my body other than hatchets, gunpowder, lighter fluid, handcuffs, duct tape, propane torches, pruning shears, kindling, barbecues, lassos, bear spray, smelling salts, whoopee cushions, whiskey, martini glasses, parachutes, meathooks, garden trowels, smart phones, antifreeze, and maple syrup.

Of course, the more manual, albeit personal, method is to go for the pat-down, in which our armpits and nether-regions, our bodily crevices and cavities, are probed, then swabbed by a woman wearing rubber gloves.

So, I'm not saying that airport travel should not occur—I'm just suggesting that our local beaches may be the preferable holiday option—and at the beach, you can take liquids in any amount.

There is also a misconception that the ideal vacation is a warm one, but for some more than others, there are times when it's not rest that we need, but rather stimulation. When this is the case, an invigorating winter beach storm (enjoyed a generous, safe distance from rogue waves) will more than suffice. All you have to do is purchase some rubber pants, boots, and hankies; tie a scarf around your ears, make sure your water-resistant coat has nice, deep pockets, and venture out on a stormy day to experience nature's beautiful volatility. Turn your face towards the blustery, steely sea—people pay a lot for fancy facial exfoliation, but a salty beach tempest is way less expensive and will awaken your senses in a superior fashion. It's fantastic physical exercise as well, trudging over the sands, arcing your body into the winds as nearby trees sway and bend, and seabirds float and hover on the surging air currents above. (Be very careful in the woods, though—the odd loose limb may come crashing down to the forest floor and break its fall on your head.)

Embracing adversity through weather can be a remarkable

psychological tonic. Think of how children become excited at the first snowfall. "Batten down the hatches" is said with an edge of glee and amusement at the first autumn windstorm. And there's the shared delight when we see those high November tides, known as king tides, crashing onto the shore, throwing down tangled, knee-deep heaps of kelp and seaweed.

We all know that we feel better when we connect with nature, but we also frequently forget this simple cure for sluggishness and lack of motivation. (I am not referring to a chemical, clinical depression, but a more general malaise that occasionally looms and lurks, just waiting for that vulnerable moment to bear down on us, often without warning.)

Even grey days are beneficial, giving us rest and time for reflection. And Mother Nature helps us forget ourselves, gently urging us to take ourselves less seriously by reminding us of our minuscule existence. What a paradox—nature can cause us to reflect and to empty our minds even while infusing our senses, our very being, with an immense inner joy.

When Peggy Lee sings, "Is this all there is?" I answer, "Well, Peggy, my friend, have you ever walked the seashore on a stormy day? For that will provide you with your answer." Yes, this *is* all there is, but what a tremendous "all there is" there is! There is nothing, and yet there is everything.

I believe we have a deep, primal instinct to be at one with nature. We are drawn to it—it is no coincidence that people are awestruck at sunrise and sundown, staring mesmerized at the pink sky streaked with gold, some with cameras, some simply sitting on a beach log lost in the beauty of the rising or fading glow.

So the next time you feel a bit down, or dare I say bored, or wonder, like Peggy Lee, "Why are we here?" get yourself to the seashore—the stormier the better (again, taking care to stay safe), and you shall feel invigorated, renewed, restored, and at one with nature, at one with the kelp, the pebbles, the wind, and those dark azure-green waves. The question of why you are here will not matter nearly as much as your time in Mother Nature's world—a world you came from and are part of. Nature does not discriminate. She is there for all of us, rain or shine, at any time of day that we choose to see her.

There's a wonderful, informative book titled *Marine Life of the Pacific Northwest* by Andy Lamb and Bernard P. Hanby. It is a fabulous compilation of sea life that you may encounter on our West Coast, whether swimming, paddling, beach-combing, or simply observing and breathing in the ocean air. I spent a delightful, amusing afternoon by the fire after a stormy beach walk, thumbing slowly through the lovely photographs in this book, taking note of the following list of sea life and creatures that reside on our beaches, in tidal pools, or squeezed into rock crevices hiding deep under the waves.

Let's begin with two beautiful names: the moon jelly and the mermaid's gloves. And now for the rather unmentionables: the retractable nipple sponge, the clapper hydroid, the tiny green balls, the humpy shrimp, the pubescent crab, the pink beach hopper, the furry and white knee hermit, and the spiny lumpsucker.

Now, for those that could be creepily lurking in the shadows like a clown behind a circus tent, I give you the hooded nudibranch, the perverse whelk, the unstable limpet, and the eccentric sand dollar!

We mustn't forget those named after household features and cloth-ing: the shag rug, the seersucker kelp, the bushy Turkish washcloth, the stiletto shrimp, and the mosshead warbonnet.

The Snowbirds

Every April, the Snowbirds migrate to Comox—no, not retired humans, nor the lovely white-feathered goose or swan, but the nimble aerobatic airplanes. They come here to practice over the great expanse of white sand, much to the delight of many local residents. Twice a day we are treated to a free spectacular air show, albeit at ear-shattering levels. The nine little red jets spend hours making hearts, spirals, plumes, circles, and crossovers from the many patterns and manoeuvres in their repertoire. Their precision and skill are such that when they fly into an arc together over the white-capped blue-green sea below and fall like arrows in perfect synchronization, the breakaway looks like petals falling from a flower. It gives the impression that there is only one plane remaining (if you're viewing from a certain angle), just a knife quietly slicing through the air until the planes all gracefully reunite, seemingly from nowhere, their engines roaring once again.

The pilots fly at close to six hundred kilometres an hour, and often only four feet apart. These experienced Canadian Air Force pilots have the squadron motto *the Hatiten Ronteriios*, meaning "Warriors of the Air." Moose Jaw, Saskatchewan, is their home base, where they train in the winter months and choreograph their amazingly precise patterns.

Every time I think of Moose Jaw, I remember how, after Dad died, Mikki and I drove his car—an enormous, ugly Toyota Venza—across Canada from Fredericton to Victoria. We stopped in Moose Jaw and had an ice cream under a huge prairie sky as we sat among the historic stone buildings on the gritty main street.

I took an underground tour called "The Chicago Connection," which iu un.ioted Al Capone's bootlegging antics from the 1920s in Moose Jaw's dark and mysterious tunnels under the city.

Mikki took the other tour, which centred on Moose Jaw's local Chinese history; this led participants through the dark tunnels and dank laundries and opium dens, a significant and melancholy part of Canadian history.

Although the Snowbirds accomplish breathtaking aerobatic feats, there have been accidents and deaths, several during live performances.

When flying upside down at great speeds at less than five feet apart, an unexpected gust of wind, or a momentary loss of concentration, a bird, or a split second of blinding glare could mean disaster.

At the Kye Bay beach in Comox, people gather with their binoculars and tripods in little groups on the hill between the parked cars, watching the twirls and whirls under the roar of the nine jet engines; others venture onto the sand to gaze upwards at the spectacle.

I am in awe of the calculations and control, the physics, the skill, and the precision, but I am simultaneously horrified at the engines' roar, not to mention the risk of a pilot perishing, as well as the shaking and shuddering of the houses and the baby blue herons in their high tree-top nests, and the terrified dogs on the sand.

On a sunny April morning, I met an elderly man on Kye Beach. It was a chilly day, with a sharp sea breeze, but even so, the man wore baggy khaki shorts over his scrawny, red knobby knees. Squinting at the little red planes about to break out of a huge, perfectly symmetrical starburst formation, he murmured, "Beautiful, absolutely beautiful."

A few minutes later, a lady in a large straw hat walked by with her little dog and said, "All that money spent on these air shows when there's so many homeless! All that fuel falling into the ecosystem—can you smell it? I can smell it! Oh, the poor birds, and right at nesting time."

And so it goes, the two views: yin and yang, comedy and tragedy, inhale and exhale, ebb and flow, good and evil, light and dark. Everywhere you go, there it is.

If you'd like to see a Snowbird jet up close, there is one at the Comox Information Centre on the main road out of town leading to the Trans-Canada Highway.

Nymph Falls

This breathtaking, spellbinding nature park is a fifteen- or twenty-minute drive out of Comox heading north. The lovely forest path will take you to the shores of the Puntledge River, where salmon ladders have been installed to assist the fish in their upriver journey. The river itself is formed from glacial runoff and winter snowpack.

After you amble through the shady woods on the impeccably maintained trails (which, I noticed, features community-made signage), you will come across the spectacular, stunning, shallow falls and rapids that thunder and cascade over extensive sandstone slabs, ledges, and bedrock shelves of various heights, creating a diversity of colour, sound, and visual awe. You may just find yourself hypnotized by the churning mass of pearly, turquoise wash and spray, which then flows into deep, dark, silent pools; here, you can swim after you sun yourself on the warm stone.

Although the water does not drop from an impressive precipice or great height, as it does at Elk Falls (farther north at Campbell River), the Nymph site is, for me, far more interesting, with its more diverse rock formations and water flow. I love the shimmering blend of blues and whites, shadows and light, and I am soothed by the sounds of the rushing water that pools and gurgles between the ledges, crevices, and boulders.

Nymph Falls is also a hydroelectric spillway, which means that there are times when the water flow is controlled from the dam upstream at Comox Lake. Apparently, when the water is allowed to flow higher and faster, a siren is set off, which indicates to any in the vicinity that there is a very real danger of being swept off the rocks, possibly falling to your death. YOU MUST EVACUATE IMMEDIATELY, the sign says.

Well, I'm not sure I could relax on those warm rocks knowing that I might meet my maker as I tumble down the river over those colossal stones, through the whitewash, and finally spill into the estuary fronting the Comox Pub, my lifeless body eventually found wedged in the mud by kayakers enjoying an afternoon paddle. That may be the reason I write down all my Little Thinks: Otherwise, if I don't hear that siren, and I have drifted off on one of those warm rocks, all that will remain will *be* my remains; all my Little Thinks would simply float away and evaporate into the universe and mingle with all the other little thoughts floating around through space and time. My Little Thinks may blend with those of my two heroes, Darwin and Catherine the Great as well!

Mount Washington

Most of us think of Mount Washington as a winter ski resort, perhaps the most popular on Vancouver Island. The Island is one of the few places where you can snowshoe through a pristine white woodland in the morning, and kayak off the Comox beaches in the afternoon; you can even swim the same day you've been in the snow, if it's a warm April day.

A forty-minute drive north from Comox (most of the drive is actually up the mountain), Mount Washington is part of the extensive, Strathcona Provincial Park. On a snowy winter day, skiing, tubing, and snowshoeing through the powder, with the view of the coastal mountains rising from the lavender mist in the distance, are fabulous, fun, and refreshing activities. A summer or autumn hike on the same mountain is just as rewarding an activity.

Part of the surprise and delight of a walk through the trails of the alpine meadows and mountain woodland, known as Paradise Meadows, is the completely unexpected landscape; one thinks that a mountain would be blanketed in pristine snow, but it is much more diverse and interesting in the warmer months. If you've never experienced an alpine scene in person, Mount Washington is the place to go. The hikes are easy—especially the Centennial Trail Loop. (Paradise Meadows was lovingly worked on by volunteers for fifteen years to make paradise barrier-free with its wheelchair-accessible gravel paths and boardwalks and lack of stairs.) In addition to beautiful trails, which are stunning and educational, there are pristine lakes along the routes in which to cool down, dip your hot toes, and to sit and have a snack while relaxing on the little wooden docks.

On your walk—and there are a variety to choose from—you will encounter our sociable and jovial national bird, the whiskey jack or grey jay. These friendly birds will fly from the branches of the hemlocks, cedars, and firs and perch confidently on your shoulders!

A highlight of the alpine landscape is the low-lying wetlands, usually referred to as the alpine meadows. Indeed, they do look like lush meadows when dry in the summer; in the autumn they are a wave of crimson, gold, and deep magenta. Often wet and marshy, they are in fact fens (not to be confused with bogs). The beautiful brochure for sale at the Wilderness Centre near the parking lot clarifies the definition of a fen as that which "receives water and/or groundwater as its source of moisture, whereas a bog receives direct precipitation." Either way, the nature of the alpine meadows are unique and spectacular.

The easiest walk is to Battleship Lake, beginning from the parking lot and the little information cabin, the "Wilderness Centre." I ambled up to the lake and back with my friend Les, and my banker, Brenda, in under two hours, taking photos of the saucy whiskey jacks and the three of us dangling our hot feet into the cool lake as we sat on a nice sturdy dock. Most of the trail is over the beautifully maintained boardwalk that winds its way around the fens and meadows, through the trees, and over streams; it is easy to follow with excellent signage.

The brochure I picked up before setting out gives directions and clear guidance on an alternative and equally easy trail named the Paradise Meadows Loop Trail; it is 3.5 kilometres in length and also starts from the Wilderness Centre. The brochure points out many natural and peculiar features such as the hanging ponds, which are ponds on higher ground "possibly due to the force of expanding ice" (presumably in the ancient past). The brochure also describes tree islands, a group of trees that grow in one fertile area, and the Old Man of the Meadows, a very elderly hemlock. You can divert off to nearby Battleship Lake as well.

It is said that Battleship Lake is so named because the young son of early explorer Clinton Wood remarked that the islands in the centre of the lake resembled battleships. Personally, I didn't see this—instead I saw fuzzy trolls. If I had my way, Three Troll Lake would make a fabulous name for this glistening, pristine, glacial delight. Whatever the name, you will experience a stunning alpine landscape here, one that is well worth the easy stroll.

Marmots

As you drive to and from Mount Washington, look out for the signs warning visitors that marmots may be crossing the road. Just like human outdoor enthusiasts, marmots could very well be heading for the spectacular hikes on this beautiful mountain, enjoying their own little amble in the alpine meadows, their preferred abode rather than heavily treed areas.

The Vancouver Island marmot is Canada's most endangered mammal (although there are fifteen other marmot species in the world). They possess two very endearing characteristics: They "box" when they play, and they greet each other by nose touching. In spring they emerge from hibernation in their deep burrows and nibble on succulent spring sedges; they pass their days by lounging on the sun-warmed mountain boulders, and, hopefully, mating. (Happily, due to the increasing numbers, this looks as though it must be true!)

When marmots sense danger, they produce a shrill whistle sound, which is why they are often called the "whistle pig," a nickname I like, as I love pigs.

Strathcona Park's adorable marmots are closely monitored and protected by dedicated volunteers, researchers, and scientists.

Approximately two hundred marmots now live in these mountainous meadows including the area around the Nanaimo Lakes and north to Mount Washington in Strathcona Park—this despite the fact that ten years ago the situation was dire with barely a marmot to be seen.

In 2018 I became a proud "marmoteer," which means I "adopted" a marmot and will receive a poster, an adoption certificate, and a newsletter. To help protect these little creatures, you can join the Marmot Recovery Foundation by visiting their website at marmots.org.

My maiden name, Bobak, is Polish; by coincidence, bobak means "marmot" in Polish. With this in mind, every Christmas I renewed Dad's membership to the Marmot Recovery Foundation. And when the city of Fredericton roasted Dad for being their local artist celebrity, I was asked to make a speech at the roast, which meant we had to publicly, though in a good-natured and humorous way, insult him. (People cracked right up—poor Dad!) In my speech, I described Dad as a nearly extinct "Polish Miramichi Marmot" (he loved fishing on the Miramichi River) with a barren daughter, so the line would be definitely be on the decline. Roasting and fishing and Polish aside, the protection of our western marmot is a serious matter and a worthy cause to support.

When I was a child, Dad carved me a beautiful box from New Brunswick pine, about the size of a small trunk. On the top he had sculpted a marmot, and on the back he had carved my date of birth.

"For your treasures," he said when he gave it to me. He knew I had some private items that I preferred to keep hidden away. I think he understood my need for privacy more than Mum. I was always a rather secretive child, and Dad never pried into my private world, but I always sensed that Mum was trying to figure out my secretive behaviour. I was very secretive about maturing, my looming approach into adulthood—growing up seemed so embarrassing. One of the first items to go into my marmot box was a hand-blown glass cup, which I had purchased from a store on Queen Street,

the main street in Fredericton where Mum loved to paint the parades and protests and small-town hustle and bustle. My cup was a secret, as I recall, because purchasing such an object was a mature choice, unlike purchasing a doll, so I kept the cup in my box until I moved to Vancouver and rented a little apartment on Harwood and Nicola near English Bay.

Dad's pine box has remained with me all my life, but nowadays it is empty and is the chosen place for a little feral black cat to sleep in every night in the basement; he arrives every evening through the cat door and has his dinner, then sleeps in the box. He's so feral that I cannot go near him—he hisses and spits at me, but he loves Dad's marmot box.

My treasures that once were secretly hidden under the lovely marmot carving are now arranged on my bookshelf, desk, and windowsill, where I glance at them before writing in the early morning hours or before falling asleep at night. The greatest treasures include my trolls, naked and pale, all lined up with their faded, fuzzy hair, like some sort of shrine.

I think everyone should have a box for treasures, for a few secret little truths, not to be shared but kept private. A little box of memories and treasures holds so much more than a digital memory stick and gives you so much more comfort.

The Vancouver Island Marmot is Canada's most endangered mammal, according to the foundation's website. This particular marmot lives only in Canada, and it may surprise you to learn that the marmot is a member of the squirrel and woodchuck family, although with his little protruding front teeth, he resembles a small beaver. They live in family groups, and since they hibernate throughout the winter, they live in lower areas where digging is possible; they do not live on frozen mountaintops. The mountain meadows are their habitat, and they eat a variety of sedges, grasses, and alpine flowers, including the beautiful wild lupines, which cover our rural slopes with a carpet of mauve cobalt during the warm summer months.

North Island

Campbell River, Elk Falls, Quadra Island, Sayward,
Woss, Port McNeill, Alert Bay, and Sointula

Campbell River

IF YOU EVER SEEK A DEEPER LEVEL OF SERENITY ON VANCOUVER
Island, visit your desired destination in the off-season—for example, in
early November (before the snow falls on the mountain passes), when the
fine, soft drizzle has begun, and the blustery weather is sweeping the delicate golden and rust leaves from the hawthorns, poplars, woodland alders,
and beech trees. You may see a wisp of smoke rising into the damp air from
a hot bonfire or distant chimney. Along the country lanes are the deep
orange of the rosehip hedgerows flecked with plump, white Styrofoam-like
snowberries; and, as always, in the distance are deep green conifer forests.

Our West Coast autumnal hues are awash in greens and ochres,
blending in with deep coppers and reddish purples, all rising into the
delicate sea mist under a silvery golden light, as if heavenly angels or a
Greek goddess is about to descend.

Although our eastern sugar maple woods are a dazzling and breathtaking display of blazing scarlets and flaming orange at this time of

year, our West Coast autumn landscapes are, to me, far more arresting and pleasing to both the mind and the eye.

One of the most enchanting moments of the autumnal day is the brief transition into dusk. Just before the sun slips beneath the snow-capped, mountainous horizon, there is a silent, motionless, divine light, an almost-opaque, cool blue-grey, like antique milk glass that seems to coat the sea, the remains of the sunlight gently streaking the water with a silver shimmer, then kissed with a chilly pale pink; finally, there is the sunless sky above the soft grey quivering water, the black, bobbing clusters of winter-migrated waterfowl resting for another day, their nightly gurgles and sleepy squawks merging with the lapping surf. Then, at last, darkness descends.

A perfect ambling, half-hour drive in such a season is north from Comox to Campbell River (on the scenic route, of course). The road winds gracefully along the shore and through the little settlements of Black Creek and Saratoga Beach until motels and newer-looking developments appear, signalling your approach to Campbell River.

I must admit, this is a town I once vaguely perceived as rather rough—that is, until I did a book reading at the beautiful seaside activity centre there. While speaking to a large, keen audience, I realized that Campbell River is, in fact, a sophisticated and art-appreciative community.

The town centre is indeed lovely, but their exquisite gem, in my opinion, is the new museum, a contemporary structure of brick and glass that sits on the western hill as you enter town. In 2014, TripAdvisor listed the museum at Campbell River as one of the top ten in Canada, unsurprising when you consider its understated, elegant craftsmanship, hands-on and interactive displays, audio and visual exhibits, dramatic presentations, models and replicas, repatriated First Nations' masks and other items, as well as fascinating, well-researched data. The outdoor areas of the museum also offer interactivity and information with indigenous vegetation, historic artifacts, and resting spots, all with a stunning view of the ocean, forest, and mountains. Although it would be easy to do so, the museum does not overwhelm visitors with too much information but, instead, provides tasteful offerings of special, unique stories and pieces. With skilful use of natural light, space, and clean, fresh-smelling wood, we can enjoy an opportunity to slip into a Little Think (as good museums entice us to do) about our place in the world

Elk Falls

Just on the other side of Campbell River is the famous Elk Falls, in Strathcona Provincial Park. It is well marked and easy to find—both the campground and the falls. The falls are well-known because they are a spectacular sight, the great white water cascading dramatically into a ravine from a rock face high above. A short walk through the woods from the parking lot takes you there, and if you are a brave soul, you might walk across the suspension bridge next to the falls to the other viewing platform. Then, of course, you must return back across.

On a drizzling autumn afternoon, my friends Lilla, Regine, Tara, and I made the excursion to the bridge. The mist hung low, just above the treetops; the woods smelled pungent as the new autumn rains dampened the dry mosses and ferns of the forest floor under the towering hemlocks and firs.

Lilla and I were terrified to cross the bridge—absolutely petrified; we are both afflicted with fear of heights. Still, we decided to white-knuckle it across, refusing to be defeated by our own selves. Gearing up with visualization exercises and with much yoga breathing, we prepared to conquer our fear and trek over the precipice where we would all tumble to our deaths, to our maker, if the bridge loosened from its steel and concrete footings.

Our little adventure began at the small interpretive centre, accessed just after we'd parked; there was a detailed display of the new generating station project on the river. I recalled reading about this massive tunnelled project, named the John Hart Replacement Project, a few years earlier. There was colossal drilling and burrowing through metres of rock far below the earth's surface in efforts to send water surging from the John Hart Lake towards the towns of Comox and Courtenay. (John Hart, the province's twenty-third premier, served British Columbia from 1941 to 1945 and was well-known for his "rural electrification" projects following the Second World War.)

Although the tunnels—a true feat of engineering brilliance—exist for practical reasons, the original, old wood-stave penstocks are an amazing sight all on their own. Huge and rotund, these gigantic wooden pipes are made from the abundant local Douglas firs, braced with steel frames painted a fading turquoise. They curve through the grasses and woodland shrubbery, a thin film of green lichen and mosses settling on their rotting surfaces. They run from the dam at the lake, at a length of over one and a half kilometres, to the generating station.

The first penstock was constructed in 1947, so it is indeed time for a replacement—hence, the tunnels. I am not an engineer, but the project fascinates me, due to its immensity.

The falls are very close to the penstocks, just a stroll through the forest. As we neared the rushing water that echoed through the trees, I began to perspire, and Lilla turned pale. We almost passed out when we rounded a bend and saw the high, narrow, slightly swaying, fragile-looking bridge high above the precipice; the falls were slightly off to one side.

After all the breathing and visualizing, the time had come. I went first, by myself—when terrified, I prefer to be alone, resisting all assistance—gingerly walking straight ahead. I did not look down. I am told that, at one point, Tara took my picture, but I don't remember anything about that. I saw neither the falls nor the scenery—I just looked straight ahead and made it to the ledge on the other side.

Lilla was next. Regine led her across, and, like me, Lilla also completely missed the view. Still, we made it. Shortly later, we briskly crossed back, which seemed to be more nerve-wracking as the second time often is. But we did it—we walked the suspension bridge at Elk Falls.

Strangely, I felt no sense of accomplishment at conquering my fear of crossing the bridge; perhaps it was because the fear was actually not conquered at all, even though the action was accomplished. I will never repeat the challenge, and the fear remains.

Quadra Island

On a fine autumn day, my friend Les and I visited Quadra Island, a community easily reached by ferry off Campbell River, only a half-hour's drive up from Comox, on the scenic route along the quieter coastal road through scattered farming communities, quiet after a busy summer of tourists. It is a most mysterious and austere time of year that reminds me of those moments just before we drift into sleep.

Quadra Island is part of the Discovery Islands, located in the waters between Campbell River and the mainland, where deep fjords cut eighty kilometres into the coastal mountains and rivers gush down into the sea through the great rainforest.

Quadra and Cortes Islands are the most familiar of the Discovery Islands; they have established active communities and are accessible by little car ferries. Thousands of tiny islets, scattered throughout this marine area, are popular with kayakers and accessible only by boat.

The ferry terminal to Quadra is easily found and well-marked in Campbell River—just drive through the town along the main street towards a great olive-green building. The ferry terminal will be on your right. As far as ferry terminals go, it is dull, not much more than a little booth and few rows of asphalt lanes. The fare was approximately forty dollars for two people and the car. This fare is for a return trip, the assumption being that one must return to civilization at some point, although many do not. The crossing itself takes only ten minutes, so there is no coffee shop on board the ferry, but you might have time to file your nails.

In a cloud-wrapped drizzling mist, the tub-like *Quadra Queen II* carried us through the choppy murky waves like a little workhorse and docked at her berth at Quathiaski Cove, tucked among numerous fishing boats bobbing at their docks, their great rose-coloured float balls and nets hauled in for the winter, and their aluminum masts clinking in the breeze. Dampness hung in the cedar and fir treetops, where two eagles slouched, maybe waiting to grab a salmon after its long, exhausting journey to spawn in a nearby creek.

With a full-time population of twenty-seven hundred, Quadra Island is not a wild, backwoods, remote settlement; rather, it is a busy and productive community with impressive shopping experiences and residents skilled in the arts, food industries, and trades. Many residents, no doubt, have occupations that see them commuting daily to their place of employment off the island, in the town of Campbell River.

The first thing to do on an island you have never visited (I had not looked at a map nor planned any route or activity, and, of course, did not have one of those GPS gizmos) is to seek out the village and/or the coffee shop. This is where the action is; at the very least, you can find a map and a helpful and talkative resident. And so, we pulled into a little shopping plaza, a row of fascinating, unique little shops, which provided us with a fabulous little buying spree. There was an art gallery displaying over seventy local artists' works; I purchased an elegant shot glass as a Christmas present for Mikki, bedecked with glass starfish and pearls. ("For wheatgrass shots," said the gallery owner, but I was thinking of an alternate use.) The health food store sold local produce; the yoga goods store displayed polished stones, handmade cards, and knitted socks; there was a library; and a bookstore called the Book Bonanza, which was one of the best bookstores I've ever visited. It was crammed with all the new bestsellers (from the last ten years) but also had stacks and shelves of books I never knew existed—a memoir by Gathie Falk, one of my favourite Vancouver artists who at one time painted enormous oil canvases of pink pavement (oh, what she could do with pink!) and vast night skies. Her sculptures were great pyramids of glossy ceramic fruit, and she did things with dresses, chairs, and fish, as I recall.

At the bottom of an enormous pile of novels was a pamphlet on nudibranchs—the name always makes me chuckle . . . nudibranch, nudibranch . . .

There was everything on every topic in this amazing bookshop!

Nudibranchs are colourful, soft-bodied molluscs—and, yes, nudi *comes from the Latin word, "naked." There are three thousand species of this naked mollusc, and they are divided into two types: aeolids and dorids. Dorids breathe by way of a plume that flows from their anus!*

Nudibranchs have exotic and flamboyant nicknames, such as the Spanish shawl, shown in a mauve, gauze-like gown on National Geographic's *website.*

Here is another interesting fact: In the nineteenth century, a Mr. Philip Henry Gosse reported that a professor had discovered that nudibranchs could be audible from twelve feet away; he said that nudibranch communication resembles the sound of a wire hitting the side of a glass.

The Aroma Coffee Shop was just up the road and served the best double espresso I have ever had anywhere, including Spain, as well as a blueberry cream scone that appeared from the kitchen on a large cookie sheet, like a massive, thick, succulent cake before it was sliced into enormous voluptuous pieces.

We found a map and a friendly man with a smelly, hairy old dog shuffling at his side; he gave us directions to our two destinations: the beautiful Rebecca Spit and the historic Heriot Bay Inn, both on the southern part of the island, which is only several kilometres across. The island is thirty-five kilometres long and much wider in the north, where there are lakes and wilderness hiking trails, beaches and bluffs, marine parks, and rugged coastlines to discover.

When exploring, it also helps to read the community notice board to get the gist of a place. By studying the café's bulletin board, I learned that Quadra Island has a seniors' program called "Stepping Up, Stepping Out," which provides social interaction, physical activity, and a variety of creative and cultural projects. They serve lunch, too, and provide transportation. Isn't that just the kindest and most compassionate endeavour, especially on an island where it is all too easy to become an isolated hermit, enveloped by the drooping damp cedars in a little wood cabin, alone with perhaps a few feral cats who you have befriended and a wood stove for heat?

I have begun to wonder what will become of me when I am elderly, as I have no family and fear my eyes will go as Mum's did—or worse, my legs will give out, or I'll have a stroke as Gran did (except mine will be on my horse, probably at the Saanich Fair in front of a thousand spectators), or I'll take a fall on the beach off a slippery log and have to drag myself across the pebbles to the nearest road as the cold surf washes over my broken ankles. I cannot envision myself in a "home," eating a little pink cake and green Jell-O in the dining room with a hundred others like me or tossing a ball to an old man next to me for exercise—I just can't see it; I've never been a team player. There must be something available where I can have martinis, my art, my stacks of books, the CBC, and lots of rescued pets, but also have a little assistance.

And so the Quadra Island Stepping Up, Stepping Out program seems like the right fit for me, as long as they don't expect me to do sing-alongs, or those annoying, gluey dexterous craft activities, or clap my hands, or blow or bang on things, or much of any other movement, plus speaking or singing. My social interaction is mostly that of an observer.

Les and I drove across the island and easily located Rebecca Spit Marine Provincial Park. Its little wooded lane off Heriot Bay Road led to a spacious parking lot with a large grassy meadow between two lovely vistas. On one side was the little cove of Heriot Bay, dotted with bobbing, moored pleasure boats, and on the other was the rollicking grey sea with the shadowy Discovery Islands in the misty distance. The ferry to Cortes Island was tossing in the waves as she approached the little terminal around the corner.

Cortes Island is also a vibrant island community widely known for Hollyhock, a health-focused getaway with a spa, yoga, nature adventures, artistic and spiritual-type courses, "transformational" programs, and the like. I'm sure they don't use fabric softener on their bedding, or artificially scented candles or air fresheners, or processed cheese, all of which give me a sore throat. The ferry journey to Cortes Island is forty-five minutes from Heriot Bay on Quadra.

The stroll around Rebecca Spit was enchanting—a gentle, easy amble along a forest path—and for me, especially peaceful in the soft and pungent wet autumn woods. An aged and tarnished metal plaque at the entrance indicates that Rebecca Spit was dedicated a park in 1959. Its original owners were a Mr. and Mrs. J. C. Clandenning—a wonderful name!

It is a short drive from the spit to the Heriot Bay Inn once you're back onto the main road, and the directions are well marked.

The inn is located at the end of the road on the sheltered bay where the little Cortes Island ferry arrives. It is a historic but nicely restored wooden building, painted white, with an old-time porch and a vast front lawn adorned with deck chairs (which on our visit were soon to be brought in for the winter) leading down to a little beach. In their brochure, they say, "We've been serving fun-loving locals and visitors for over a hundred years."

As soon as we entered on that damp, drizzly November day, I fell in love with the warmth and coziness: the quaint entrance greets you with original wood floors, a fireplace, and large overstuffed red velvet sofas. We sat in a corner overlooking the sea and had delicious bowls of clam chowder, not too thick, and full of wild salmon.

There's a fun and crammed gift shop as well where I purchased a few Christmas presents, including a biodegradable toothbrush. I wondered which would last longer: this hemp-bristled brush or my teeth?

Unique and original local art by two women adorned the walls; one artist in particular, Elena Mason, a Mexican artist, had designed and painstakingly created beautiful mosaic frames around mirrors. I wonder how it came to be that a Mexican artist ended up on a northern Canadian Pacific island, creating mosaics now displayed on the walls of the Heriot Bay Inn.

To the south—back towards the shopping centre and the coffee shop—is an additional site to visit, although Les and I ran out of time and had to return home, but I made a note to return to Quadra Island in the spring to visit Cape Mudge, a well-known First Nations community and the location of the Nuyumbalees Cultural Centre, which houses and preserves crucial and historic potlatch artifacts, including stunning masks, tools, ceremonial and spiritual objects and shawls, repatriated years after the potlatch was outlawed and after the dismal residential schools were closed. That period was a sad and shameful time in our history, as we now know. (The museum at Campbell River and the U'mista Cultural Centre at Alert Bay on Cormorant Island also display numerous repatriated items.)

Cape Mudge—so named after Captain George Vancouver's first lieutenant, Zachary Mudge—is also the site of a historic lighthouse originally built in 1898. Along with the First Nations village, the area has a significant history in that it was where Captain George Vancouver landed in 1792 and paid a friendly visit to the Coast Salish community. However, Vancouver was not impressed with the voyage through the treacherous, churning whirlpools of what is now known as the Seymour Narrows, calling it "one of the most vile stretches of water in the world." A little farther north, there was a more hazardous challenge: Ripple Rock.

Ripple Rock

In 1959, our government took heed of Captain Vancouver's view that travelling the marine passage north among the hundreds of islands and through the narrow channels was extremely treacherous. Indeed, many a shipwreck lay between the lurking, submerged rock ridges and reefs beneath the green landscape and serene beauty of these capes, clamshell bays, and scattered islands. As idyllic as it looks, there are turbulent and tumultuous vortices below waiting to swallow any vessel endeavouring to traverse these waters. This precarious passage was a crucial route to strategic trading locations along the Pacific coast, including Alaska.

At one specific location, a few kilometres north of Campbell River, one of the largest marine blasting projects ever attempted was to take place: the removal of the top of the infamous Ripple Rock, an underwater mountain where, at low tide, the two peaks were only nine feet beneath the surface. The currents that violently churned around the rock were equally hazardous and often brought a ship and its crew to its death and destruction before even hitting the obstruction.

The great explosive event was broadcast live across the country on CBC; debris landed on both sides of the channel, but the deed was successful. The Ripple Rock blast is well documented, and the photographs can be seen at local museums (and, of course, on the Internet).

Today, there is a lovely wooded path from the road to the Ripple Rock site; it's a pleasant, easy hike and takes a couple of hours there and back. Driving north from Campbell River, there is signage in two locations; the first is simply a viewpoint with a plaque, but a few hundred metres along is the Ripple Rock parking lot and trail.

The road north

From Ripple Rock onwards, the island is distinctively remote and presents a picture of the wild wooded coast of years gone by, with very few tiny seaside or forest communities, some only accessible by dirt roads; sad little logging camps appear every so often between the dark green mist-filled valleys where nothing but the cold grey peaks are visible against the white sky; the only signs of civilization for miles are forest fire signage or a black skid mark on the pavement. As we drove, I truly felt, with a slight anxiety, that civilization remained behind us, but a couple of hundred kilometres beyond was our destination, the fascinating island communities of Alert Bay and Sointula. There were lengthy stretches of poor radio reception, and I think I must have wondered aloud, "What if we break down" a million times, my voice weaker with every mention. (We had a lovely strong vehicle, but that's what anxiety is all about—the *what ifs*.) What a grand relief it was to finally see a sign of life far ahead, which turned out to be the Crossroads Restaurant and Pub at the entrance to the village of Sayward.

"Let's stop," I suggested to Mikki, before the next, even-longer stretch and even more remote journey continued. I needed a rest, and I wasn't even driving! I was so stressed that I ate a huge plate of thick, white spongy French toast, and I'd only had breakfast two hours ago. We were the only patrons, except for a grizzly old logger who was voraciously eating bacon and eggs in a corner under a canopy of plastic plants. The place was cozy, and the fire was blazing. The server had just made a batch of immense cinnamon buns and colossal lemon cookies, which sat in a tall jar on the counter.

The short drive into Sayward was pleasant; there are ambling streams and rivers, small farms and a dear little community with a school, a post office, and a public park. Towards the end is the Salmon River Estuary, which flows into Salmon Bay and then into the Johnstone Strait. There's even an information centre, a small gift shop and gallery at Kelsey Bay, and a café at the end of the road.

Although it looks small and nondescript, Sayward has a few claims to fame, all described in a slick brochure that I read as I ate my French toast. There's a multitude of hiking trails that follow the original First Nations trading routes and feature many river locations from which to launch canoes; these spots are called put-ins. One route is forty-seven kilometres in length and is described like this:

"The Sayward Valley canoe route runs through Amour, Twin, Mohun, Lawier, Higgins, Gosling, Lower Campbell, Fry, Grey, Brewster and Surprise Lakes . . . and takes a week to complete."

The brochure makes it clear that these activities are "do-it-yourself adventures," so perhaps I would need to hire a guide, considering the stress I had just experienced driving (or, being driven as a passenger) on the highway.

Other features of note: Sayward also hosts a stop on the Tour de Rock bicycle journey for the Cops for Cancer, and the movie *The Scarlet Letter* was filmed nearby at White River Provincial Park in 1994. And there is one more endearing feature of little Sayward: its two-thousand-year-old yellow cedar named Sergeant RandAlly. This tree was the world's largest yellow cedar until it fell in 2004! Even toppled, however, it is an incredible sight. A clever leaflet depicts the growth of trees like this through history, beginning with the crucifix-ion, the invention of book printing and gunpowder, Ivan the Terrible, abolishment of slavery, and finally ending with the Olympic Games in Whistler. The yellow cedar is a member of the cypress family with distinguished flattened needles. In the case of Sergeant RandAlly, this enormous fallen champion boasts a diameter of 4.16 metres and rests protected deep in the forest within the Sayward area; if you are inclined towards a possible overnight hike to visit the sergeant, you can embark on the thirty-four-kilometre, one-way visit by starting out on the trail at the Sayward waterfront and then heading south. The Sayward tree protectors have also lovingly and amusingly named two other significantly enormous trees Admiral Broeren (the *new* reigning champion) and General Buxton.

Sayward has numerous bed and breakfasts which you might plan to visit if driving the very long distance to the north island from Victoria.

So, the next time you pass a little town that simply looks as if it is nothing but a few houses along a meandering stream, consider what possibly is in store for you if you take the time to stop; look for the local café, and pick up a brochure—there may be a few surprises in store for you!

Woss and Port McNeill

From Sayward, the road took a lengthy turn inland, winding its way through mountain valleys heavy with fog and dotted with dark little lakes; there were no autumn colours here, just the dark green coniferous forests stretching as far as the eye could see and the cold mottled grey trunks and bare limbs of maples and alders lining the roadside.

Our first sign of life and civilization as we know it was the Hoomak Lake rest stop; it looked intriguing with all its informative billboards, so we pulled over. It was by the far the most well-kept rest stop I have ever encountered: The composting toilets were spotless, and there was even an explanation of how they work. There was a beautiful trail down to the lake, so Archie and I took a stroll—he needed to have a drink, and I needed to stretch my stiff, aching legs. (This was the first year that I wore compression stockings on an airplane—a true sign of approaching seniorhood. You'll know I've reached full-blown seniorhood when I wear them with shorts to the liquor store, probably in just a few more years.)

The signage described the history and culture of all the north island communities. At this location, you are in the First Nation territory of the Nimpkish Valley. Here, backcountry wilderness activities abound: caving, rock climbing, camping, fishing, and hiking across the Island from east to west on the ancient First Nation trading route trails.

There was a little nondescript sign in the parking lot that asked that visitors not remain for longer than eight hours.

We pushed on as Woss, established originally as a logging camp, was just around the corner and arrived at a tired looking gas station and convenience store.

We filled the car and bought a stale sausage roll, which Archie and I ate in the chilly, damp mountain air beside the gas pump. There was a grizzly looking fellow sitting on a tree stump beside a phone booth (yes, a real phone booth with a working phone). He had one red boot on, and a blue boot on the other foot.

"Is this Woss?" I asked him.

"What's it look like?" he growled. Then, a bit more affably, he added, "You can charge your car down the road to the left."

"Well, we don't have an electric car yet."

"Well, in case you ever do, there's a charging station down the road and to the left."

Online, you can find an aerial image of Woss that shows a slightly larger community of approximately two hundred people, with several roads and groups of structures carved into the forest. Wikipedia also states, to my amusement, that Woss has regular telephone service (hence the phone booth) and at one time had an elementary school, which is now closed. The school's principal, the late Tage Wickstrom, was a local hero, having organized the construction of a running track. The main tourist attraction is a working steam-powered engine originally used to heat the lumbermen's bunkhouses.

According to another website (VancouverIsland.com), Woss also has the longest working logging railway in North America at 122 kilometres.

There's something melancholy about this little community, which has clearly seen happier times and better days, sitting all alone in the fog with its telephone booth and old steam engine hoping that a tourist will take an interest in it; perhaps when it receives attention, the old steam engine, with great effort, will squirt a bit of steam like it did in its heyday. After learning more about this community, I regret that I didn't venture down the road to the left, past the electric charger, to the Tage Wickstrom running track. I would have taken a jog (with Archie), purely out of empathy for what used to be and is no longer.

Soon Mikki, Archie, and I embarked on the next leg of our journey to Port McNeill, seventy-five kilometres down the road, where the ferry would carry us to our final destination.

I never thought I'd be so relieved to see a bowling alley and a Canadian Tire, but that is what I felt when we came upon Port McNeill. These comforting, familiar signs of modern life appeared to us as we emerged from the cold, forest mists in the rugged mountains into the glowing sunshine, the sparkling sea dotted with little islands—the Broughton Archipelago—glistening at the bottom of the hill. We drove over the hill and down towards the busy waterfront just in time to catch the little ferry to Alert Bay on Cormorant Island.

Civilization never felt so good—there were flowers along the boardwalk, a bustling coffee shop, a jovial fisherman cleaning his boat, a smiling cheerful ferry worker, two elegant merganser ducks with their upswept ginger hairstyles paddling among the dark, floating kelp beds, and a little yellow warbler on the white, freshly painted railing.

I realized that although solitude and retreat from the world is often attractive, I am not a hermit, and could never be, at least not in the woods.

From the little freshly painted blue-and-white terminal, the ferry travels to either the village of Sointula on Malcolm Island, seen as a line of minuscule roofs in the hazy blue distance to the left, or to Alert Bay, the village on Cormorant Island to the right and around the dark, coniferous corner. The ferry schedule is good, and the boat travels back and forth throughout the day.

Alert Bay

Cormorant Island is primarily a First Nations community. The street signs are both in English and the traditional First Nation language of the 'Namgis. Shaped a bit like a cashew, the island is very small; if you were inclined, you could stroll through the forest trails around the perimeter, which is approximately eight kilometres.

There is an arch that greets visitors to Alert Bay and welcomes them—Gilakas'la—to 'Namgis First Nation. And although the hub of activity is basically along one waterfront street, Front Street, there is plenty to do, learn, discover, reflect upon, observe, and enjoy in several other areas.

We arrived at lunchtime and followed directions from Maxine, the owner of our accommodation, the historic Customs House. Our directions were to drive off the ferry, turn right, and go past the general store; the blue painted Customs House would be on the left.

With deep awe and respect, I observed this rather rustic, quiet, misty coastal island village. The water side of the street was lined with aged fishing piers and salt-whipped, tin-roofed, abandoned boat sheds; on the left, there were a few little businesses that supply the community with its basic needs.

So far removed from the bustling life that most of us are used to, Alert Bay has retained an elegant, dignified, but rugged old-time West Coast seafaring charm. It is the oldest community established off north Vancouver Island, and remnants of its busy coastal fishing industry can be seen at every turn.

We met Maxine's son on the side lawn of Customs House, which was built in 1917, and he presented us with a key and a special Customs House pen. (I love pens and markers, and this particular pen had a lovely smooth feel, a good weight, and easy movement.) Our abode for the one evening was on the top floor, so we climbed the narrow stairs. When we reached the top, we were met with a quaint and cozy, warm and homey little residence, with plush furniture, a sparkling clean bathroom, a fully supplied kitchen, a view of the sea, lots of lamps and carpets and cushions, and numerous knick-knacks on the window sills and walls.

No Hilton, Ritz, or five-star hotel has ever made me feel this welcome or comfortable. I would have loved to just put my feet up and read books with a glass of wine, but we had to head out before the early November dusk descended. Alas, we were only there for the afternoon and evening.

Our first excursion was a lovely walk through the Alert Bay Ecological Park, a brief uphill walk from Front Street, but if you prefer to drive, there is a parking lot at the park as well as a spacious campsite in a pretty meadow.

The park has an abundance of gentle wooded trails; it is impossible to get lost, and the signage is excellent. The highlight is the well-maintained boardwalk that stretches over a beautiful bog full of reeds, grasses, and marshy crimson shrubbery; towering snags reach into the white sky with sage-green mosses hanging from their dry, bare, brittle old limbs.

Bogs are the most fascinating and mysterious ecosystems—most of what they are composed of are concealed beneath a diverse mat of vegetation. This bog, according to a little brochure I picked up at the Alert Bay post office, is fed not only by precipitation but by numerous underground streams. It's a little gem in the woods where you can sit peacefully on one of the benches and listen to the silence of the surrounding woods and marsh reeds.

Following our amble through the forest and over the bog, we visited the U'mista Cultural Centre, easily located at the far end of Front Street on a slope overlooking the village. This beautiful centre is not to be missed. U'mista means "the return of something important," and in this case this refers to the return of the traditional and cultural tools, masks, and other items, many deeply spiritual, that the First Nation peoples used to celebrate and perform in their potlatch ceremonies. In our colonist past, which we recognize now as shameful, the potlatch was outlawed, and the ceremonial items were removed and sent to various museums as exhibits.

Next to the U'mista Cultural Centre is a bare, wide-open field, the site of what was a massive red brick residential school, the source of many atrocities. The school was torn down and demolished a few years ago as an act of reconciliation.

The barren field is a powerful symbol in itself. There are times when nothing means everything. Monuments may be informative, but empty space evokes thought, and so I found the bare field very moving.

Inside the centre are displays, the repatriated treasures, and informative exhibits, beautifully and tastefully presented. As soon as you walk through the fragrant cedar entrance, there is a sense of calm that invites you to stay awhile. You can sit with a cup of coffee and watch a wonderful short film on the potlatch—the masks, some enormous heads of hairy, snapping animals or skilfully carved birds, and the dancing that accompanies the spirits, are true works of art and, in my view, are more powerful than staring at the *Mona Lisa*. My heart was pounding when the film ended.

Another gallery paid tribute to the well-known First Nations advocate and Member of the Order of Canada, Chief Dan George. An Academy Award–nominated actor, poet, and activist, he was recognizable by his long, flowing grey hair and a gentle face that was lovely and expressive—a face which had lived through a thousand challenges as well as glories. Chief Dan George also wrote several bestselling books, the most popular being *My Heart Soars*, a collection of memories and poetry. He died in 1981 in North Vancouver.

From the U'mista Cultural Centre, we took a walk along Front Street back towards the village. Dusk was approaching over the charcoal sea under the hazy glow of the setting sun in the slate-coloured sky. Our stroll along the boardwalk took us past the old cannery, a cold, tarnished, weather-beaten tin building, atop an intricate row of black pilings, jutting out into the cool, lapping bay. Piles of netting and little white sponge floats sat on the end of the dock. Alert Bay was built for the fishing industry; in 1870, the building was originally a fish saltery but became a cannery in 1881. At the time, the community's fresh water came from underground springs in the nearby bog and was regulated by way of a dam. Fish canning took place until 1941, and then the building was (and still is) used as a net loft by the 'Namgis fishermen. Here they construct, store, and repair their nets, and an informative plaque on the waterfront explains net making, an intricate and time-consuming craft involving precise knot measurements calculated by using a special stool (yes, a stool, not a tool).

I strolled beyond our cozy abode at Customs House and came upon the 'Namgis burial grounds, a grassy slope dotted with beautiful sun–bleached weathered totem poles, several sinking back into the ground as if in a deep and peaceful sleep, returning to where they once grew out of the earth.

It is quite crucial that you do not walk through this special place but instead look from afar, from the road. The totem poles are beautiful symbols from the 'Namgis culture—some have gracefully collapsed into the grass, others still stand with enormous dignity; perhaps a wing or an ear has been taken by the wind or by other natural means. When you observe these ancient poles, remember that concepts such as rot, mildew, and death are accepted, and perhaps even celebrated, as having a place in the circle of life. And so the poles lie there with a grand dignity and contentment (you can almost hear them sigh) for having been in the world, then letting go with ease and gratitude. What a difficult thing it is to hang on to life and not let go—but the poles let go with such grace.

Across the road sit old boat sheds and little wooden tugs and vessels, with their blue or red paint peeling; they are anchored with seaweed-covered ropes between slanted and neglected wooden structures, pilings, and crumbling, unused fishing docks. Like the totems across the road on the hill, they do not resist at the end and stoically remain as nature takes her course.

I cannot finish my story about our visit to Alert Bay without mentioning the Pass'n Thyme Inn and Restaurant, also on Front Street. Warm and delightfully friendly, with early Christmas lights sparkling around the windows, and flower boxes of withering geraniums brought in for the winter, the fresh halibut burger was amazing, and the apple pie—homemade by Wendy, our cheerful server—was to die for!

If you find yourself in Alert Bay for a few hours, visit the Pass'n Thyme and nosh down (as they say in all the trendy food articles in the *New York Times*) a piece of Wendy's pie!

Heading home via Sointula

Alert Bay was silent and empty under a cold starry sky. The town was still asleep when we boarded the little ferry under a few copper glowing street lights in the early pre-waking hours. We sat, still half awake, in the warm lounge above the decks on the worn brown vinyl seats as the vessel chugged through the cold choppy waters, its engines gently humming below, to Sointula and back to Port McNeill.

In the chilly blue dawn that had begun to appear, I stood on the cold, wet deck while we gently rocked into the Sointula dock, engines deeply idling with their distinctive hum. The village had just begun to stir. A few cars appeared on the narrow road behind the curved bay of little red-and-silver tin roofs, and there were wisps of smoke from a few chimneys. There was the co-op store at the wharf, which no doubt supplied the community with everything, from rubber boots to cow udder creams, candles to canning jars to chimney cleaning brooms— everything you need to live off the grid. I love these types of stores on the West Coast; those island stores are your lifeline, and they have everything you need. The Sointula Co-operative Store Association is the oldest in the province, having been started up in 1909 by early residents.

These initial residents have given Sointula a unique and fascinating history. In the late 1800s, crowds of European immigrants arrived in Canada to begin a new life, a better life with more freedom and opportunity. Many made their way out west, and many on Vancouver Island took on the harsh work in the coal mines and lumber industries.

This work was tough, filthy, and extremely hazardous, and in 1901, a group of Finns, led by a "utopian socialist" by the name of Matti Kurikka established an isolated utopian colony on Malcolm Island with the goal of living in an idealistic commune, a free and healthy existence of sharing and equality, away from the stresses, and capitalistic injustices of the rest of the world. They named their new community Sointula, which means "place of harmony." The energetic Finns established a sawmill, foundry, brickyard, and blacksmith shop, plus they even published a newspaper. The compulsory arts and physical health regimens played a large and vital role as well.

Alas, regimented commune life—and the inevitability of internal politics—took its toll and things eventually fell apart in 1905, when Kurikka dissolved the colony and left for Vancouver with half the colonists. (It is perhaps a bit ironic that Malcolm Island today has its own conflict management and dispute resolution facilitator.) Those who remained carried on as a community, weathering the hardships that all small communities endure—fire, shifts of industry, financial stresses—and even thrived at times. Today strong Finnish roots remain, and the little village is a hive of activity with tourism, fishing, and a variety of local agriculture. There's even a handmade bra shop! (I always thought that off-the-grid, West Coast islanders didn't wear bras, but alas, I was wrong.) And slight idiosyncrasies still exist: Local cats and dogs have the right of way and a sleeping person must not be disturbed, no matter where they chose to snooze—according to the brochure on Sointula, "if you come across one sleeping on the road, let it sleep and go around."

I stood on the deck and watched as several Island pickup trucks jolted onto the cold steel ramp below; I took a quiet joy in watching the town awakening to the light dawning over the distant layers of dark trees and hills as far as the eye could see. The slate-grey sea splashed the ferry's wake onto the pebbled waterfront.

I did not immediately disembark. So frequently, observation from afar rewards us with a deeper aesthetic appreciation than the actual physical setting forth.

Thoughts heading home

Although these little communities are remote and isolated from mainland activity, Alert Bay is, by far, one of the most profoundly thought-provoking places I have ever visited. It's a lovely, serene blend of our West Coast rainforests and the cold, grey-green sea and offers an example of how life used to be (and still can be). It possesses a rich traditional culture, a grace and dignity, and even a bit of melancholy. The long drive was worth every minute, and it was a fitting end to my travels throughout Vancouver Island.

As Proust suggests, the real voyage of discovery consists not of seeing new lands, but seeing with new eyes. I may not be an academic, a scholar, a Nobel Prize winner, a scientist, or a brilliant novelist such as Proust, Tolstoy, or Jane Austen, but I know what I feel, what I observe, and how our perceptions can be altered, soothed, or exhilarated just by noticing a tidal pool, a one-eyed owl, a line of wet and tangled red dresses after a winter storm, or a disintegrating totem pole in the grass.

My hope is that when you venture out on a little excursion of your own—wherever it may be, no matter the distance or how trivial or remote—you will embrace a new thought, a meaningful reflection, perhaps experience a profound memory, a Little Think, or simply learn something new about yourself, or the place. This is what travel and journey is all about: the remarkable experience of journeying within ourselves.

If you'd like to share your own Little Thinks and stories of your journeys, please feel free to contact Anny by either snail mail or email via touchwoodeditions.com.

Acknowledgements

First and foremost, I must thank my wonderful, patient publishers, Pat Touchie and Taryn Boyd, at Touchwood Editions; my editor, Renée Layberry, without whom there would be no journey described in this book; my partner, Mikki, who knows how to work a computer *really* well.

Thanks as well to chef Bill Jones for the pickled herring recipe, and Anne Gardner for the Comox forest walk and talk, to Pam Bjornson for the Nanoose excursion, and to Tracey Kraemer who took the time to explain the hiking skills and thrills of the West Coast Trail. Thanks to my friends who accompanied me on our numerous adventures, which enabled me to write about our fabulous Island home: Yumi, Lilla, Regine, and Tara, and my friend and fellow camper, Sarah Hein.

I am also grateful to Caila Holbrook from Project Watershed for her information on Kus-kus-sum. Thanks as well to the Union Bay Historical Society for their helpful suggestions.

A special thank you to Lesley Henderson for her support, friendship, humour, knowledge, and positivity. And, of course, to Archie, who was always patiently ready to embark on a new journey.

Finally, thanks to the little English schoolboy I met so many years ago, who was the original inspiration for seeking out the Little Thinks that I engage in daily—and will continue to do until I take my final breath.